MODERN
AMERICAN
HISTORY ★ A
Garland
Series

Edited by
FRANK FREIDEL
Harvard University

THE INSURGENT PROGRESSIVES IN THE UNITED STATES SENATE AND THE NEW DEAL, 1933–1939

Ronald A. Mulder

Garland Publishing, Inc.
New York & London ★ 1979

Library of Congress Cataloging in Publication Data

Mulder, Ronald A
    The insurgent progressives in the United States Senate
and the New Deal, 1933–1939.

    (Modern American history)
    Originally presented as the author's thesis, University
of Michigan, 1970.
    Bibliography: p.
    Includes index.
    1. United States—Politics and government—
1933–1945. 2. Progressivism (United States politics).
I. Title. II. Series.
E806.M84   1979   320.9'73'0917   78-62389
ISBN 0-8240-3637-9

All volumes in this series are printed on acid-free,
250-year-life paper.
Printed in the United States of America

To my wife, Sandra

PREFACE

During the Taft and Wilson administrations a group of
Western and Midwestern progressives, known as Insurgents,
formed an informal coalition in the United States Congress
to promote the enactment of reform measures and to protect
American agriculture from the encroachments of industrialism
and urbanism. In 1933 a loosely organized Progressive or
Insurgent bloc consisting of William E. Borah of Idaho,
Arthur Capper of Kansas, Edward P. Costigan of Colorado,
James Couzens of Michigan, Bronson M. Cutting of New Mexico,
Lynn J. Frazier of North Dakota, Hiram W. Johnson of
California, Robert M. LaFollette, Jr., of Wisconsin, Peter
Norbeck of South Dakota, George W. Norris of Nebraska,
Gerald P. Nye of North Dakota, Henrik Shipstead of Minnesota,
and Burton K. Wheeler of Montana still remained in the United
States Senate. Politically, most of these Insurgents were
dissident Republicans; ideologically, they were opposed to
concentrated economic and political power; and personally,
they were extremely self-righteous and pugnaciously independent.
This study, based largely on the private papers of the Insurgents
and on pertinent material in the Franklin D. Roosevelt Library
and in the Library of Congress, explores the Insurgents' views

of President Roosevelt, the interrelationships between the
primarily agrarian-based progressivism of the Insurgents
and the increasingly urban-oriented liberalism of the New
Deal, and the congressional-executive cooperation and
rivalry generated by the federal government's response to
the Great Depression.

Believing that the policies of the Republican party
in the 1920's had been disastrous, many of the Insurgents
campaigned for the Democratic Roosevelt in 1932 and hailed
his ensuing election as a prelude to the revival of progressivism. In the main, however, the legislation of the so-called
First New Deal, with its emphasis on a business-government
partnership to achieve economic recovery, disappointed the
Insurgents. Despite their disenchantment with some early New
Deal programs, the Insurgents retained a high regard for
Franklin D. Roosevelt and continued to urge the President to
move against large concentrations of corporate and personal
wealth. In 1935 when the alleged Second New Deal adopted an
antimonopolistic approach, the Insurgents, their advice
apparently followed, responded with enthusiasm. Ironically,
however, at the same time the New Deal pleased the Insurgents
by its attack on economic monopoly, it also disturbed many of
them by its resultant increase in governmental power.

Many of the Insurgents supported Roosevelt's bid for reelection in 1936, although with much less fervor and confidence than they had exhibited in 1932. The immediate post-election worry of most Insurgents was that the President, because of his overwhelming electoral victory and a huge Democratic majority in Congress, would consider himself free from traditional restraints in the exercise of executive authority. In February 1937, Roosevelt's announced plan to "pack" the Supreme Court confirmed Insurgent fears about his abuse of presidential power. The subsequent Court fight revealed some stark differences between Insurgent progressivism and New Deal liberalism. It also resulted in most of the Insurgents losing their faith in Roosevelt, for it indicated to them the extent to which the President and other New Dealers were willing to go to lodge political power in the executive branch of the federal government.

Among the Insurgents only Robert M. LaFollette, Jr., and George W. Norris were consistent supporters of New Deal proposals during Roosevelt's second term. For the other Insurgents who claimed loyalty to the same progressive creed that they had embraced in their early political careers, the New Deal constituted a marked departure from past American reform movements. They believed that the New Deal's reliance

on welfare-state liberalism and broker-state politics, with
its accompanying augmentation of the federal bureaucracy,
large increases in governmental spending, and massive
governmental intervention into people's daily lives, was
harmful to the American character and to democratic government. The voting records of these Insurgents for the years
1937-1939 clearly indicate that they not only did not regard
the New Deal as a "rendezvous with destiny," but that they
were also associated with a bipartisan coalition of congressional conservatives which effectively blocked expansion of
the New Deal during this period.

This work concentrates on the Insurgents' efforts in
the domestic arena. This, of course, does not mean that they
were not intensely interested in New Deal foreign policy.
In fact, their isolationistic views generally prevailed during
this era--an aspect of Insurgent progressivism that previously
has been documented well by several outstanding historians
and political scientists. By the time foreign affairs became
a major national concern in 1939, however, most of the
Insurgents already had decided that the New Deal was quite
incompatible with their view of reform. Furthermore, this
analysis deals only with the Insurgent Progressives in the
United States Senate. The reasons for this are numerous:

v

first, by the 1930's most of the prominent remaining
Insurgents were Senators; second, the Insurgents in the
Senate provide a small and a rather cohesive control group
which makes this case study more manageable and its con-
clusions more accurate; third, in most instances during
the presidency of Franklin D. Roosevelt the Senate was more
influential in policy formation than the House was; and
finally, the long six-year terms enjoyed by Senators, the
practice of nearly unlimited senatorial debate, and the
informality and intimacy of the smaller Upper Chamber allow
for both a greater continuity of personnel and a more
thorough airing of issues in the Senate than in the House
of Representatives.

For help in preparation of this study, I am indebted to
many individuals and institutions. I am grateful to the
librarians and archivists at the many libraries and historical
societies visited during my research. Special thanks are due
to the staffs at the Bancroft library, the Franklin D. Roosevelt Library, the Harlan H. Hatcher Library at the University
of Michigan, the Manuscripts Division of the Library of Congress,
and the Muskingum College Library. The Eleanor Roosevelt
Institute, the History Department at the University of Michigan,
the Mack Foundation of Indiana, Pennsylvania, and the Horace H.

Rackham School of Graduate Studies at the University of
Michigan granted financial support. I particularly wish
to acknowledge Muskingum College whose generous granting
of my sabbatical leave coincided with the final months of
research and writing. Frank Freidel of Harvard University,
the editor of the Garland series in Modern American History,
and the staff of Garland Publishing, Inc., especially Senior
Editor Ralph Carlson, provided assistance and encouragement.
Barbara George was a careful research assistant, and Marjorie
Hawkenberry typed parts of the manuscript with her usual
proficiency.

In its original form the project was a doctoral disser-
tation at the University of Michigan under the direction of
Sidney Fine, Andrew Dickson White Professor of History. To
him I owe an incalculable debt for professional guidance and
personal friendship. I have received invaluable aid from
Professor Robert M. Warner, Director of the Michigan Historical
Collections at the University of Michigan, Larry D. Engelmann
of San Jose State University, William W. Freehling of The Johns
Hopkins University, Joseph R. Kallenbach of the University of
Michigan, Shaw Livermore of the University of Michigan, and
Bernard Sternsher of Bowling Green State University of Ohio
read portions of the manuscript, and I benefited from their

suggestions. My History Department colleagues at Muskingum College, especially fellow American historian Joe L. Dubbert with whom I have taught the United States History Survey courses for the past five years and David R. Sturtevant who provided an exemplary model of professionalism, served, sometimes quite unwittingly, as sounding-boards, critics, and advisors. While gratefully recognizing the important contributions of many friends and associates, the author is solely responsible for any errors of fact or interpretation which may remain.

A preliminary summary of this research was presented at the Ohio Academy of History Spring Meeting in 1971. Major portions of chapters II and III have appeared previously as articles in Capitol Studies (Winter 1974) and in Mid-America (April 1975) respectively and are used here with their per-mission.

My wife, Sandra Cady Mulder, greatly improved the manus-cript by her intelligent reading and editing. Her tolerance, understanding and assistance were indispensable from the in-ception of this project to its completion. The dedication of this book to her is both a token of my affection and a recognition of her partnership in its creation.

Ronald A. Mulder

New Concord, Ohio

June 1978

TABLE OF CONTENTS

CHAPTER I

INTRODUCTION: INSURGENCY BEFORE 1933

Much has been written concerning the continuity or discontinuity between progressivism and the New Deal, and,
needless to say, historians have reached opposing conclu-
sions regarding the interrelationship of these two reform
movements. One uncompromising advocate of the thesis that
the New Deal was a lineal descendant of progressivism, Henry
Steele Commager, has written, "After a lapse of a decade and
a half, Franklin D. Roosevelt took up once more the program
of the Populists and Progressives and carried it to its
logical conclusion." Challenging Commager's view, Otis L.
Graham, Jr., has stated that "most progressives who survived
decided, after an initial enthusiasm, that the New Deal was
destructive of their political and social hopes for America."
Most historians, however, have avoided extreme positions on
the question and have emphasized that the New Deal both borrowed a great deal from progressivism and at the same time
differed from it in many important respects.[1]

Anyone undertaking a study of progressivism is likely
to be impressed by the widespread appeal of its reform impulse.

---

[1]Henry Steele Commager, The American Mind (New Haven,
1950), p. 347; Otis L. Graham, Jr., An Encore for Reform: The
Old Progressives and the New Deal (New York, 1967), chapt. VI.

1

In the first decade and a half of the twentieth century,
many Americans considered themselves "progressives." Such
disparate groups as Mugwumps, heads of large corporations,
owners of small businesses, trust-busters, advocates of government regulation of big business, politicians at all
levels of government, social workers, members of the various
professions, farmers, residents of small towns, and, to a
lesser extent, poor urban dwellers all seemingly enrolled
in the giant progressive crusade "to make America over."
Because of progressivism's widespread appeal, historians,
in their attempts to analyze the connection between progressivism and the New Deal, have increasingly confined their
research to the reactions to the New Deal of progressives
who survived into the 1930's and witnessed Franklin D.
Roosevelt's version of American liberalism. For example,
Sidney Fine, in his <u>Laissez Faire and the General-Welfare
State</u>, notes that certain Theodore Roosevelt-New Nationalist
progressives accepted much of the New Deal. Paul L. Silver,
on the other hand, finds that six Woodrow Wilson-New Freedom
progressives opposed the New Deal. In an article dealing
with Mary Dewson, James M. Patterson contends that many progressive social workers demonstrated a strong affinity for
New Deal reformism. Otis L. Graham, Jr., in his <u>An Encore
for Reform: The Old Progressives and the New Deal</u>, supports
Patterson's findings about social workers, but Graham contends that most progressives ultimately regarded the New
Deal's liberalism as distasteful. In his <u>Midwestern Progressive Politics</u>, Russel B. Nye concludes that the New

3

Deal's "spirit and methods" seemed "to ring false" for most
agrarian progressives.[2]

Among the American historians who have explored the in-
terconnections between progressivism and the New Deal, only
James T. Patterson has carefully studied the Congressional
careers of progressives whose tenure in office continued
into the New Deal period. Patterson, who primarily concerns
himself with the reaction to the New Deal of members of the
Democratic party, concludes that old Woodrow Wilson progressives in Congress were generally careful to disassociate
themselves from Franklin D. Roosevelt liberals. "I think
I am a progressive and I hope a sound progressive," John N.
Garner thus declared in the 1930's, "/but_7 there is a vast
difference between progressivism and /New Deal_7 makeshift."[3]

Following Patterson's example, this study seeks to
ascertain the degree of compatibility between New Deal liberalism and the progressivism of the Insurgents, a group of
primarily Republican Senators who still served in Congress during the 1930's. Insurgent Senators represented, in the main,
the states of the Pacific Northwest and the Middlewest; most
of them came from the predominantly agrarian North-Central

---

[2] Sidney Fine, Laissez Faire and the General-Welfare
State (Ann Arbor, 1956), chapt. XI; Paul L. Silver, "Wil-
sonians and the New Deal" (Ph.D. Thesis, University of Penn-
sylvania, 1964), passim.; James M. Patterson, "Mary Dewson
and the American Minimum Wage Movement," Labor History, V
(Spring, 1964), 134-44; Graham, An Encore for Reform, passim.;
Russel B. Nye, Midwestern Progressive Politics (East Lansing,
Mich., 1951), pp. 327-49.

[3] James T. Patterson, Congressional Conservatism and
the New Deal (Lexington, Ky., 1967), chapt. IV.

4

states—the Dakotas, Iowa, Kansas, Minnesota, Montana, Nebraska, and Wisconsin. During the Taft and Wilson years, the Insurgents banded together in an informal Congressional coalition to champion progressive causes and to protect the interests of American agriculture against the encroachments of industrialism.[4] Senate members of the Insurgent group at one time or another during these years included William E. Borah of Idaho, Jonathan Bourne of Oregon, Joseph L. Bristow and Arthur Capper of Kansas, Moses Clapp of Minnesota, Coe I. Crawford of South Dakota, Albert B. Cummins, Jonathan Dolliver and William S. Kenyon of Iowa, Joseph M. Dixon and Thomas J. Walsh of Montana, Asle J. Gronna of North Dakota, Robert M. LaFollette, Sr., of Wisconsin, George W. Norris of Nebraska, and John D. Works and Hiram W. Johnson of California.[5] Later, during the years of the "Republican Ascendancy" in the 1920's, John J. Blaine and Robert M. LaFollette, Jr., of Wisconsin, Smith W. Brookhart of Iowa, Edward P. Costigan of Colorado, James Couzens of Michigan, Bronson M. Cutting of New Mexico, Robert V. Howell of Nebraska, Edwin Ladd, Lynn J. Frazier, and Gerald P. Nye of North Dakota, Peter Norbeck of South Dakota, Henrik

---

[4]For brief accounts of the interrelationships between Insurgent progressivism and New Deal liberalism, see James Holt, Congressional Insurgents and the Party System, 1909-1916 (Cambridge, Mass., 1967), pp. 168-70; Kenneth Hechler, Insurgency: Personalities and Politics of the Taft Era (New York, 1940), pp. 220-26; Nye, Midwestern Progressive Politics, pp. 327-49; and Kenneth Campbell MacKay, The Progressive Movement of 1924 (New York, 1947), pp. 243-63.

[5]Among this original group of Insurgents, Borah, Capper, Johnson, and Norris were still members of the United States Senate in 1933.

Shipstead of Minnesota, and Burton K. Wheeler of Montana joined the ranks of the Insurgent Senators.[6]

According to the journalist Ray Tucker, the Insurgents possessed an instinctive sympathy for the underprivileged members of American society. Tucker's characterization applies especially to George W. Norris. As a Republican judge in Nebraska in the 1890's, Norris had an opportunity to observe the sad effects of economic deprivation on the farmers of his circuit. "During the seven years I served as a district judge," the Nebraska Insurgent later recalled, "my sympathies were broadened, my understanding of life enriched, and my conceptions of simple justice strengthened." Although Norris did not formulate any particular political philosophy, his natural concern for the economically and socially deprived led him throughout his political career to advocate government intervention to alleviate poverty whether it existed on the arid farms of the Great Plains or on the crowded sidewalks of New York City. "He is a perambulatory Declaration of Independence," Arthur Capper said of Norris.[7]

Robert M. LaFollette, Jr. gained his political experience serving as an assistant to his illustrious father.

---

[6]Among the group of Insurgents elected in the 1920's, Costigan, Couzens, Cutting, Frazier, LaFollette, Norbeck, Nye, Shipstead, and Wheeler were still members of the United States Senate in 1933.

[7]Ray Tucker and Frederick R. Barkley, Sons of the Wild Jackass (Boston, 1932), p. 6; George W. Norris, Fighting Liberal: The Autobiography of George W. Norris (Collier Books Edition: New York, 1961), p. 85; Time, XXIX (Jan. 11, 1937), 16-19.

"Young Bob" became a close personal friend of Norris, and
he shared the Nebraska Insurgent's humane sympathy for the
poor. Unlike Norris, however, LaFollette embraced a political philosophy similar to what was to become the welfare-
state liberalism of the New Deal. Early in his Senatorial
career, he advocated economic planning, national unemployment insurance, federally financed public-works projects,
and federal relief in time of economic recession. Although
one political observer critized most of the Insurgents for
their selfish interest "in grabbing for western agricultural interests a place at the federal trough," he praised
LaFollette as one of the few Insurgents who had "reshaped
and reoriented his progressive policies until they may now
be said to be national in scope."[8]

William E. Borah was probably the most independent of
the Insurgents. "There are four distinct political factions
in the United States Senate—Republicans, Democrats, Progressives, and William Edgar Borah," one pundit wrote in
1932. Although he espoused many liberal causes in his lifetime, the Idaho Senator never departed from his progressive
creed of 1907-1916—a belief that the protection of individual liberty necessitated the destruction of collective
power, economic and political. Even this outdated brand of
Jeffersonian liberalism was, however, tempered by Borah's
deep reverence for social stability. From the time of his
unsuccessful prosecution of Big Bill Haywood for his alleged

---

[8]Tucker and Barkley, Sons of the Wild Jackass, pp. 46,
152; William T. Evjue, "Young Bob," Nation, CLXXVI (March 7,
1953), 200.

murder of Frank Steunenberg in 1906 to his indictment of some
New Deal reform programs for their alleged subversion of the
traditional American political system, Borah wrapped himself
in the mantle of law and order. "During two decades when
some men grieved for lynched Negroes, German Jews, or the
peddlers of Dedham," the historian Otis L. Graham has written, "Borah grieved for the Constitution."[9]

Like the liberalism of Borah, the liberalism of two
other prominent Insurgents, Hiram W. Johnson and Burton K.
Wheeler, did not change perceptibly after 1918 from the
progressive creed that each man had espoused at the beginning of his political career. Beginning with their assaults
against big business in the Progressive Era, Johnson against
the Southern Pacific Railroad in California and Wheeler
against the Anaconda Copper Company in Montana, both men
continued in the 1920's and in the 1930's to champion the
individual and to rail against concentrated power. "In all
my political life," Johnson boasted in 1937, "I have pursued
one course,. . .and I would not if I could alter that
course."[10]

More than any of the other Insurgents, Johnson and
Wheeler enjoyed the politics of controversy. Each loved to

[9]Tucker and Barkley, Sons of the Wild Jackass, p. 70;
Jay Franklin, "The Nullification of Senator Borah," Vanity
Fair, XL (June, 1933), 16, 57, 59; Claudius O. Johnson, Borah
of Idaho (American Library Edition: Seattle, 1967), chapt.
V; Graham, An Encore for Reform, p. 182.

[10]George E. Mowry, The California Progressives (Berkeley,
1951), chapts. I-III; Burton K. Wheeler, Yankee from the West
(Garden City, N. Y., 1962), chapt. IV; Johnson to H. L. Bag-
gerly, Sept. 24, 1937, Hiram W. Johnson Papers, Part III, Box
17, Bancroft Library, University of California, Berkeley.

imagine himself fighting grandly alone against almost impossible odds to destroy all forms of collective power.
Also, both men often identified issues with personalities
and were capable of feeling deep hatred for individuals
whose liberalism, in the view of these two Insurgents, did
not measure up to their own standards. Johnson and Wheeler
were both extremely self-righteous, extraordinarily individualistic, and highly ambitious and irascible. The Progressive of the Johnson-Wheeler type, according to the historian George E. Mowry, was marked by intolerance "of opposition either within or without his own ranks. After
/each/ had held his first important office, he seemed to
demand fealty from his supporters which they were often
unable or unwilling to give."[11]

Most of the Insurgents had lived their entire lives
before they came to Washington in rural areas or in small
towns. Most of them received law degrees from midwestern
or western universities; and a small-town legal practice
usually preceded their election to Congress. Capper, Cutting, and Nye as newspaper publishers, Couzens as a wealthy
corporation executive for the Ford Motor Company, Frazier
as a farmer, Norbeck as a well-driller, and Shipstead as a
dentist were the non-lawyers in the group. Also, most of
the Insurgents had gained political experience on the state
or local level before they began their Congressional careers.
Capper, Frazier, Johnson, and Norbeck were governors of their

[11]Graham, Encore for Reform, pp. 113-16; Mowry, California Progressives, pp. 291-92.

respective states; Shipstead and Wheeler were one-term state
legislators; Norris was a Nebraska state judge; Couzens
served as police commissioner and later as mayor of Detroit;
and the other five Insurgents still serving in the Senate
in 1933 had been active in the political affairs of their
states in one capacity or another.[12]

Politically, the term "insurgent" usually referred to
the dissident Republicans in the United States Senate.
Costigan and Wheeler, who were Democrats, and Shipstead,
who was a Minnesota Farmer-Laborite, were exceptions to
this generalization. Even though numerous residents of
their states had embraced the doctrines of the Populists,
only Borah among the Insurgents had joined the Silver Republicans to support William Jennings Bryan's campaign for
the presidency in 1896. The other Insurgents, appalled by
the Great Commoner's "radicalism," chose to remain Republicans and to support the party's conservative presidential
nominee, William McKinley of Ohio. This fact is not so surprising, for in the 1890's regular Republicanism in the Insurgents' home states was still regarded with a reverence
usually reserved for religious creeds. "The men who do the
work of piety and charity in the churches," one political
analyst wrote in 1890, "the men who administer our school
systems, the men who own and till their own farms, the men
who perform skilled labor in the shops,. . .the men who went

---

[12]For brief biographical sketches of the Insurgents,
see the __Biographical__ __Directory__ __of__ __the__ __American__ __Congress__,
__1774-1949__, House Document 607, 81st Cong., 2nd Sess.

to war and stayed all through, the men who paid their debts
and kept the currency sound. . .naturally find their place
in the Republican Party. While the old slave-owner, the
saloon-keeper, the ballot-box stuffer, the Kuklux, the crim-
inal classes of the great cities. . .find their congenial
place in the Democratic Party." In the 1890's even George
Norris, who in 1936 would drop all pretense of party affiliation and would run for reelection as an Independent,
subscribed to this theory. "I then thought the Republican
Party was perfect," the Nebraska Insurgent later recalled.[13]

Although the Insurgents in the 1890's refused to abandon their commitment to Republicanism, the Populist programs
designed to alleviate rural poverty had a significant im-
pact on their thinking. As GOP office holders at the state
level during the first two decades of the twentieth century,
the Insurgents implemented many of the Populist ideas by
transforming their state Republican parties into vehicles
for progressive reform. Johnson as governor of California,
Frazier as governor of North Dakota, and LaFollette as
governor of Wisconsin supported programs of reform that included the regulation of railroads and grain exchanges,
the taxation of corporate property and gross earnings, fair-
trade and corrupt-practices laws, and the regulation of
public utilities, banks, and insurance companies. The resulting legislation seemed to validate William Allen White's

---

[13]Leonard Woolsey Bacon, "A Political Paradox,"
Forum, VIII (Feb., 1890), 676; Norris, Fighting Liberal,
p. 13.

claim that the Republican Insurgents "caught the Populists in swimming and stole all of their clothing except the frayed underdrawers of free silver."[14]

Like the Populists, the Insurgents were especially concerned about the problem of monopoly. To the Insurgents, the emergence of giant industrial and financial organizations and the accompanying concentration of wealth in the hands of the few, the growth of absentee controls and impersonal corporate relationships, and the decline of a self-employed middle class represented a perversion of American ideals. The Insurgents believed that democracy could best exist if the values of pre-industrial America, a society dominated by independent yeoman and prosperous small businessmen, were retained. If monopoly were allowed to continue its uninterrupted growth, they warned, the inevitable result would be the destruction of democratic government and individual freedom. "Monopoly is at war with democratic institutions," Borah declared in 1913, "and the conflict is as irrepressible as was the conflict between freedom and slavery."[15]

The Insurgent solution to the trust question was simple but completely impractical and totally unrealistic. Because of the grave threat monopoly presented to the American way of life, the Insurgents recommended that the national government should divide big corporations into

---

[14]Quoted in Hechler, _Insurgency_, pp. 21-22.

[15]Quoted in John M. Cooper, "William E. Borah: Political Thespian," _Pacific Northwest Quarterly_, LVI (Oct., 1965), 149.

smaller units. Ignoring all the evidence indicating that
unregulated competition had led to the formation of trusts,
the Insurgents contended that increased competition would
rid the country of the evils of monopoly. The Insurgents
argued that, by using corrupt practices and taking advantage of special privileges, big businessmen and Eastern
bankers had perverted the natural competitive processes.
The Insurgents consequently favored the enforcement of the
Sherman Antitrust Act—the 1890 statute forbidding "all
combinations in restraint of trade"—as the first step in
slowing down the trend toward the consolidation of industry.
They also called for new legislation to eliminate the unfair advantages enjoyed by concentrated wealth and to restore the beneficent reign of free competition.[16]

For the most part, the Insurgents championed what one
historian has called a rural or traditional brand of progressivism. "These progressives," said Theodore Roosevelt
in accurately describing the Insurgents in 1911, "are
really representative of a kind of rural toryism, which
wishes to attempt the impossible task of returning to the
economic conditions that obtained sixty years ago." The
Insurgents were fervent exponents of the excellence of
rural life, and they were disturbed by the threats that
industrialization and urbanization posed to an agrarian
society. They lionized the farmer as the "man who represents

---

[16]For an excellent account of Insurgent attitudes on
the trust question, see John Braeman, "Seven Progressives,"
Business History Review, XXV (Winter, 1961), 588-92.

13

the primary industry of the United States without which the
republic could not exist." On the other hand, they saw most
of the dangers to the nation as emanating from the great
cities. The urban East not only was the home of the pluto-
crats who conspired to defraud the farmer of the fruits of
his labor but was also the locus of the "new" immigrants,
the machine politicians, and the labor unionists who chal-
lenged the moral values espoused by the noble yeomen. "The
overcrowded city has always been the breeding place of crime
and immorality," one Insuregent declared in 1912. "The
slums of the cities are the places where the anarchist
thrives and where there is a lack not only of patriotism
for the country, but a lack of morality, of honesty, and of
respectability." Since they held cities and their residents
in such low esteem, the Insurgents were not likely to look
favorably upon the urban-oriented legislation of the New
Deal.[17]

Since the Insurgents believed that monopoly must be
exterminated, they were reluctant supporters of Theodore
Roosevelt's bid for the Republican presidential nomination
in 1912. Roosevelt's New Nationalism, which called for a
recognition of the inevitability of combinations in business
and for a corresponding increase in governmental power to
control large corporations, did not appeal to the Insurgents.
They supported Robert M. LaFollette, Sr., until it became

---

[17]Ibid., p. 582; George E. Mowry, The Era of Theodore
Roosevelt, 1900-1912 (New York, 1958), p. 55; William E.
Borah, "The Farmer's Enemy," Colliers, XCVII (Feb. 1, 1936)
12; Holt, Congressional Insurgents, p. 9.

evident that Roosevelt had a better chance to defeat the incumbent, William Howard Taft, for the Republican nomination.
"No man was more enthusiastic in his support of LaFollette
than I was, and yet. . .in the present contest the people
seemed to want Roosevelt," George Norris declared in ex-
plantion of the Insurgent switch to Roosevelt in 1912.[18]

Although the Insurgents endorsed Roosevelt for the
Republican nomination, most of them did not follow the
former Rough Rider into his new Progressive party after
he failed to wrest the GOP nomination from Taft. Only Hiram
Johnson, who was the vice-presidential candidate of the Bull
Moose party, Edward Costigan, and Bronson Cutting among the
later New Deal Insurgents transferred their allegiance to
the new party. The other Insurgents reasoned that there was
no point in establishing a third party in states where they
already controlled the GOP, and they realized that if they
bolted the Republican party, the party machinery in their
states would fall under the sway of the conservative Republicans. Also, the Progressive platform's espousal of the
regulation of monopoly, its acceptance of a powerful national government, and its paternalistic approach to reform
were hardly consistent with the trust-busting, states-
rights, and individualistic doctrines of the Insurgents.

The split in the Republican party in 1912 paved the
way for the election of Woodrow Wilson, the Democratic presidential candidate. Since Wilson's so-called New Freedom

---

[18]Holt, *Congressional Insurgents*, p. 55.

appeared to be an enunciation of the Insurgents' political

principles, many Washington observers predicted an alliance

between the Republican and Democratic progressives in sup-

port of the President's legislative program. This alliance,

however, did not materialize in the enactment of the four

principal measures of the New Freedom, the Underwood Tariff,

the Federal Reserve Act, the Clayton Antitrust Act, and the

Federal Trade Commission Act. James Holt has maintained

that the Insurgent failure to support the New Freedom legis-

lation in Congress was motivated primarily by intense par-

tisanship. Holt's assessment is partially correct, but there

were also substantial ideological differences between Insur-

gent progressivism and New Freedom reformism as it evolved

in Congress in 1913-1914.[19]

In explaining their reasons for not supporting the

fundamental reform measures of the New Freedom, the Insur-

gents used arguments very much like they were later to use

in opposing portions of the New Deal. The Insurgent crit-

icism of the Underwood Tariff because it allegedly discrim-

inated against agriculture in favor of the manufacturing

interests was to be repeated in the Insurgent censure of

the New Deal's reciprocal trade agreements program two decades

later. The Insurgents complained that the Federal Reserve

Act left the nation's banking system in the hands of the

bankers, and they were later to make similar charges against

---

[19]Ibid., pp. 81-120; Howard W. Allen, "Geography
and Politics: Voting on Reform Issues in the United States
Senate, 1911-1916," Journal of Southern History, XXVII (May,
1961), 216-26.

the Emergency Banking Act of 1933 and the Banking Act of
1935. Insurgent apprehension over the Clayton Act and the
Federal Trade Commission Act, the core of the New Freedom
reform program, was matched by identical doubts regarding
the National Industrial Recovery Act and the proliferation
of the federal bureaucracy under the New Deal.

Contemporary political observers were at a loss to
explain Insurgent criticism of the Clayton and Federal Trade
Commission Acts. The Insurgents, however, regarded both
measures as a "sell-out" to the monopolists. They complained that such provisions of the Clayton Act as the ban
on interlocking directorates and intercorporate stockholdings
had been so diluted by conservatives in the Senate that it
was safe to conclude that the Wilson administration was
abjectly subservient to Wall Street. The Insurgents opposed the Federal Trade Commission Act because it seemed
to them to be accepting the New Nationalism's solution for
the trust question in its acceptance of a powerful regulatory commission.[20]

The Insurgents not only opposed the Federal Trade
Commission Act because they feared that it called for the
regulation of trusts rather than for their destruction, but
they also maintained that the new trade commission would
remove government from the people and would grant excessive
power to the federal government. Faith in popular government was a vital component of Insurgent progressivism.

---

[20]*Congressional Record*, 63rd Cong., 2nd Sess., pp.
16043-56; Arthur S. Link, *Woodrow Wilson and the Progressive
Era, 1910-1917* (New York, 1954), p. 70.

Their campaign against House Speaker Joseph G. Cannon in 1909-1910 and their support of such electoral techniques as the direct primary, the direct election of Senators, the initiative, recall, and referendum were predicated upon the thesis that the extension of "peoples' rule" would rid the nation of the clandestine "private interests." It is not surprising, therefore, that the Insurgents did not look kindly upon a measure that called for the creation of a commission of non-elected officials to regulate trusts. The Insurgents similarly favored the use of the Sherman Antitrust Act to destroy monopoly because this could theo-retically be accomplished without creating new federal agencies. They regarded a powerful state to be as dangerous a threat to individual liberty as private monopoly was. "Their central fear was a fear of power," Walter Lippmann wrote of the Insurgents. "They opposed all concentrations of power,. . .private privilege and private monopoly /as well as7 political bureaucracy and centralized government."[21]

The Insurgents not only criticized the legislation of the New Freedom, but they were also critical of Wilson's performance as president. In criticizing Wilson's behavior as president, they used arguments which they were to repeat in the 1930's when Franklin D. Roosevelt was the nation's Chief Executive. The Insurgents complained that Wilson was not a true progressive, that he filled government posts with party henchmen, and that he relied on the conservative Democratic leadership to guide his program through Congress.

---

[21]Cooper, "Borah," p. 148.

Many Insurgents claimed that Wilson did not consult Congress
at all but rather dictated his program to the legislators.
"Wilson. . .rules with an arbitrariness no other President
has ever approached," one Insurgent lamented. "His program,
whatever, it may be, must be carried out by Congress to the
letter."[22]

The Insurgents were especially critical of Wilson's
foreign policy, of his conduct both in war and peace. The
isolationist-minded Insurgents were fundamentally opposed
to American involvement in the European conflict, and they
also were suspicious of Wilson's reasons for leading the
nation into war. "Wilson," Hiram Johnson wrote in 1918,
"sees himself. . .as the savior of mankind, as a ruler who
freed all nations, and established world democracy. . . .
But in my opinion, he has taken us into war with one thought—
to have history write him the greatest man of all time. . . .
I do not think it at all exaggerative to say that he regards himself exactly as Louis XIV regarded himself, and
that while he doesn't say it aloud, to himself he often
repeats, 'I am the state.'"[23]

Many historians have contended that progressivism was
a casualty of America's entry into World War I. These
scholars have concluded that the disillusionment resulting
from the war and the Versailles Treaty led Americans to reject Wilson's idealism in favor of Harding's "normalcy."

[22]Johnson to Hiram Johnson, Jr., and Archibald Johnson, April 6, 1917, Johnson Papers, Part IV, Box 1.

[23]Johnson to Hiram Johnson, Jr., and Archibald Johnson, Jan. 26, 1918, Johnson Papers, Part IV, Box 1.

The record of the United States in the 1920's seemed to substantiate the view that the progressive reform impulse was indeed dead.[24]

Although conceding that the mass hysteria and the deep hatreds generated by the war contributed to the "liquidation of the progressive spirit," Richard Hofstadter has maintained that a "dark" side of progressivism flourished during the 1920's. According to Hofstadter, immigration restriction, the Scopes Trial, and prohibition were supported by the "rural-evangelical" progressives who were trying to protect the old-time morality from the encroachments of aliens, industrialization, and urbanization. In Hofstadter's opinion, the progressive "successes" of the 1920's revealed that reform objectives often were not synonymous with liberal objectives.[25]

Since the Insurgents were rural progressives who supported immigration restriction and, with a few exceptions, favored prohibition, they apparently qualify as representatives of the "dark" side of progressivism. The Insurgents, however, denied that either of these two movements was repressive in intent. They contended that the exclusion of certain types of immigrants and the adoption of prohibition would help to improve the quality of American life.[26] Quite

---

[24]William E. Leuchtenberg, The Perils of Prosperity, 1914-32 (Chicago, 1958), pp. 120-39.

[25]Richard Hofstadter, The Age of Reform: From Bryan to F.D.R. (New York, 1955), pp. 272-302.

[26]Lawrence W. Levine, Defender of the Faith; William Jennings Bryan: The Last Decade, 1915-1925 (New York, 1965); Arthur S. Link, "What Happened to the Progressive Movement

apart from this, in their efforts to pass new farm legislation, expose corruption in government, maintain a graduated
taxation policy, and create a government-operated power
system in the Tennessee Valley, they demonstrated that there
was another dimension to their progressivism.[27]

For the majority of American farmers the decade of
the 1920's was largely one of economic depression. Agriculture's problems could be traced back to the war, when the
farmers had expanded their output to feed much of Europe.
The loss of these European markets after the war led to the
accumulation of a large surplus of agricultural products.
Continued overproduction contributed to a decline in
the price of agricultural commodities; from 1919 to 1921
gross farm income fell by about $7 billion. The Wilson
administration failed to do anything decisive to halt the
downward plunge of farm prices, and the business-dominated
Republican administrations of the 1920's did not come to
grips with the problem either. Irked that they could not
gain the legislation they desired from Washington and
believing that America was being industrialized and urbanized
at their expense, many farmers, especially those in the
wheat-producing states of the Great Plains, turned to protest activities. Agricultural discontent and a postwar
recession placed Norbeck in the Senate in 1920, and he was

---

in the 1920's?" American Historical Review, LXIV (July, 1959),
833-51.

[27]David Burner, The Politics of Provincialism: The
Democratic Party in Transition, 1918-1932 (New York, 1968),
chapt. VI, maintains that the Insurgents were the most progressive members in the Congresses of the 1920's.

later joined by Brookhart, Couzens, Frazier, "Young Bob"
LaFollette, Nye, Shipstead, and Wheeler.[28]

Although most of the Insurgents would later complain
that the New Deal catered to special-interest groups instead
of legislating in the national interest, they spent much of
their time and energy in the 1920's securing favorable
legislation for American agriculture.[29] On May 9, 1921,
most of the Insurgents met with a bipartisan group of Senators in the Washington office of the American Farm Bureau
Federation to organize the Farm Bloc to secure the passage
of agricultural legislation. From 1921-1924 the Farm Bloc,
often despite opposition from within the Harding and
Coolidge administrations, succeeded in enacting measures
designed to benefit agriculture. Congress approved high
tariffs on farm products, federal regulation of stock yards,
packing houses, and grain exchanges, the exemption of agricultural cooperatives from the provisions of the antitrust
laws, the stimulation of the export of farm commodities,
and a government system to provide intermediate rural credit.[30]

---

[28]Seward W. Livermore, "The Sectional Issue in the 1918
Congressional Elections," Mississippi Valley Historical Re-
view, XXXV (June, 1948), 29-60; Arthur S. Link, "The Federal
Reserve Policy and the Agricultural Depression of 1920-1921,"
Agricultural History, XX (July, 1946), 166-75; Robert L.
Morlan, Political Prairie Fire: The Nonpartisan League, 1915-
1922 (Minneapolis, 1955).

[29]Of course, the Insurgents maintained that since agriculture was the country's basic industry, farm subsidies were
really in the national interest.

[30]Arthur Capper, The Agricultural Bloc (New York, 1922);
James H. Shideler, Farm Crisis, 1919-1923 (Berkeley, Calif.,
1957).

The agricultural legislation of 1921-1924 failed,
however, to restore farm prosperity, and most of the Insurgents consequently lent their support to a new farm relief
plan authored by George Peek. The basic idea behind the
Peek proposal was the concept of "parity"—the economic
equality of agriculture and industry. The plan called for
the federal government to establish a two-price system for
American agricultural products. The "fair exchange" or the
"parity" price was the price that would be achieved for
farm commodities in the American market. It was assumed
that the price for individual farm commodities would increase to the extent afforded by the tariff on those commodities if the surplus of such crops could be absorbed by
the government from the domestic market and disposed of
abroad at the world price. The loss the government incurred
in selling the surplus abroad at the "export price" was to
be made up by some form of equalization tax imposed upon the
farmers. The general scheme was embodied in the so-called
McNary-Haugen bills of the 1920's, versions of which were
approved by Congress in 1927 and 1928. Both bills, however,
were vetoed by Coolidge on the grounds that price fixing
was economically unsound and blatantly un-American.[31]

The Insurgents scoffed at Coolidge's contention that
McNary-Haugenism was economically unsound. "The fact of
the matter is," Hiram Johnson declared, "Coolidge would not
know an economic policy if he met it on the street." The

---

[31]For an excellent account of the battle for McNary-
Haugenism in the 1920's, see Gilbert C. Fite, George N.
Peek and the Fight for Farm Parity (Norman, Okla., 1954).

Insurgents believed that the farmers and other distressed groups could not receive aid from a government so inbred with the ideology of businessmen. Secretary of Commerce Herbert Hoover and Secretary of the Treasury Andrew Mellon, after all, were quick to point out to Coolidge that the actions of the Farm Bloc might be potentially harmful to the administration's more urgent objective of aiding business.[32]

The Coolidge administration's attempt to establish a business-government alliance was most evident in the Treasury Department, where Andrew Mellon campaigned vigorously to reduce the tax on large personal and corporate incomes. Shortly after accepting his cabinet post, Mellon announced that his department would be "run on business principles." This meant paying off the national debt, balancing the budget, and, most important, reducing the rate of taxation on high incomes. In 1921, at Mellon's instigation, Congress repealed the wartime excess-profits tax, but an Insurgent-Democratic coalition managed to retain the existing tax rates in the higher income brackets. Insisting that existing taxes on wealth were confiscatory, the Secretary of the Treasury succeeded in 1924 in persuading Congress to cut the maximum surtax rate from 65 to 40 per cent. The 1924 tax bill, however, also contained some provisions which represented significant victories for the

[32]Johnson to Hiram Johnson, Jr., and Archibald Johnson, July 2, 1926, Johnson Papers, Part IV, Box 2; Robert K. Murray, The Harding Era (Minneapolis, 1969), chapt. VII.

Insurgents. They persuaded Congress to levy the highest
estate tax in American history, to impose a new gift tax,
and to make tax returns available for public scrutiny.
Mellon, however, persevered, and his efforts were largely
successful. The Treasury Department covertly gave rebates
to wealthy taxpayers and advised them how to avoid paying
certain taxes. The Revenue Act of 1926 eliminated the gift
tax, cut the estate tax in half, and reduced the maximum
surtax rate from 40 to 20 per cent. In 1928, finally, Congress lowered corporation taxes.[33]

LaFollette detested the Mellon tax program, contending
that it demonstrated that "wealth will not and cannot be
made to bear its full share of taxation." In their struggle against Mellon, however, the Insurgents were hampered
by the fact that their arguments for the retention of high
tax rates were largely negative in character. In advocating
graduated tax rates on high incomes, the primary objective
of the Insurgents was to deflate "swollen fortunes." Although many of the Insurgents favored a redistribution of
wealth, they failed, apart from their espousal of farm
subsidies, to formulate social and economic programs that
would augment consumer purchasing power. Also, as during
the New Deal period, most of the Insurgents in the 1920's
favored a balanced budget. Since the Insurgents failed to

[33]See Arthur M. Schlesinger, Jr., The Crisis of the
Old Order, 1919-1933 (Boston, 1957), Part II; Sidney Ratner,
American Taxation: Its History as a Social Force in Demo-
cracy (New York, 1942).

devise programs for large-scale government spending to distribute the mounting Treasury surplus, their arguments for
high tax rates proved vulnerable to Mellon's appeal for
lower taxes.[34]

In addition to farm subsidies, the Insurgents favored
an expansion of federal authority and an increase in public
spending in the area of hydro-electric power. The most
significant Insurgent legislative accomplishment of the
1920's was probably their successful fight to prevent the
Republican presidents from turning over to private interests
the federal power site at Muscle Shoals in the Tennessee
Valley. During World War I, the government built two power
plants at Muscle Shoals and began the construction of Wilson
Dam in order to convert nitrates into explosives. When he
became president, Harding ordered all construction on Wilson
Dam halted and announced his intention to sell the entire
Muscle Shoals project to private enterprise. In response
to the government's request, Henry Ford offered to lease
the project for a fraction of the cost of the original in-
vestment. Herbert Hoover praised Ford's offer as a display
of "real business courage," but George Norris referred to
it as an attempt to defraud the government. From 1921 to
1925 Norris, as chairman of the Senate Agriculture Committee,
almost single-handedly blocked the attempt to sell the Muscle Shoals development to Ford. Norris himself sponsored

---

[34]Quoted in John D. Hicks, Republican Ascendancy,
1921-1933 (New York, 1960), p. 53; Leuchtenberg, Perils of
Prosperity, pp. 136-39.

the creation of a government corporation to develop the
power site for the benefit of the people of the area. The
Nebraska Senator was twice able to get his plan through Congress, but Coolidge pocket-vetoed the first Norris bill in
1928, and Hoover vetoed a similar measure in 1929 as "a
negation of the ideals upon which our civilization is
based."[35]

Despite their opposition to many of the policies of
the Harding and Coolidge administrations, few of the Insurgents renounced their loyalty to the Republican party in
the 1920's. Only Lynn Frazier, George Norris, and Gerald
Nye among the Republican Insurgents supported Robert
LaFollette's 1924 bid for the presidency on the Progressive
party ticket.[36] When Herbert Hoover, the chief proponent
of a businessman's government and the chief opponent of
both McNary-Haugenism and what became the Tennessee Valley
Authority (TVA), captured the GOP nomination in 1928, only
Norris among the Republican Insurgents bolted his party to
support Al Smith, the Democratic candidate. Many of Norris'
fellow GOP Insurgents did not favor Hoover's election, but
they could not bring themselves to endorse Smith. "I agree
that the Republican party deserves a thorough whipping,"

---

[35]Richard Lowitt, "A Neglected Aspect of the Progressive Movement: George W. Norris and the Public Control of
Hydro-electric Power, 1913-1919," The Historian, LVII (May,
1965), 350-65; Preston J. Hubbard, Origins of the TVA: The
Muscle Shoals Controversy, 1920-1932 (Nashville, Tenn.,
1961).

[36]MacKay, The Progressive Movement of 1924, chapt. X.
Burton K. Wheeler, a Democratic Insurgent, served as
LaFollette's vice-presidential candidate.

Nye wrote, "but if I must help administer that whipping at
the expense of rewarding Smith and Tammany I must postpone
that whipping." Nye's views suggest that Smith was not an
appealing candidate for rural Americans, but the farm states
nevertheless gave him more votes than they had given any
Democratic presidential nominee since Woodrow Wilson in
1916.[37]

Once he assumed the presidency, Hoover quickly pro-
ceeded to alienate what little Insurgent support he possessed.
Some of the Insurgents, most notably William E. Borah, had
endorsed Hoover because he promised to seek the enactment
of a new farm program.[38] To redeem a campaign pledge to
Borah, Hoover called a special session of Congress in 1929
to deal with the crisis in American agriculture. The Agricultural Marketing Act that was enacted by the special session did not, however, please the Insurgents, who maintained
that it was more beneficial to the manufacturing interests
than to the farmers. Borah felt betrayed, and he joined
other Insurgents and some Democratic Senators in opposition
to what he called a "standpat" measure.[39]

---

[37]Gilbert C. Fite, "The Agricultural Issue in the
Presidential Campaign of 1928," Mississippi Valley Historical Review, XXVII (March, 1951), p. 668; Richard Hofstadter, "Could a Protestant Have Beaten Hoover in 1928?"
Reporter, March 17, 1960, pp. 31-3.

[38]Borah had been the only Insurgent opposed to the
McNary-Haugen plan for agriculture. See Darrel LeRoy Ashby,
"Progressivism Against Itself: The Senate Western Bloc in
the 1920's," Mid-America Historical Review, L (October,
1968), 291-304.

[39]Claudius O. Johnson, Borah, chapt. XXII.

The Hoover administration's response to the 1929 stock market crash and the ensuing depression disappointed the Insurgents further. Hoover initially contended that the depression was nothing more than a temporary aberration in an otherwise healthy economy, and, consequently, he did nothing to combat it. As the economic slump deepened, however, he advised the Federal Reserve Board to relax its credit controls, urged the Farm Board to buy up surplus agricultural commodities, urged state and local governments to expand the construction of public works, invited employers to Washington to importune them not to reduce wages or to discharge employees, and predicted that "prosperity was just around the corner." Hiram Johnson could not fathom Hoover's reaction to the depression. "The President is the prince of the bunk artists," the California Senator wrote his sons. "He calls those here who have much and have lost little. They make speeches from the White House steps that business is sound, . . . that prosperity is with us, and tell those who have lost their all that it is quite for the best, and they will soon recover it."[40]

As the depression continued, it became apparent to the Insurgents that the economy was far from sound, and they realized that "pep talks" did not feed hungry people or restore lost jobs. To alleviate the economic crisis, LaFollette and Costigan sponsored a federal relief bill, and Cutting advocated a program of federally financed public

---

[40]Johnson to Hiram Johnson, Jr., Nov. 23, 1929, Johnson Papers, Part IV, Box 3.

works. Both of these relief measures, however, were defeated by Congressional supporters of the Hoover administration. The President, who favored local relief efforts even though most communities were financially insolvent, maintained that federal relief would bankrupt the national government, under-mine local self-government, and destroy individual initia-tive. The Insurgents themselves shared many of Hoover's concerns, but they believed that it was more important to feed the hungry than to uphold the principles the President was allegedly defending. Costigan wondered what "curious alchemy" led Hoover to conclude that federal relief was more destructive of individual initiative than was local relief.[41]

Hoover recognized the need for some kind of federal relief by the middle of 1931, but he did not favor the type of relief being urged by the Insurgents. Since the President was a firm believer in the beneficence of business, he recommended that the government come to the aid of private enterprise. Hoover reasoned that if business recovered, the ensuing prosperity would "trickle down" to the masses. In January, 1932, Congress, in response to the President's request, created the Reconstruction Finance Corporation (RFC) and authorized it to loan $2 billion to banks, cor-porations, and railroads. Hiram Johnson called the RFC appropriation a "dole to the bankers." LaFollette deplored

---

[41]For a good legislative history of the LaFollette-Costigan relief bills in the 72nd Congress, see Fred Green-baum, "Edward Prentis Costigan: Study of a Progressive" (Ph.D. Thesis, University of Colorado, 1962), pp. 331-56.

what he called a double standard: "rugged individualism"
for corporations and "ragged individualism" for destitute
Americans. The Wisconsin Senator renewed his efforts to
provide federal relief for individuals, and an Insurgent-
Democratic coalition pushed through the Emergency Relief
and Construction Act later in 1932 authorizing the RFC to
loan $300 million to the states for relief. Although the
RFC provided much needed aid to some states, by the end of
the year it had alloted only one-tenth of its relief
money.[42]

The Insurgents by 1931 were completely dissatisfied
with the Hoover administration's efforts to combat the depression. "Our President is in such complete sympathy with
monopoly and organized wealth that. . .the common individual can expect no help from the White House," George Norris
declared. To remedy what they regarded as a deplorable
state of affairs, the Insurgents recommended that the Republican party replace Hoover with a progressive candidate in
1932. It soon became evident, however, that the conservative GOP leadership had no intention of deposing Hoover to
placate the Insurgents. "He is more unpopular than Judas
Iscariot," a frustrated Hiram Johnson wrote of Hoover in
December, 1931. "Practically nobody thinks he can be

[42]Mauritz H. Hallgren, "Young Bob LaFollette," Nation,
CXXXII (March 4, 1931), 235-37; Schlesinger, Crisis of the
Old Order, pp. 236-41.

31

re-elected, /but/ the Republicans in their hysterical mad-
ness will take their orders and renominate him."[43]

Realizing the impossibility of persuading the Republican party to rid itself of Herbert Hoover, many Insurgents
began to look to the Democratic party for a progressive
presidential candidate in 1932. George Norris had stated,
as early as 1930, that "we of the progressive faith must
look to the Democratic party." At a conference of Progressives on March 11-12, 1931, in Washington, Norris revealed
that Governor Franklin D. Roosevelt of New York was the
Democratic candidate he preferred. The Nebraska Insurgent
told a cheering audience, "What the country needs is. . .
another Roosevelt."[44] Hiram Johnson agreed and cited
Roosevelt's fight against the private utility magnates and
in behalf of public electric power as evidence of his progressivism. "The one thing that draws to Roosevelt those
of us who believe in real democracy is the character of
the opposition against him," the California Senator wrote.
"This opposition embraces all who believe in the right to
exploit government for their own selfish advantages." The
Insurgents were also satisfied that Roosevelt understood
the urgent necessity for federal unemployment relief and
for greater government efforts to deal with the problems

---

[43]Norris to J. D. Ream, March 24, 1931, George W.
Norris Papers, Tray 8, Box 4, Library of Congress, Washing-
ton, D. C.; Johnson to Charles K. McClatchy, Dec. 1, 1931,
Johnson Papers, Part III, Box 13.

[44]Alfred Lief, Democracy's Norris (New York, 1939)
pp. 388-94; Proceedings of a Conference of Progressives.
Held at Washington, D. C., March 11 and 12, 1931 (Washington, D. C.), p. 127.

of agriculture. George Peek, the chief exponent of the McNary-Haugen farm program, predicted that American farmers were "doomed to peasantry" if Roosevelt were not elected president in 1932.[45]

For his part, Roosevelt did everything that he could to cultivate Insurgent support. He praised Insurgent support of progressive legislation in the 72nd Congress, renounced any intention to sponsor American entry into the League of Nations, and endorsed government development of the Muscle Shoals power sites. Recognizing the low opinion that the Insurgents and other disaffected Republicans had of the Democratic party, Roosevelt promised to run as a progressive rather than solely as a Democrat. This pledge led George Norris to form a nonpartisan organization to marshal liberal Republican and independent voters behind Roosevelt—the National Progressive Republican League to Support Franklin D. Roosevelt for President in 1932 (NPL). Costigan, Cutting, LaFollette, Johnson, Shipstead, and Wheeler worked with Norris through the NPL to support Roosevelt. Couzens, Frazier, Norbeck, and Nye did not join the NPL or endorse Roosevelt, but each of them announced that he did not favor Hoover's reelection. Only Borah and Capper among the Insurgents endorsed Hoover in 1932.[46]

---

[45] Johnson to Hiram Johnson, Jr., and Archibald Johnson, May 1, 1932, Johnson Papers, Part IV, Box 3; Fite, Peek, p. 239.

[46] Paul Y. Anderson, "Roosevelt Woos the Progressives: Insurgency Goes Democratic," Nation, CXXXV (Oct. 12, 1932), 331; New York Times, Sept. 24, 1932, p. 1; Marty Hamilton, "Bull Moose Plays an Encore: Hiram Johnson and the

Roosevelt swept the traditionally Republican states
of the Middlewest and West enroute to capturing the presidency from Hoover in the 1932 election. Most of the Insurgents were jubilant over Roosevelt's triumph; Norris told
reporters that he had not been so happy over the outcome of
a national election since Theodore Roosevelt's victory in
1904. Pleased with the part the NPL had played in lining
up liberal Republican votes for the Democratic Roosevelt,
Norris desired to keep the League in operation as part of
an Insurgent effort to secure the enactment of progressive
legislation and to promote the election of progressive
candidates. In line with this view, a conference of progressives convened in Washington in February, 1933, to discuss the feasibility of forming a permanent progressive
organization. The endeavor failed, however, largely, as
Norris indicated, because the Insurgents "refused to play
follow the leader." Most of the Insurgents believed that
to join such an organization would somehow limit their independence in the United States Senate; they preferred to
make their individual judgment on issues and candidates
rather than to be bound by the wishes of any organization.
"I am very glad to be a bloc of one," Hiram Johnson declared, "and in the remainder of my official life I shall
continue a bloc of one." Seasoned political observers concluded that the personality of the President-elect was the
only real tie between many of the Insurgents and the new

administration, and they predicted that progressive support
for the proposed "new deal" would disappear if the Insurgents ever lost their trust in Roosevelt.[47]

[47]Richard L. Neuberger, and Stephen B. Kahn, Integrity:
The Life of George W. Norris (New York, 1937), p. 307;
Donald R. McCoy, "The Progressive National Committee of
1936," Western Political Quarterly, IX (June, 1956), pp.
454-57; Johnson to Charles K. McClatchy, Dec. 1, 1932, Johnson Papers, Part III, Box 13; Nye, Midwestern Progressive
Politics, pp. 325-26.

CHAPTER II

INSURGENT PROGRESSIVISM AND THE FIRST NEW DEAL, 1933-1934

At a critical moment in history, American voters had
armed Franklin D. Roosevelt with a mandate to alleviate the
country's economic woes. William Allen White, respected
editor of the Emporia Gazette, recognized the new President
as America's only hope and asserted that "democracy is sick
abed. . ./and/ needs a shot in the arm of temporarily centralized power. . . ." Former New York Governor Al Smith
was quick to point out that the depression was more of an
emergency than "the great war of 1917 and 1918. . ./and/ in
the World War we took our Constitution, wrapped it up and
laid it on the shelf and left it there until it was over."
After receiving Roosevelt's assurance that he desired to
maintain cordial relations with the Insurgents, Hiram
Johnson suggested that the President "have his program
ready, present it with a bang, and if he believed in it,
shove it through at all hazards."[1]

---

[1]White to Allen Nevins, March 15, 1933, quoted in
Walter Johnson (ed.), Selected Letters of William Allen
White, 1899-1943 (New York, 1945), pp. 330-31; New York
Times, Feb. 8, 1933, p. 1; Johnson to Charles K. McClatchy,
Jan. 29, 1933, Hiram W. Johnson Papers, Part III, Box 14,
Bancroft Library, University of California, Berkeley.
Johnson was worried, however. "If by the time Roosevelt's
special session meets," he wrote to his son, "there has not
been some little improvement, my guess is that you will see

35

Roosevelt acted on Johnson's advice, and his performance received commendation from all but his most extreme opponents. Endowed with substantial Democratic majorities in both Houses of Congress, the President encountered no effective partisan opposition. In fact, all but the most reactionary Republicans expressed a desire to help him whenever possible. The House Republican leader, Bertrand H. Snell of New York, announced that his party's policy would be "to stand squarely behind the Democratic Administration in support of legislation to better conditions."[2]

The Republican party in Congress was, as a matter of fact, badly divided, especially in the Senate, where many of the Progressive group had openly supported Roosevelt's 1932 election. Indicative of Republican weakness was the GOP's refusal to expel Insurgent bolters from the party or bar them from committee assignments, as it had done when some of these same men endorsed Robert LaFollette, Sr's., candidacy on the Progressive party ticket in 1924. The new minority leader in the Senate, Charles L. McNary from Oregon, realized that the Republicans' enfeebled position called for a new party strategy. Instead of appearing to

---

some of the most bizarre and fantastic legislation that was ever enacted. The Democrats have already been submitting some plan by which dictatorial powers would be given to the President. . . . We are. . .much closer to a sort of dictatorship in this country than we have ever been during any of our lives." Johnson to Archibald Johnson, Feb. 12, 1933, Johnson Papers, Part IV, Box 4.

[2]Quoted in E. Pendleton Herring, "First Session of the 73rd Congress," American Political Science Review, XVIII (Feb., 1934), 67.

ignore the election returns by making a frontal attack on
Roosevelt's legislative program, McNary wisely persuaded his
charges to follow a policy of silent cooperation. To
columnist Arthur Krock, who feared the passing of two-party
government, McNary's strategy of cooperation with the
Democrats appeared to be self-defeating. "These 'liberal'
Republicans are not working for the ultimate reorganization
of the Republican party but for its more complete disor-
ganization," Krock concluded.[3]

The most influential weapon in the Democratic arsenal
to combat the depression was probably Roosevelt himself.
His affable personality and his unique sense of political
timing charmed friend and foe alike. "You'll never know
the appeal of that man Roosevelt, individually and personally; the hardest man in the world to say 'no' to who ever
lived," recalled Gerald P. Nye. Hiram Johnson thought that
Roosevelt had been the recipient of some supernatural dis-
pensation. "The Lord gave him a remarkable disposition,"
the Senator reported. "I don't think he has any nervous

---

[3]Hiram Johnson, for one, expected the Regular
Republicans to get rid of the Insurgents. "If I were in
charge of the Republican Party I would eliminate immediately
those who would not bow to its discipline, and while I will
raise Cain with the gentlemen who are managing the present
movement, I have a sort of feeling that they are justified
in their activities." Johnson to Charles K. McClatchy,
Feb. 26, 1933, Johnson Papers, Part III, Box 14. For an
elaboration of McNary's role, see Walter K. Roberts, "The
Political Career of Charles Linza McNary, 1924-1944" (Ph.D.
Thesis, University of North Carolina, 1953), pp. 172-77.
Roberts correctly concluded that McNary, "by effectively
leading the small group of Republicans to follow his tactics,
was later credited with the political salvation of the national organization," p. 172. Krock's remark is found in the
New York Times, Dec. 31, 1934, p. 12.

system. If he has, there is no evidence it disturbs under
any circumstances at any time his serenity."[4]

Even though his party clearly possessed an extraordi-
nary President, Nevada's Senator Key Pittman had predicted
that Democrats, since they had been out of power for so long,
would not easily play follow the leader. By 1939, however,
Pittman, too, was convinced. "No President. . .ever had
thrust upon him any more crucial problems than you have
struggled with under the most adverse conditions for six
long years," he wrote to Roosevelt. "I marvel at your great
mental and physical strength that has sustained you in the
heart-rending fight." If personal charm failed, the President fell back on his finely attuned political senses, as
exhibited repeatedly during the "first hundred days." "We
thought that the President's cousin, Theodore, in some
degree was able at this sort of thing," exclaimed the
Saturday Evening Post, "but he was a mere amateur compared
to this super-politician now in the White House." Finally,
Roosevelt used the iron club of patronage to force job-
hungry Congressmen into line.[5] Armed with such personal

---

[4]Gerald P. Nye Lecture Series, "North Dakota and the
New Deal" (University of North Dakota, Nov. 15, 1967), Tape
MR 69 (1), Franklin D. Roosevelt Papers, Franklin D. Roose-
velt Library, Hyde Park, New York; Johnson to Hiram Johnson,
Jr., and Archibald Johnson, Feb. 19, 1933, Johnson Papers,
Part IV, Box 4.

[5]James T. Patterson, Congressional Conservatism and
the New Deal (Lexington, Ky., 1967), p. 1; Pittman to
Roosevelt, August 9, 1939, Roosevelt Papers, President's
Secretary File (PSF) 62; Samuel G. Blythe, "New Deal
Politics," Saturday Evening Post, CCVII (Sept. 22, 1934),
94. See Raymond Moley, After Seven Years (New York, 1939),

and political assets, Roosevelt, on March 4, 1933, appeared
certain to dominate the upcoming special session of Congress.

As Roosevelt took the oath of office, Arthur Krock
reported that the atmosphere in Washington was like that
"in a beleaguered capital in war time." Inauguration Day,
March 4, 1933, was not very pleasant; the dark, dreary
weather seemed symbolic of the nation's economic future.
After accepting the reins of government from a disconsolate
Herbert Hoover, the new President, however, asserted his
firm belief that "the only thing we have to fear is fear
itself" and promised vigorous leadership because "this Nation
asks for action and action now."[6]

The New Deal's first target was the banking system.
The depression had exposed the fragility of the country's
banking structure, and subsequent investigations had revealed the malpractices of many prominent financiers. As
bank after bank closed its doors, jittery depositors with-
drew their savings from those institutions that still remained open. Aggravating this already disastrous state of
affairs was the absence of adequate federal supervision.
Predictably, Washington was besieged with pleas for governmental intervention. Equipped with the somewhat dubious
authority Attorney General Homer Cummings had found for
him in the Trading with the Enemy Act of 1917, Roosevelt, on

---

pp. 127-28, for a description of the administration's handling of patronage.

[6]New York Times, March 5, 1933, p. 1; Samuel Rosenman
(ed.), The Public Papers and Addresses of Franklin D.
Roosevelt (13 vols., New York, 1938-1950), II, 11-16.

Sunday, March 5, responded by proclaiming a national bank
holiday. At the same time he called for Congress to convene
in special session on March 9, presumably to ratify some
sort of emergency banking measure.

The President commissioned his Secretary of the Treasury, William Woodin, to draft the appropriate banking
legislation. Working around the clock for nearly five con-
secutive days, Woodin finally completed his task. "Yes, it's
finished," he quipped to newspapermen. "Both bills are
finished. You know my name is Bill and I'm finished too."
On the eve of the opening of Congress, Roosevelt scheduled
a White House meeting to explain the bill to a select group
of Congressional leaders. Among them was Hiram Johnson,
who, although agreeing to vote for the bill, was chagrined
by its failure to punish the bankers. "I have one fundamental view," Johnson wrote to a friend, "that we can allay
the present fear and restore the confidence of our people if
the whole Wall Street crew is neck and crock thrown into the
street. . . . This was my contribution to the meeting Wed-
nesday night." Unscheduled visitors of the President that
same evening included Insurgent Senators Edward P. Costigan
and Robert M. LaFollette, Jr., both of whom implored Roosevelt to use the opportunity before him to establish a truly
national banking system. The President, however, would not
listen. "That isn't necessary at all," LaFollette later
recalled his saying. "I've just had every assurance of cooperation from the bankers."[7]

---

[7]Ernest K. Lindley, The Roosevelt Revolution (New
York, 1933), p. 87; Johnson to John Francis Neylan, March 10,

The following afternoon the banking bill was introduced in the House of Representatives. Since there had not
been enough time to have copies printed, no one other than
the few leaders present at the White House the night before
had even seen the legislation. Minority Leader Snell,
nevertheless, immediately asked for Republican support and
declared, "The House is burning down, and the President of
the United States says this is the way to put out the fire."[8]
This touched off cries of "vote, vote!" and only thirty-
eight minutes after it had been introduced, the bill passed
the House by acclamation and was whisked on to the Senate.

The Senate approved the banking bill a few hours
after receiving the measure, and the President signed it into
law that same evening. Six Insurgents either voted against
or announced against the bill, while three others, Cutting,
Frazier, and Wheeler, chose not to record their protests.
The Insurgents were in the minority, however, as most Americans hailed Roosevelt as the savior of capitalism. Also
important was the fact that the President's quick and decisive action served as a morale booster to a despondent
populace. "In one week," observed Walter Lippmann, "the
nation, which had lost confidence in every thing and everybody, has regained confidence in the government and in
itself." Although the Insurgents praised Roosevelt's
courageous leadership, they left no doubt about their

1933, Johnson Papers, Part III, Box 14; Arthur M. Schlesinger,
Jr., The Coming of the New Deal (Boston, 1958), p. 5.

[8]Quoted in Herring, "First Session of the 73rd Congress," p. 70.

42

dissatisfaction with the first legislative product of the
New Deal. North Dakota Congressman William Lemke angrily
complained that the first thing Congress did "was to open
the printing presses for the banks that had all but wrecked
the Nation." Hiram Johnson noted that in the Senate "there
is a distinct, nasty undercurrent of feeling. . .that a
fast one has been put over."[9]

To the Insurgents, probably the most objectionable
feature of the Emergency Banking Act was that it did not
nationalize the banking system. "I think back to the events
of March 4, 1933, with a sick heart," Bronson Cutting later
wrote. "For then, with even the bankers thinking the whole
economic system had crashed to ruins, the nationalization of
the banks by President Roosevelt could have been accomplished
without a word of protest. It was President Roosevelt's
great mistake." The President's failure to nationalize the
banking system, according to LaFollette, guaranteed the
solvent New York banks a virtual dictatorship over the nation's other banks. To a frustrated William Lemke it appeared as though "the President drove the money-changers
out of the capital on March 4th—and they were back on the
9th."[10]

---

[9]Schlesinger, Coming of the New Deal, p. 13; Lemke to
A. J. Nygaard, March 18, 1933, William Lemke Papers, Box 11, The
Orin G. Libby Manuscript Collection, University of North Dakota
Library, Grand Forks, North Dakota; Johnson to John Francis
Neylan, March 10, 1933, Johnson Papers, Part III, Box 14.

[10]Bronson Cutting, "Is Private Banking Doomed?" Liberty,
March 31, 1934, reprinted in the Congressional Record, 73rd
Cong. 2nd Sess., pp. 8051-53; Progressive, March 18, 1933,
p. 1; William E. Leuchtenberg, Franklin D. Roosevelt and the
New Deal, 1932-1940 (New York, 1963), p. 44.

Peter Norbeck was convinced that the banking bill discriminated against both state banks and some of the smaller
national banks. In his attempts to exempt such institutions
from the bill's provisions, he encountered the stubborn opposition of Senator Carter Glass of Virginia. "The Federal
Reserve Bank is his baby," wrote Norbeck to a concerned
constituent. "Senator Glass's banking creed is his religion—and while he may write you a nice letter, he will not
yield an inch nor a fraction of an inch—at least this is
my view after a close association with him for twelve years."
George Norris was critical of the banking act because it did
not insure deposits, a guarantee that was, however, provided
in the Glass-Steagall Banking Act, which was passed some
months later. In what was to become an almost standard Insurgent objection to New Deal legislation, Senator William E.
Borah disapproved of the new statute because Congress had
unconstitutionally delegated its authority by conferring
"autocratic" powers upon the President. The stubbornly independent Borah also resented the manner in which the administration had rushed the act through Congress. "Even if
I had been in favor of the bill," he complained, "I would
not have voted for it under such circumstances. I decline
to be an intellectual slave, even when I am being lashed in
the direction in which I want to go."[11]

---

[11]Norbeck to W. L. Baker, March 21, 1933, Peter Norbeck
Papers, Drawer 25, Richardson Archives, University of South
Dakota Library, Vermillion, South Dakota; Claudius O. Johnson,
Borah of Idaho , (Seattle, 1936), p. 469.

Pleased over his success in obtaining bank relief
legislation, Roosevelt decided to keep Congress in session
to pass other emergency measures. On March 10, he requested
authority to make arbitrary reductions in government expenditures. Specifically, he wished to cut the budget by
slashing payments to veterans and federal employees. "Too
often in recent history," the President warned, "liberal
governments have been wrecked on the rocks of loose fiscal
policy." Although the Insurgents agreed with this assessment, they thought that Roosevelt was balancing the budget
at the expense of the wrong people. Senator Henrik Shipstead said that what the President proposed played directly
into the hands of big business, which, while organizing raids
upon the Federal Treasury, covered its deeds by "propaganda
against the veterans and against government employees making
people believe that the disabled veterans are the people
who caused the Treasury deficit."[12]

Althoug its final approval was never in doubt, the
so-called Economy Act was forced to withstand a sharp attack
in the Senate. Both LaFollette and Borah futilely attempted
to amend the harsher provisions of the measure by seeking
to impose a limit beyond which pensions and salaries could
not be cut. Among the Insurgents, only Capper and Johnson
voted for the bill, and within a few months both were re-
penting their decision. Congressman Lemke complained that

---

[12]Rosenman (ed.), Public Papers of FDR, II, 50; Henrik
Shipstead, "Who Looted the Federal Treasury?" Dec. 12, 1934,
Henrik Shipstead Papers, Box 22, Minnesota Historical
Society, St. Paul, Minnesota.

it was the same bill that for many years had been sponsored
by the "Raskob gang" and the "Wall Street gangsters."
LaFollette considered it an incredibly ignorant way to fight
the depression or to balance the budget, for not only was
the bill a deflationary and regressive measure that would
remove purchasing power from those who most needed it, but
it was obvious that practically every veteran sliced from
the federal rolls would immediately become an applicant for
unemployment relief.[13]

The Insurgents were especially reluctant to grant the
Chief Executive control over veterans' pensions. Since most
of them believed that American entry into World War I had
benefited only the munitions makers and the bankers, they
considered it their special responsibility to preserve at
least some remuneration for former soldiers. "Believing as
I do that the war was wrong, and that we never should have
entered it," Norris explained, ". . .the soldier boys who
went, and who suffered wounds, and who died on the battle-
field are in my judgment entitled to the same respect, the
same honor, and the same considerations, as though we believe
the war to have been justified." Bronson Cutting, who became
the champion of veterans' rights in the Senate, urged Congress

---

[13]"The trouble with the situation," wrote Hiram Johnson,
"has been the administration of the Economy Act. A young man
named Lewis Douglas /the Director of the Budget/, who was
born to the purple, but who has a heart of stone, instead of
administering the law fairly and justly, took a real pleasure
out of the suffering of men who deserved consideration."
Johnson to Hiram Johnson, Jr., June 18, 1933, Johnson Papers,
Part IV, Box 4. Lemke to A. J. Nygaard, March 18, 1933,
Lemke Papers, Box 11; Progressive, August 19, 1933, p. 1.

to "stand to its guns" and rebuke the administration "principle" that "these men who fought for their country did not
fight for a pension, and as a result. . .must die as ex-
peditiously as possible." The Insurgents were also per-
turbed over Congress' abdication of one of its most treasured
prerogatives—control of the nation's purse strings. Borah
snapped that he was not willing to disregard the "most fundamental principles of this blessed old Republic" and vote
for such presidential powers. The authority the President
sought was not only blatantly unconstitutional but would
foster an extravagant bureaucracy, "the most demoralizing
instrumentality of government that was ever created by the
mind of man." In the same vein, Burton K. Wheeler warned
his fellow Senators that the President could not possibly
handle all requests personally. Wheeler, for one, was not
willing to see the veterans "sacrificed because some little
expert in the Veterans Administration says that we have
got to do this or we have got to do that."[14]

Roosevelt's first week in office left the country
breathless, and the Insurgents bewildered. To be sure, he
had demonstrated magnificent leadership, but his victories
were achievements that even Herbert Hoover would have been
proud to claim. James Couzens thought that the President's
emergency program clearly indicated that "this Government
is. . .a government of money lenders rather than a government

---

[14]George W. Norris to Fern McBride, April 7, 1934,
George W. Norris Papers, Tray 12, Box 2, Library of Congress,
Washington, D. C.; Congressional Record, 73rd Cong., 1st
Sess., pp. 5743, 417, 420, 6011-12.

of the people." An irritated Hiram Johnson vowed that
"Roosevelt's honeymoon legislative period is. . .at an end."
The California Senator promised that "measures will be
scrutinized now with much more care, and they will not be
passed with the same celerity which characterized those of
the financial crisis."[15]

The President did not wait very long to give Congressmen their chance to "scrutinize" his proposals: on March 16
he sent his suggestions for farm legislation to Capitol Hill.
The Insurgents believed that federal intervention to alleviate agricultural distress was long overdue, and they
assumed that agriculture's problems had to be solved before
the nation could escape the grasp of the depression. They
were still believers, in the main, in "moral agrarianism,"
a view that agriculture was more than just a vocation and
that its preservation was of fundamental importance to the
stability of American society. George W. Norris wrote in
his autobiography as late as 1944 that "the permanent stability and security of agriculture is of utmost concern to
the United States. Agriculture is more than just the food
which it contributes to satisfying the hunger of the United
States and of the world; it has made invaluable contributions
to the design of American living and of democratic government
itself." The depression of the 1920's and 1930's had added
an economic facet to this idyllic agrarianism, and during

---

[15]*Congressional Record*, 73rd Cong., 1st Sess., p. 346;
Johnson to Hiram Johnson, Jr., March 25, 1933, Johnson
Papers, Part IV, Box 4.

the New Deal years the Insurgents argued that agriculture
was the country's most vital occupation since the farmers'
purchasing power was essential to national prosperity. Borah
urged the government to do everything in its power to prevent falling farm prices. "When the farmers lose their
buying power," the Senator warned, "then industry and city
workers begin to feel the pinch; orders diminish; payrolls
and wage rates are reduced, sometimes to the vanishing
point; the unemployed cease to buy and taxes are raised to
feed the hungry."[16]

The farmers, of course, had been badly hurt by the
depression. According to one source, "agricultural prices
fell first, fell fastest, and fell farthest." Between 1929
and 1932 prices of farm commodities dropped more than 50
per cent, but agriculture had already been in grave trouble
in the early 1920's. "The East is so ignorant of the situation," an indignant Peter Norbeck wrote in 1933. "They
still speak of the depression as being three years old; they
think it started in the fall of '29. We know it started in
the fall of '19 and began to hurt a great deal in 1920."
George Norris, who had begged Congress in the 1920's "to do

---

[16]George W. Norris, Fighting Liberal: The Autobiography
of George W. Norris (New York, 1945), p. 365. Richard
Hofstadter calls this "moral agrarianism" the "agrarian myth."
See Richard Hofstadter, The Age of Reform (New York, 1955),
chapter 1. For a discussion of the "secularization" of
"moral agrarianism" into an economic creed, see Clifford B.
Anderson, "Metamorphosis of American Agrarian Idealism in
the 1920's and the 1930's," Agricultural History, XXXV
(October 1961), 182-88.

something for stricken agriculture or face the greatest panic
the world has ever known," recalled that his voice had gone
unheeded. "I was called unpatriotic and was denounced as
one who was standing in the way of human progress."[17] By
March, 1933, however, although lawmakers still expressed
sharp differences over agricultural policy, they were nearly
unanimous in the view that the federal government would have
to come to the aid of the farmer.

Roosevelt was aware of the need for farm legislation,
but he could not move quickly enough to prevent the situation
from getting out of hand. In 1932 Hiram Johnson had been
convinced that the farmers' respect for the law had up to
that time saved the country from outright rebellion. As
the economic spiral continued downward, a pessimistic Johnson
feared the farmer would "reach the depths of despair of the
urban dweller in this country, and when feeling as the city
unemployed do, he unites with them we can say goodnight to
the present government." In some sections of the country
it was evident that farmers had already reached "the depths
of despair" and had forgotten about their respect for "law
and order." Groups of men in the Farm Belt banded together
to protect their homes and property from the mortgage companies. With rifles in hand, they drove bankers, tax col-
lectors, insurance agents, and county sheriffs off their

---

[17]Clarence A. Wiley, *Agriculture* and *the* *Business* *Cycle*
Since *1920* (Madison, Wisconsin, 1930), p. 14; Norbeck to
First National Bank, White Rock, South Dakota, May 8, 1933,
Norbeck Papers, Drawer 25; Norris to Mr. and Mrs. W. E.
Buckelheide, Dec. 14, 1934, Norris Papers, Tray 12, Box 2.

land. In LeMars, Iowa, farmers nearly lynched Judge Charles
C. Bradley, who had refused to suspend foreclosure proceedings in his area. And rebellious farmers boldly marched
into the capital cities of Nebraska and Iowa, and in Wisconsin they staged a sit-in in the State Assembly building.
Edward A. O'Neal, president of the conservatively oriented
American Farm Bureau Federation, warned the Senate Agriculture Committee in January, 1933, that unless something was
done there would be a "revolt of property owners" in the
countryside in less than twelve months.[18]

Roosevelt planned to nip agrarian unrest in the bud
by the swift enactment of his farm program. The President
candidly admitted that his proposals were novel and experi-
mental, but he contended that "an unprecedented condition
calls for the trial of new means."[19] The heart of his proposed bill was the domestic allotment plan, by which the
Secretary of Agriculture hoped to persuade farmers to restrict their production in exchange for direct benefit payments, which were to be financed by a tax on the processors
of agricultural commodities. The objective of the measure
was to raise farm prices to "parity," which would give the
farmer the purchasing power he had possessed during the so-
called "Golden Age," from 1909 to 1914.

The Insurgents agreed with Roosevelt on the necessity
of raising farm prices, but they were quite certain that the

[18]Johnson to Charles K. McClatchy, June 19, 1932,
Johnson Papers, Part III, Box 13; Lindley, Roosevelt Revolution, p. 69.

[19]Rosenman (ed.), Public Papers of FDR, II, 74.

domestic allotment plan would not accomplish the desired end.
One Insurgent called it "the most bizarre thing that was ever
suggested to a set of sentient beings. If it were not for
the feeling most of us have toward the President, it would
not have a corporal's guard supporting it in the Senate."
Despite their respect for Roosevelt, five Insurgents voted
against the farm bill. The others reluctantly went along
with it, but only after they had unsuccessfully attempted
to attach a number of amendments that would have altered
the entire direction of farm policy.[20]

The Insurgents never accepted that portion of the New
Deal farm program which restricted production, for they
could not tolerate a policy that tended to promote scarcity
amidst poverty. Not only did they regard crop restriction
as undesirable from a humanitarian viewpoint, but they also
believed that the policy could simply not be enforced. To
implement the bill's provisions, they feared the Secretary
of Agriculture would require an army of agents to police
every farm. "I think this is bureaucracy gone mad," Borah
exclaimed. "I contend that you can help the American farmer
to solve the present difficulties without taking away his
personal liberty, his judgment, his opinion, his view as to
how he should run his farm." The former Iowa Insurgent,

[20]Johnson to Hiram Johnson, Jr., and Archibald Johnson,
April 16, 1933, Johnson Papers, Part IV, Box 4. The five
Insurgents who voted against the administration's agricul-
tural bill were Borah, Costigan, Frazier, Nye, and Wheeler.
For an excellent account of the Insurgent effort to rewrite
the agricultural bill, see John L. Shover, "Populism in the
1930's: The Battle for the AAA," Agricultural History, XXXIX
(January, 1965), 17-24.

Smith W. Brookhart, suggested that the bill must have been
the product of the "brainless brain trusters" in the Department of Agriculture because it could never work. For the
plan to succeed, he wrote Roosevelt, "it is necessary to
control world production, and nobody can do that. It is
also necessary to have a contract with the Almighty for the
weather, and he will not sign up."[21]

Since the ultimate purpose of the agricultural bill
was price-fixing, the Insurgents argued that a more direct
approach was preferable. Senator Norris introduced an
amendment allowing the Secretary of Agriculture to guarantee
the farmer the cost of production. This approach was largely
the brainchild of John A. Simpson, whose militant National
Farmers' Union was the dominant organization among many
of the Insurgents' constituents. The plan's appeal lay in its
apparent simplicity. The farmer was to be guaranteed a
fixed price on that portion of his crop sold in the domestic
market, and the government would market the surplus. Although
Secretary of Agriculture Henry A. Wallace correctly maintained
that, due to regional differences and other intangibles, it
would be virtually impossible to determine prices accurately,
the Insurgents saw many advantages in the cost-of-production
plan. First of all, fixed prices would presumably guarantee

[21]New York Times, August 10, 1934, p. 2; Brookhart to
Roosevelt, March 6, 1940, Roosevelt Papers, Official File
(OF)., 2971. George Norris later wrote: "I have never agreed
with the idea that was followed of killing hogs and destroying food products at a time when the world was suffering for
enough to eat, and enough to wear." Norris to August Stohl-
mann, March 2, 1934, Norris Papers, Tray 12, Box 2.

53

the farmer a fair profit without restricting his production.
Second, although the plan called for substantial expansion
of federal power over marketing, it involved no direct regulation of the individual farmer. Norris defended cost of
production mainly for this reason, insisting that it could
be implemented without having "a whole lot of detectives to
go around and trail the farmers of America so as to prevent
them from going somewhere and secretly selling their wheat
at less than the price the Secretary of Agriculture shall
have fixed."[22]

The Senate incorporated the so-called Norris-Simpson
amendment into the farm bill by a vote of 47 to 41, with all
of the Insurgents voting in the affirmative. Under heavy
administration pressure, however, the House refused to
accept the amendment, and it was then thrown out in conference. This action prompted the Insurgents to protest that
agricultural policy should be made by Congress, not by the
Executive. Wheeler revealed a particular antagonism toward
the "experts" who "never saw a bushel of wheat in their
lives." The Senator declared that Congressmen would not
be puppets of the "professors" who "say to us, 'jump through
the hoop and vote for this bill, do not cross a "t" or dot
an "i";' and ask that we shall give the Secretary of Agriculture the greatest amount of power that has ever been
granted in any bill in the history of the United States."[23]

---

[22]Congressional Record, 73rd Cong., 1st Sess., p. 1567.
[23]Ibid., p. 1569.

After their defeat on the cost-of-production plan, the
Insurgents sought to attach a number of inflationary proposals as riders to the farm bill. "Inflation and the farm
bill are logically and inevitably connected," reasoned Borah.
"In my opinion we shall not succeed in raising the price of
commodities permanently except through some system of inflation." Norris surmised that an expansion of the currency
would be of "greater assistance than anything contained in
the Agricultural Relief bill." For the most part, however,
the Insurgents were to be disappointed once again. Senator
Lynn J. Frazier's call for a refinancing of farm mortgages at
$1\frac{1}{2}$ per cent interest by issuing fiat money was easily defeated. Then Wheeler, espousing the panacea of his boyhood hero,
William Jennings Bryan, advocated the free and unlimited
coinage of silver at 16 to 1, but this proposal lost by the
margin of 33 to 45. Following this defeat it became evident
that a majority of Senators would unite around an omnibus
inflationary measure sponsored by Elmer Thomas of Oklahoma.
Since the administration wanted neither mandatory nor uncontrolled inflation, Roosevelt ordered his advisors to
seek a compromise with Thomas. After the wild inflationary
schemes and all the mandatory provisions had been eliminated,
the revised Thomas amendment passed the Senate, 64 to 20,
with all the Insurgents favoring it.[24]

---

[24]Ibid., p. 1831; Norris to H. Hoppe, May 20, 1933,
Norris Papers, Tray 38, Box 4; Burton K. Wheeler, Yankee
From the West (New York, 1962), pp. 41-42; Moley, After Seven
Years, pp. 156-161.

Despite their failure to revise the measure, eight of the Insurgents voted for the final farm bill. None of them, except possibly Arthur Capper of Kansas, thought it an especially attractive bill, but most of them regarded it as being better than nothing at all. "Frankly, I have not been insisting on any other plan," summarized Peter Norbeck, "because I felt that even though it might not be the best plan, it was the one that had the best chance of enactment."[25]

If the Insurgents were none too happy with the Farm Relief and Inflation Act, they were openly hostile toward the administration's corresponding measure for industry, the National Industrial Recovery Act (NIRA). Preoccupied with the banking, economy and agricultural bills, the President in early April still had developed no program to stimulate industrial recovery. In part, the reason for this was that there were so many ideas for recovery floating around that businessmen could not unite on any single plan. One observer noted that the country "was fairly crawling with plans. . . . You couldn't touch the Department of Economics in any American university without routing out a half-dozen schemes for an automatic society. You could even find plans in the sacred precincts of Wall Street and the Chamber of Commerce." To Roosevelt's chagrin, the Congress had a plan of its own: on April 6, the Senate passed a thirty-hour work week bill, and at the same time Senators Costigan, LaFollette, and Wagner renewed their demands for federal

---

[25]Norbeck to C. S. Harrison, April 16, 1933, Norbeck Papers, Drawer 25.

public works. "It was," reported newspaperman Ernest K.
Lindley, "a revolution boiling up from the bottom."[26]

Prodded by Congress, Roosevelt directed Raymond Moley,
his chief advisor, to sift through the morass of suggestions and to draft appropriate legislation. The measure
that emerged represented a major victory for the "planners"
in the administration and became the chief vehicle for
government-business cooperation during the early New Deal.
The bill, an ideological combination of the New Nationalism
and the Associational Activities of the 1920's, contained
something for everyone. Business received the authority
to draft code agreements exempt from the antitrust laws;
labor got the famous Section 7 (a), which guaranteed employees the right of collective bargaining free from employer interference and stipulated that the codes should set
minimum wages and maximum hours; and, finally, the advocates
of federally financed public works won a $3.3 billion ap-
propriation. Business Week left no doubt about which group
had obtained the most: it claimed that the measure was
essentially what industry had been requesting ever since
the Senate "first confronted it with rigid control from
above." The House passed the President's recovery bill
almost immediately, but it encountered stiff opposition in
the Senate. After much heated debate, the Upper House

---

[26]John Franklin Carter, The New Dealers (New York,
1934), p. 30; Schlesinger, Coming of the New Deal, p. 95.

approved the measure by a vote of 46 to 39. Among the Insurgents, only Arthur Capper cast his ballot in its favor.[27]

It was the National Industrial Recovery Act's suspen-
sion of the antitrust laws that most troubled the Insurgents.
To them it seemed as though the very monopolies which they
believed had caused the depression were now being given
governmental sanction. Since the Insurgents believed that
corporations had grown in size because they enjoyed special
privileges rather than because of their efficiency, they
wanted to remove the causes of monopoly, to eliminate unfair
practices, and to restore free competition. For the Insurgents, competition, equal opportunity, and democracy were
interrelated and essential ingredients of the American system. To preserve these values and to penalize monopolistic
exploitation most of them continued to advocate a literal
application of the Sherman Antitrust Act, which would curb
bigness by actually breaking up the "trusts" rather than by
regulating them. They believed that regulation could never
be effective because it was impossible to differentiate
between "good" and "bad" trusts. "You may just as well talk
about good kidnappers and bad kidnappers," quipped Borah.[28]

Asserting that all trusts were "economic Hitlers" and
that "John Sherman painted the picture a half century ago

---

[27]Ellis W. Hawley, The New Deal and the Problem of
Monopoly (Princeton, 1966), p. 26; Congressional Record,
73rd Cong., 1st Sess., p. 5861. For the best accounts of
the origins and drafting of the industrial recovery bill,
see Schlesinger, Coming of the New Deal, chapter 6; Moley,
After Seven Years, pp. 184-190; and Hugh S. Johnson, The Blue
Eagle From Egg to Earth (Garden City, N. Y., 1935), chapter 18.

[28]New York Times, Feb. 25, 1935, p. 2.

58

just as it is now," the Lion of Idaho led the fight on the
Senate floor to restore the antitrust laws. He persuaded
his fellow Senators to add a proviso to the recovery bill
that no code should "permit combinations in restraint of
trade, price-fixing, or other monopolistic practices."
Businessmen and administration spokesmen, however, insisted
that such an amendment was contrary to the intent of the
measure. The conference committee, consequently, removed the
prohibition on price-fixing and forbade only "monopolies or
monopolistic practices." This concession infuriated the
Insurgents because it was now definite that the codes of
"fair competition" might include anything upon which businessmen could agree and the government would approve. As
a parting salvo, Borah indicated that the bill had been
misnamed. Considering that it did not even attempt to protect the consumer or the small, independent businessman,
he maintained the act should have been entitled: "A bill
to promote and make secure monopoly."[29]

The Insurgents contended that the NIRA discriminated
against the farmer both in theory and practice. Still
smarting from their failure to add a price-fixing amendment
to the AAA, they resented the fact that industry had obtained this privilege under the NIRA. Wheeler castigated
those Senators from industrial states "who say we must not

---

[29]Congressional Record, 73rd Cong., 1st Sess., p. 5836.
"When the time comes," Borah maintained, "when the interests
in an industry, gathered together for the purpose of making
a code, do not dominate the situation but permit the small
independent to write the code for the large industry, the
millenium will have been here for many years." Ibid., pp.
5164-65.

give the farmer the cost of production, because if we do
that, it will bring about over production and will burden
our industries; and in less than two weeks' time those same
Senators are here insisting upon the cost of production for
the manufacturers of the country." In addition, the Insurgents disapproved of the selection of Hugh Johnson as the
head of the National Recovery Administration (NRA). Wheeler
believed that Johnson was so closely associated with the
country's financial interests that he could not adequately
protect the public interest. Hiram Johnson detested the
Administrator's emphasis on ballyhoo to popularize the NRA.
"What a sad commentary on our intelligence," the California
Senator wrote his son, "when we must be driven into a policy
by signs and symbols and the beating of tom toms, and our
screaming the 'We do our part,' and with the tattooing of
eagles on our anatomy and with putting eagles on our wind-
shields and in our windows."[30]

Although they probably would have supported a similar
plan for agriculture, the Insurgents honestly believed that
the NIRA was really un-American. By condoning industrial
monopoly, the bill, in their view, was a grave threat to
American democracy. Burton K. Wheeler ominously predicted
that it was "an impossibility to have a dictatorship of
industry work satisfactorily in a democracy." Claiming that
there was not even a sufficient number of Democrats to staff
the bureaucracy required by the bill, Borah forecast the

---

[30]Ibid., pp. 5241, 5839; Johnson to Hiram Johnson,
Jr., June 2, 1935, Johnson Papers, Part IV, Box 4.

complete regimentation of American life. Also, since the
bill added significantly to the already enormous power of
the President, the Senator from Idaho was none too sure that
democracy existed any longer in the United States. "I am
still old-fashioned enough," he stated, "to believe that
there are two other departments of Government besides the
executive—the legislative which abdicates, and the judiciary, which is disregarded in this bill."[31]

The passage of the NIRA brought the special session of
Congress to a close. This was none too soon, according to
one Insurgent who remarked that the industrial recovery bill
had nearly precipitated a revolt in Congress. He reported
that some Senators who had been "mute" in the past had now
reached the limit of their tolerance. Roosevelt, apparently,
sensed that fact, and he wanted Congress to adjourn before
there was an actual outbreak of hostilities between himself
and the fatigued legislators. Hiram Johnson indicated that,
for the most part, he was pleased with the performance of
the man in the White House, but he believed that "it would
be a very bold man who could prophesy the outcome of what
we are trying to do—we can only hope and pray."[32]

These remarks typified the ambivalent attitude of most
Insurgents toward the early New Deal. They usually chose to

---

[31]Congressional Record, 73rd Cong., 1st Sess., pp.
5146, 5841.

[32]Johnson to Hiram Johnson, Jr., and Archibald
Johnson, June 4, 1933, Johnson Papers, Part IV, Box 4;
Johnson to Peter Norbeck, Sept. 22, 1933, Johnson Papers,
Part III, Box 15.

separate the President from his legislative program: although
they were enthusiastic about Roosevelt's leadership, they
were concerned about the wisdom of his program. This is not
to say that the Insurgents took a dim view of every piece of
New Deal legislation, for they believed that some of the
measures had helped to restore purchasing power and to check
the influence of monopolies. They were especially pleased
with the Federal Emergency Relief Act and the act creating
the Tennessee Valley Authority (TVA). In pushing the TVA,
the President had gone even further than the Insurgents had
believed he would. George Norris was delighted that his
fondest dreams had come true, and Hiram Johnson conceded
that Roosevelt had taken "such a remarkable position on
Muscle Shoals that we can forgive him many other things."[33]
In addition, the Insurgents were pleased that at least an
effort had been made to solve some of the nation's fundamental economic problems, and they hoped that the legislation dealing with agriculture, banks, and the stock exchanges would be perfected in future sessions. The over-
riding sentiment among them, however, was that the major
New Deal measures had been too conciliatory toward big
business and Wall Street and had failed to relieve the distress of the people in an appreciable manner.

Prior to the second session of the 73rd Congress,
Robert LaFollette announced that he was for "pulling the
throttle wide open in a concerted effort to drive 'old man

[33]Johnson to Charles K. McClatchy, Feb. 4, 1933,
Johnson Papers, Part III, Box 14.

depression' from our midst." Specifically, the Wisconsin
Senator called for an expanded public-works program, increased inheritance and income taxes, cost of production for
the farmer, increased wages for the laborer, payment of the
veterans' bonus, and expansion of the currency. Borah
thought that the "money question" presented the most serious
problem; the Idaho Senator was certain that the nation was
courting disaster by pursuing a deflationary course.[34]
During the 1934 session the Insurgents, with Roosevelt sometimes in opposition, were successful in their efforts to
pump more money into the economy through silver inflation
and the restoration of certain veterans' pensions, but they
were defeated in their attempts to increase appropriations
for public works and work relief.

The debate over the agricultural relief bill in 1933
had revealed a strong inflationary sentiment in Congress.
Because of the slow start of the AAA and the President's
refusal to use the discretionary powers provided in the
Thomas amendment, unrest mounted in the Farm Belt. John A.
Simpson hastily dispatched to Roosevelt a formula to restore
prosperity within twenty-four hours. "The minute you remonetize silver by proclamation, the minute you cut the
dollar in two by proclamation," he advised, "the next
morning. . .prices of farm products will go back to what
they were in May, 1920." After a two-week tour of his state,

[34]*Progressive*, Dec. 30, 1933, p. 1; William E. Borah to
Colonel Raymond Robins, Dec. 1, 1933, Raymond Robins Papers,
Box 26, State Historical Society of Wisconsin, Madison, Wis.

George Norris wired the President that expansion of the currency was necessary so that those in debt could "pay what
they owe in dollars of the same value as they borrowed when
they went into debt." Convinced that some concessions to
inflation would have to be made, Roosevelt asked Congress in
January, 1934, for power to devalue the dollar by fixing the
gold content of the dollar at no more than 60 per cent of
its existing weight. Although this request sent conservatives like Carter Glass into paroxysms of rage, it did not
go far enough to please the Insurgents. "I can understand
how it can put more money into banks, but it will not put
more money into circulation among the people. We have enough
money in banks now," Borah contended.[35] The passage of the
Gold Reserve Act on January 30 only whetted the appetite of
the inflationists.

In the Senate, inflationary sentiment centered around
the use of silver. Wheeler reintroduced his 16-1 amendment,
which was narrowly defeated by a vote of 43 to 45. This
prompted Charles E. Coughlin, the radio priest from Royal
Oak, Michigan, to broadcast in behalf of "20,000,000 inar-
ticulate taxpayers" and to ask God's blessing upon the
Congress so that it would remonetize silver and undo the

---

[35]Simpson to Roosevelt, Oct. 23, 1933, Roosevelt Papers,
President's Personal File (PPF), 471; Progressive, Nov. 4,
1933, p. 1; Congressional Record, 73rd Cong., 2nd Sess., p.
1235. "I cast the deciding vote that permitted President
Roosevelt to reduce the content of the gold dollar nearly
forty per cent—that is, I cast it in the Banking Committee,
when Conservative Democrats like McAdoo, Glass and Gore were
even against it; even their own Democratic Chairman of the
Committee voted against the President." Norbeck to Eino H.
Groop, Feb. 16, 1935, Norbeck Papers, Drawer 27.

crime of Good Friday, 1917, "when the American citizenry was
crucified between two thieves, Gold and Greed." Moving
quickly, Roosevelt called a group of silver Senators to the
White House and attempted to persuade them to tone down their
demands. The silverites, however, were not in a compromising
mood; Wheeler refused to attend, and Borah walked out of the
parley. The Idaho Senator told waiting newsmen that the
President just wanted "another measure of avoidance," and
he threatened to take the issue to the country in the 1934
elections. Following this statement, White House resistance
crumbled, and Roosevelt agreed "to do something for silver."
The result was the Pittman Silver Purchase Act, by which the
Secretary of the Treasury was directed to buy silver until
it comprised one-quarter of the nation's monetary reserve
or until the world price of the metal reached $1.29 an
ounce. All of the Insurgents voted for the measure.[36] The
act, in effect, was a subsidy to the silver mine operators
and resulted in little inflation, but it did succeed in
mollifying all but the most rabid inflationists.[37]

---

[36]_Time_, XXIII (Jan. 15, 1934), 15. Henrik Shipstead
castigated the critics of the President's monetary policy.
"They seem to forget that our monetary system was wrecked
before President Roosevelt was inaugurated into office. I
believe that all his critics supported the insane creation
of credit policies that prevailed up until the crash of 1929.
That was uncontrollable inflation by the banks and the so-
called orthodox economists. After the crash they all supported uncontrolled, deflation which resulted in the closing
of every bank in the United States." Undated Speech, Shipstead Papers, Box 22.

[37]Herbert Bratter, "The Silver Episode," _Journal of
Political Economy_, XLVI (Oct., Dec., 1938), 609-52, 802-37.
Burton K. Wheeler, piqued by the President's refusal to back
his 16-1 proposal, claimed that "the remonetization of silver

Congress also triumphed over the President in restoring certain cuts made under the 1933 Economy Act. The Insurgents played the prominent role in this battle. Bronson Cutting won approval for an increase in payments to Spanish-American War veterans, and Borah gained a similar increase for certain classes of government employees. Even though this added only a paltry amount to federal spending, Roosevelt threatened the "spendthrift" Congressmen with a veto. "I refuse to be driven from what I believe my duty by the threat of a veto, even if it comes from my own father," was the angry retort of George Norris. When Congress passed the appropriation, the President kept his word and vetoed the measure. The Insurgents regarded the veto as wholly unnecessary. "It is simply impossible. . .to understand his mental processes in presenting the veto message that he did," Hiram Johnson wrote of the President, "but it has left a very bad taste with many men here."[38]

Congress "stuck to its guns" and overrode the President. Peter Norbeck, who was so ill that he had not been in the Senate chamber for weeks, appeared in order to strike a blow for Congressional independence. Hiram Johnson dubbed it "the event of the week," and Harold Ickes conceded that "the President had suffered his first serious political setback." In the Senate, an unlikely coalition of liberal

---

was the only way to take thousands of people off relief and put them into legitimate industry. New York Times, August 13, 1934, p. 2.

[38]Congressional Record, 73rd Cong., 2nd Sess., p. 5996; Johnson to John Francis Neylan, March 30, 1934, Johnson Papers, Part III, Box 16.

Democrats, Insurgents, and regular Republicans contributed to Roosevelt's defeat on the 1934 bonus bill. It was the action of normally economy-minded GOP Senators that puzzled political observers. "In all of this business the Republicans seem to be reversing the experience of Saul," editorialized the New York Times." "He went out to search for an ass and found a kingdom. They are searching eagerly for a kingdom, but seem to be able to turn up only a lot of asses."[39]

Although the Insurgents were largely successful in their effort to increase veterans' payments and to enact measures designed to stimulate inflation, they achieved only a partial victory with regard to relief legislation. Norris had already indicated in June, 1933, that he favored greater governmental appropriations for relief so that the unemployed might receive jobs rather than charity. The Civil Works Emergency Appropriation Act of 1934 placed an emphasis on work relief, but the Insurgents contended that the program was not funded substantially enough to provide a living wage for those on the relief rolls. To obtain what he called "the local prevailing wage rate" for the unemployed, LaFollette had attempted to affix to the administration's $3.45 million relief bill an amendment allowing for a $500 million increase in expenditures. However, both this and a

---

[39] Time, XXIII (April 9, 1934), 15; Johnson to Hiram Johnson, Jr., March 31, 1934, Johnson Papers, Part IV, Box 4; Harold L. Ickes, The Secret Diary of Harold L. Ickes, I (New York, 1953), 158; New York Times, Feb. 28, 1934, p. 18.

$1.5 billion relief measure, sponsored by Bronson Cutting,
met defeat in the Senate, largely because Roosevelt insisted
that adequate funds existed to meet the government's relief
obligations.[40]

Eight of the Insurgents voted for additional relief
expenditures but only in the hope that this spending would
be coupled with drastic changes in the country's tax laws.
"It can only be a temporary palliative," Henrik Shipstead
said of relief spending, "to give us a chance to inaugurate
policies that will. . .enable a start to be made toward a
redistribution of the national income to the great mass of
the people." Norris concurred with the Minnesota Senator's
assessment. "It is a crime," the Nebraskan believed, "to
have millions of people starving and hungry while a few
others, who neither toil nor do they spin, are living in
luxury." Demonstrating that his crusade to redistribute the
nation's wealth was motivated in part by a desire to balance
the government's budget, Lafollette promised "to fight for
increased inheritance and income taxes—the likes of which
we have never heard of—so that those with huge incomes will
have to cough up to help pay for this /relief/ program."[41]

---

[40]Norris to H. H. Harper, June 19, 1933, Norris Papers,
Tray 15, Box 3; Progressive, Dec. 30, 1933, p. 1. Roosevelt
did not want to spend the extra money just prior to the 1934
elections, but by 1935 he was hoping to substitute work for
relief. Roosevelt to Colonel E. M. House, Nov. 27, 1934,
Roosevelt Papers, PPF 222.

[41]Congressional Record, 73rd Cong., 2nd Sess., pp.
2184-85; Norris to L. D. Cole, March 17, 1934, Norris Papers,
Tray 13, Box 2; Progressive, Dec. 30, 1933, p. 1.

It is not surprising that the Insurgents were in the forefront of the battle for progressive taxation. Some of them had played a prominent role in the campaign leading to the adoption of the Sixteenth Amendment, and others among them, in the hostile environment of the 1920's, had successfully defended the principle of the graduated income tax. Many of them believed that the taxing power could be used both to redistribute wealth and to attack monopoly. "It is idle to say we are helpless," Brandeis stated. "By taxation bigness can be destroyed."[42]

In their effort to secure tax reform, the Insurgents sustained their most bitter defeat of the session. They attempted to rewrite the administration's tax bill on the Senate floor, but they met with failure. In Brandeisian fashion, LaFollette contended that history demonstrated "that the concentration of wealth as has taken place in the United States is inimical to the perpetuity of democratic institutions." This fact alone, the Wisconsin Senator maintained, justified an increase in the graduated income tax schedule, but the amendments he sponsored along this line were defeated. The Insurgents then directed their efforts to closing the many tax loopholes available to wealthy taxpayers and corporations. Borah introduced an amendment designed to eliminate consolidated corporation returns and to prevent holding companies from avoiding taxes on income derived from their affiliates. "Frankly, I would like to tax them all out of existence," one Insurgent exclaimed.

---

[42]Quoted in Hawley, The New Deal and Monopoly, p. 344.

Norris led a movement to levy a tax upon previously exempt capital gains and government securities, but both his and Borah's efforts in this direction were unavailing. The Senate finally approved a measure calling for a 10 per cent increase in the surtax, a moderate increase in estate and gift taxes (". . .only because the dead couldn't be here to object," quipped Lafollette), and publicity for income tax returns. What had started out as an Insurgent attempt to "soak the rich" thus ended as a revenue bill soaking all taxpayers. The Progressive, the LaFollette newspaper in Wisconsin, warned that Roosevelt's failure to support progressive tax reform was "a challenge to the liberalism of the New Deal."[43]

The New Deal effort to regulate the stock exchanges met with Insurgent approval, but the legislation devised was not as stringent as they would have preferred. The Insurgents had long looked with disfavor upon the stock exchanges as agents of the "money power." At the request of Herbert Hoover, Peter Norbeck had begun an investigation in 1932 into "the speculation with other people's money." Norbeck subsequently hired Ferdinand Pecora, the peppery Italian-American lawyer from New York City, to head the probe, and Pecora exposed what Norbeck called "the worst crap game in the country." The first legislative product of the Pecora investigation was the Securities Act of 1933, essentially a truth-in-lending measure that did nothing to

---

[43]Congressional Record, 73rd Cong., 2nd Sess., p. 5974; Ibid., p. 6470; Progressive, Feb. 16, 1935, p. 4.

guarantee the soundness of securities. The Insurgents, nevertheless, regarded "Norbeck's legislation" as an important first-step in reducing the influence of Wall Street. "He must come first in any distribution of awards for the results," journalist John T. Flynn reported, and he praised Norbeck as "one of those prairie-state Republicans—half-Democrat, half other ingredients, but less than one-half of one per cent Republican."[44]

As the Pecora investigation continued into 1934, under the chairmanship of Florida's Senator Duncan Fletcher, it became clear that the stock exchanges had not yet been reformed. Roosevelt, therefore, sent Congress early in February the draft of a measure designed to police the exchanges. The Fletcher-Rayburn bill, as the proposal was dubbed, immediately produced a chorus of denunciations from the business and financial communities. Richard Whitney, president of the New York Stock Exchange, asserted that the exchange was a perfect institution and quite capable of regulating itself. The rest of the country knew better, however. "Those old Wall Street boys are putting up an awful fight to keep the government from putting a cop on their corner," concluded Will Rogers.[45]

In the Senate, argument centered around two features of the bill: the provision creating a new federal agency to administer the measure and the section providing for

---

[44]Quoted in Gilbert C. Fite, <u>Peter Norbeck: Prairie Statesman</u> (Columbia, Mo., 1948), pp. 176, 182.

[45]Quoted in Schlesinger, <u>Coming of the New Deal</u>, p. 464.

statutory margin requirements. With regard to the administrative question, Carter Glass persuaded the Senate Banking and Currency Committee to vest discretionary regulatory powers in a new Securities Exchange Commission (SEC). On the floor, however, the Insurgents fought to assign administrative responsibility for the bill to the Federal Trade Commission. Not only would this save the public approximately half-a-million dollars a year, they reasoned, but it would also serve to check the spread of an already swollen bureaucracy. The Insurgents, moreover, doubted that the proposed new commission could be an impartial one. Since "it is really Richard Whitney's idea," declared Edward P. Costigan, "it is a fair inference that in recommending another supervisory body it was the purpose of the New York Stock Exchange to go as far as it could to gain a firm foothold to regulate the official regulators to be established by this law." The Senate, however, followed Glass's suggestion and voted to establish the SEC as the administering agency of the measure.[46]

As for the issue of statutory margin requirements, the Insurgents failed to secure Senatorial approval for an amendment that would have severely restricted stock brokers from loaning money to speculators who offered the securities they were purchasing as collateral. Norris, who considered the adoption of this principle the essence of any measure regulating the stock exchanges, held that a poker game was respectable compared to buying stocks on the margin, for at

---

[46]*Congressional Record*, 73rd Cong., 2nd Sess., p. 8399.

least "when one engages in a poker game he used his own money
or puts his own security right on the table in the presence
of everybody." Though Norris would later designate the
Securities Exchange Act as one which represented "a great
improvement in American life," the Insurgents at the time
believed that they had suffered significant setbacks with
regard to both the administration of the securities law and
the provision for establishing fixed margin requirements.[47]

The voting records of the Insurgents during the 73rd
Congress not only reveal their dissatisfaction with some
major New Deal legislation but also present clear evidence
that they were not "rubber stamps" of the President. Since
the Insurgents were renowned for their independence, the
fact that they did not become Presidential puppets is not
too surprising. At the beginning of the Congress, Hiram
Johnson had announced that he would be "delighted to render
any assistance. . .and to go forward in behalf of any
presidential program if it does not violate fundamental
ideas of my own." At the close of the Congress, James
Couzens reminded his colleagues that he still had "a voice
in the matter of legislation" and would "not swallow everything the Democrats saw fit to offer."[48] On roll calls
where the final votes on bills were the decisive ones,
only 47.1 per cent of the total Insurgent vote was recorded

---

[47] Ibid., p. 8362; Norris, Fighting Liberal, p. 367.

[48] Johnson to Hiram Johnson, Jr., and Archibald Johnson,
March 19, 1933, Johnson Papers, Part IV, Box 4; Congressional
Record, 73rd Cong., 2nd Sess., p. 11634.

in favor of the New Deal.[49] On final roll calls that did
not constitute the crucial vote on major bills the Insurgents
voted for the New Deal 83.3 per cent of the time.[50] To be
sure, this figure indicates Insurgent support for much of
the New Deal, but their assent to many of these administration measures was only given reluctantly. The Insurgents
had their own legislative ideas about aiding agriculture
and industry, providing for unemployment relief, stimulating
inflation, guaranteeing a fairer distribution of the tax
load, and regulating the stock exchanges. In many instances
they either sponsored or supported amendments embodying
their views which, if adopted, would have considerably
changed the resulting New Deal legislation. They finally
voted for the measures in question only because they preferred these bills to no legislation at all.[51]

As indicated previously, the Insurgents enthusiastically endorsed some of the domestic accomplishments of
the New Deal. They also supported its nationalistic approach

---

[49]The measures included are the Emergency Banking Act,
the Economy Act, the Federal Emergency Relief Act, the TVA,
the NIRA, and the Independent Offices Appropriations Act
(1934). The Insurgents voted unanimously for both the FERA
and the TVA. If one eliminates these two roll calls from
consideration, they favored the New Deal only 22.2 per cent
of the time. (All figures include both the actual votes and
the announced votes.)

[50]The measures included are the AAA, the Gold Reserve
Act, the Civil Works Emergency Relief Act, the Securities
Exchange Act, the Silver Purchase Act, the Internal Revenue
Act (1934), and the Reciprocal Trade Agreements Act.

[51]See Appendix A. for a tabulation of Insurgent votes
on selective amendments. This computation reveals that the
Insurgents voted to change administration-sponsored bills
84.7 per cent of the time.

to foreign affairs. When Roosevelt sabotaged the London
Economic Conference, the Progressive approvingly noted that
"the government is looking out first and foremost for the
interest of its own citizens, and it is doing it in what
seems to be a hard-boiled and effective manner." Finally,
although the Insurgents were not automatic allies of the
President, they were quite certain that he meant well.
James Couzens wrote that, of the four Presidents under whom
he had served, Roosevelt was "the only one who has indicated a keen interest in the common people whom Lincoln
pleaded for." Rather than criticizing the President, the
Insurgents often blamed the President's advisors or the
Democratic party leadership for New Deal legislation that
displeased them. "As far as Franklin D. is concerned,"
William Lemke typically wrote, "I am inclined to believe
that he is far more progressive than the reactionary Democratic Machine. I am not sure where he is going, but he
has certainly done things that no other person would have
done."[52]

The Insurgents believed that the New Deal had many
shortcomings. Prominent among Insurgent complaints was the
enormous growth of presidential authority. Borah felt that
this trend endangered the republican form of government;
and he pleaded with his colleagues to meet their obligation

[52]Progressive, July 8, 1933, p. 4; Christopher Lindley,
"Franklin D. Roosevelt and the Politics of Isolationism,
1932-1936" (Ph.D. Thesis, Cornell University, 1963), passim.;
Couzens to Charles L. McNary, Oct. 5, 1934, Charles L. Mc-
Nary Papers, Box 5, Library of Congress, Washington, D. C.:
Lemke to Covington Hall, Feb. 8, 1934, Lemke Papers, Box 11.

as legislators by refusing to delegate additional power to the President. Hiram Johnson worried over the effect such power might have on Roosevelt. "He is sitting on top of the world," the Senator confided to his son, "and I fear him becoming conscious of it, just as Wilson did when he went abroad, and all the peoples of the world looked to him, and he forgot his own."[53]

The Insurgents often indiscriminately coupled their hostility towards centralization with a concern about a burgeoning federal bureaucracy. The Insurgents believed that bureaucracies were inimical to individual liberty since they permitted vital decisions affecting the lives of people to be made by non-elected officials. What was most distressing about the New Deal bureaucrats, as the Insurgents saw it, was that many of them appeared to be party hacks. Lemke suggested that the administration had "accepted Andrew Jackson as its patron saint and with him the spoils system with a vengeance." Most of the Insurgents blamed Postmaster General James A. Farley for the apparent elevation of partisanship above liberalism. "Two-job Jim," they called him, and they urged Roosevelt to dismiss Farley or otherwise bear the onus for hindering national recovery. "My opposition to Mr. Farley is. . .fundamental," announced Norris.

---

[53]Congressional Record, 73rd Cong., 1st Sess., pp. 4658-59; Johnson to Hiram Johnson, Jr., Feb. 8, 1934, Johnson Papers, Part IV, Box 4.

"I do not believe any man who is in the Cabinet should be the chairman or any other official of a great national party."[54]

The Insurgents were also troubled because they believed that Roosevelt was uncertain about the final destination of his program. William Allen White called "the President the greatest hitchhiker since Andrew Johnson, going a little piece down the road with anyone, backward and forward, zig zagging, covering and recovering." Hiram Johnson observed that the growing sentiment in Congress was that Roosevelt was "just continuing to shoot in the dark and advancing upon a way. . .which may lead in a direction other than he intends to go." All this confusion so exasperated James Couzens that he issued a public plea to the President to declare a definite policy that would be subject to change only in dire emergency.[55]

The Insurgents believed that Roosevelt's uncertainty about his goals was reflected in the inconsistency of some New Deal legislation. To them a blatant example of this inconsistency was the conflicting relationship of the New

---

[54]Lemke to Covington Hall, Feb. 3, 1934, Lemke Papers, Box 11; Norris to C. A. Randall, Dec. 12, 1934, Norris Papers, Tray 13, Box 6. The Progressive editorialized that "the people voted for a new deal in politics by an over-whelming mandate. They are not getting it when the spoils system is permitted to subvert the purposes of the recovery program, and the recovery agencies are made convenient vehicles for rewarding party henchmen." May 19, 1934, p. 4.

[55]White to Allen Nevins, May 24, 1934, quoted in Johnson, Selected Letters of William Allen White, p. 345; Johnson to Hiram Johnson, Jr., April 15, 1934, Johnson Papers, Part IV, Box 4; Couzens to Amos Pinchot, Sept. 5, 1934, James Couzens Papers, Box 104, Library of Congress, Washington, D. C.

Deal's agricultural program and the Reciprocal Trade Agreements Act of 1934, which empowered the President to negotiate lower tariffs without requiring him to submit the ensuing "treaties" to the Senate for ratification. "It must seem cockeyed to the American farmer," declared Arthur Capper, "when the Government is bearing down on him to cut production, to have that same Government making tariff agreements and concessions with other nations which will make it easier for agricultural products to be imported from abroad." Actually, though, the Insurgents were probably more concerned about providing tariff protection for American agricultural products than they were about the alleged inconsistency of the measure with the New Deal's farm program. Always staunch protectionists when it came to agriculture, they worried that reciprocity would flood the American market with foodstuffs produced in foreign countries. The Insurgents also objected to the surrender of Congressional prerogatives that the statute embodied. After Democrats rejected amendments forbidding tariff reductions on agricultural products and requiring Senatorial approval of all trade agreements, eight of the Insurgents reluctantly supported the proposal. Norris justified it as an emergency measure, and Norbeck hoped that it might do something to lower the disastrously high trade barriers that had been erected by the United States. All of the Insurgents, however, agreed with Arthur Capper, who qualified his vote for the bill by warning Roosevelt that the agricultural states

would hold him responsible if their interests were not protected.[56]

The Reciprocal Trade Agreements Act was an example of
"fundamentally unsound legislation" to Bronson Cutting. The
New Mexico Senator recommended that the administration "get
down to bedrock and do something for the people of our own
country and their internal purchasing power." The other
Insurgents agreed that the New Deal had not gone far enough
in this direction. In fact, they believed that some of the
major New Deal legislation seemed to favor the vested interests at the expense of the common people. Wheeler remarked that the AAA helped the "commuting farmer" but did
nothing to help the "dirt farmer." The most flagrant example of inequitable legislation to the Insurgents, however,
was the NIRA. Borah and Nye carried on a successful campaign to exempt some small businessmen from certain code
provisions, and they also persuaded Roosevelt to create the
National Recovery Review Board, headed by the aging Clarence
Darrow, to investigate charges of monopoly against the NRA.
Although Darrow's committee returned a verdict of "guilty"
against the NRA, it still remained as of 1934 the primary

---

[56]Arthur Capper Speech, undated speech, Arthur Capper
Papers, Agriculture, Reciprocal Trade-Wheat, Kansas State
Historical Society, Topeka, Kansas; Congressional Record,
73rd Cong., 2nd Sess., p. 9955; Norbeck to E. J. Wipf,
Feb. 4, 1935, Norbeck Papers, Drawer 26; Congressional
Record, 73rd Cong., 2nd Sess., p. 10380. "I really believe,"
wrote Hiram Johnson, "that to submit our tariffs to Messrs.
Wallace and Hull (both ardent internationalists and free-
traders) may actually imperil the prosperity of agriculture."
Johnson to Charles K. McClatchy, March 25, 1934, Johnson
Papers, Part III, Box 16.

recovery agency of the New Deal. Nye claimed that "the same monopolists who were guiding the destinies of America's economic structure. . .up to the days of the new deal. . . were really behind the national recovery program." Most of the Insurgents echoed Nye's sentiments, and they believed that the New Deal would have to abandon the NRA philosophy of coddling big business if economic prosperity were to be restored. "All this CWA, PWA, and all other letters of the alphabet are doomed to failure," William Lemke warned, "unless something more substantial is done to get rid of the Wall Street Crowd."[57] It was clear that Roosevelt would have to challenge the power of concentrated wealth if he were to receive strong Insurgent support for his New Deal.

---

[57]Congressional Record, 73rd Cong., 1st Sess., p. 10089; interview with Burton K. Wheeler, Nov. 22, 1968; Congressional Record, 73rd Cong., 1st Sess., p. 9235; Lemke to Covington Hall, March 7, 1934, Lemke Papers, Box 11. For the Insurgent assault on the NRA, see Hawley, The New Deal and Monopoly, pp. 91-129.

CHAPTER III

INSURGENT PROGRESSIVISM AND THE SECOND NEW DEAL, 1935-1936

Although the Insurgents were aware that some of the
major New Deal legislation was as inadequate as that of the
"old deal," they remained optimistic that they could convince Roosevelt to alter his course. The President, to be
sure, gave them every opportunity to present their views
by continuing to invite Johnson, LaFollette, and Norris to
the White House for informal policy and social chats—a
practice that proved highly flattering to these Insurgents.
"Through it all," noted Hiram Johnson, "the President has
been kindly, considerate and generous, and while I may dis-
agree with him on some policies, I have for him the greatest
admiration and respect."[1]

In addition to granting the Insurgents visiting privileges, the President had offered some of them cabinet positions. Before the old Bull Mooser Harold Ickes had consented
to head the Interior Department, Roosevelt had first tendered
the post to Bronson Cutting and then to Hiram Johnson. Since
it would appear that they were being rewarded for supporting
the President in 1932, the Insurgents had agreed to refuse

---

[1] Johnson to Irving Martin, May 28, 1933, Hiram W.
Johnson Papers, Part III, Box 14, Bancroft Library, University of California, Berkeley.

all cabinet-level appointments. Another, and probably more
important, reason for their decision was that acceptance of
an administration post would have placed severe limits upon
their independent political activities. "I cannot quite see
myself. . .with my peculiar temperament and singlular independence, which I prize above all things," explained Hiram
Johnson, "going into any President's cabinet."[2] James
Couzens did, however, accept the sub-cabinet position of
delegate to the London Economic Conference, after both
LaFollette and Johnson had refused the appointment. The
President also appointed many Progressive friends of the
Insurgents to lesser administrative posts. This led many
Democrats to protest that Roosevelt had not been partisan
enough in his appointments. "I fully recognize that it was
morally incumbent upon the President to recognize those
leading Progressive Republicans who so courageously and
loyally supported him during the campaign. . . . But this
is not a coalition government," complained Key Pittman, "this
is a Democratic government."[3]

James MacGregor Burns has accurately argued that
during 1933 and 1934 Roosevelt "took the role of a national
father, of bipartisan leader, of President of all the people." In keeping with this role, the President declined
to speak on traditional Democratic holidays. "My best

[2]Johnson to Charles K. McClatchy, Dec. 11, 1932,
Johnson Papers, Part III, Box 13.

[3]Pittman to Louis M. Howe, August 28, 1933, Franklin
D. Roosevelt Papers, PPF 745, Franklin D. Roosevelt Library,
Hyde Park, New York.

judgment is that I should take part in no Jefferson Day
celebrations this year," he wrote to Colonel House in 1934.
"Our strongest plea to the country. . .is that the recovery
and reconstruction program is being accomplished by men and
women of all parties." Speculation arose that the President
was assuming his non-partisan stance as a first step toward
restructuring the two-party system along liberal-conserva-
tive lines. There were many indications that this, indeed,
was his intention. At Hyde Park in 1932, Roosevelt thus
told Rexford G. Tugwell, a charter member of the Brains
Trust, that party realignment was his "fondest hope." "Rex,"
Tugwell recalled Roosevelt's saying, "We shall have eight
years in Washington. At the end of that time we may or may
not have a Democratic party; but we will have a Progressive
one." Ernest K. Lindley wrote in 1933 that it had long been
the President's desire "to form a new liberal party by at-
taching the Republican Progressives and miscellaneous liberals to the Democratic party."[4]

Among the Insurgents there seemed to be no lack of
advocates for the idea of party realignment. One of them
thought that Roosevelt eventually would "have to separate
the goats from the sheep and quit fooling around with any
of the old buccaneers, whether they are Democratic John
Davises or old Hoover bootleggers." "Why not do it now?"

---

[4]James MacGregor Burns, Roosevelt: The Lion and the
Fox (New York, 1956), p. 183; Franklin D. Roosevelt to Edwin
M. House, March 10, 1934, Roosevelt Papers, PPF 222; Arthur
M. Schlesinger, Jr., The Coming of the New Deal (Boston,
1958), p. 504; Ernest K. Lindley, The Roosevelt Revolution
(New York, 1933), p. 10.

Smith W. Brookhart urged the President. The former Iowa
Insurgent thought that the 1934 reelection campaigns of
Johnson, LaFollette, and Shipstead presented the first op-
portunity "for a realignment of political issues since
Lincoln was elected President."[5] Roosevelt appeared to heed
Brookhart's advice, at least with regard to these three
Insurgents, as he called for the election of "the right kind
of people" regardless of party label.[6]

Roosevelt's endorsement of Hiram Johnson involved
little difficulty for the administration. The Senator was
very popular in California and had backed Roosevelt in 1932.
In January, 1934, Farley authorized the release of a statement calling Johnson "a true champion of human rights" and
urging his reelection.[7] Not wanting to miss out on a sure
winner, the California Republican, Progressive, and Commonwealth parties jumped onto the crowded bandwagon and also
nominated the Senator. Running as a "Progressive-Republican-
Roosevelt man," Johnson swept to an easy victory in November.

Henrik Shipstead of Minnesota proved to be much more
of a problem for the administration. The Minnesota Democratic

---

[5]Johnson to Harold L. Ickes, Nov. 24, 1933, Johnson
Papers, Part III, Box 15; Brookhart to Roosevelt, August 28,
1934, Roosevelt Papers, Official File (OF) 419A.

[6]Other Insurgents up for reelection in 1934 were Wheeler,
Frazier, and Cutting. Surprisingly, Roosevelt did nothing to
aid Wheeler and, not too surprisingly, nothing to aid Frazier.
The President, however, collaborated with Farley and New
Mexico Democrats against Cutting—an action which angered the
other Insurgents.

[7]John J. McGrath to Roosevelt, Jan. 24, 1934, Roosevelt
Papers, OF 126.

party was weak and factionalized, and a pro-New Deal third
party, the Farmer-Labor party, dominated state politics.
The President and Farley were at odds in deciding how to
deal with the situation. The Postmaster General announced
support for the entire Democratic ticket "from top to bottom." Roosevelt, however, invited Shipstead aboard the
presidential train during a Western campaign trip; and the
President wrote Farley: "In Minnesota hands off—don't
encourage opposition to Shipstead."[8] In the end, both
Shipstead and Floyd B. Olson, the Farmer-Labor gubernatorial
candidate, won handsomely.

Wisconsin presented the most ticklish situation for
the administration. Young Bob LaFollette was up for reelection, and the LaFollette name had become a fixture in
Badger State politics. In addition, the Wisconsin Senator
had worked arduously to persuade other Progressive Republicans to campaign for Roosevelt in 1932. The President
confided that he hoped there was "some way of sending Bob
LaFollette back here." Matters were complicated for
Roosevelt, however, when LaFollette and his younger brother,
Phil, collaborated on May 19, 1934, to form the Independent
Progressive party. Also, Wisconsin Democrats, who in 1932
had succeeded in obtaining some major state offices for the
first time in nearly forty years, asserted that they deserved Roosevelt's support in 1934. Democratic Governor

---

[8]New York Times, Oct. 17, 1934, p. 16; Sister Mary
Rene Lorentz, "Henrik Shipstead: Minnesota Independent,
1923-1946" (Ph.D. Thesis, Catholic University of America,
1963), p. 51; Burns, Roosevelt, p. 202; Roosevelt Papers,
OF 300 (Minnesota Politics).

Albert G. Schmedeman warned that Presidential endorsement
of LaFollette "would be a serious mistake as it would
handicap our party." The Insurgents, however, wanting to
make the Wisconsin elections a test of Roosevelt's liberalism, flooded the President with telegrams pleading for his
intervention in LaFollette's behalf, and Costigan, Frazier,
Norris, Nye, and Wheeler volunteered for campaign duty.
In this difficult situation Roosevelt took what he hoped
state Democrats would recognize as a neutral stand. Speaking at Green Bay in early August, he expressed gratitude to
both LaFollette and Democratic Senator F. Ryan Duffy.
LaFollette and most other Progressive candidates emerged
victorious in November, and Duffy left no doubt as to who
was responsible for his party's reverses. "Your apparent
attitude of favoritism toward the Progressives," he wrote
Roosevelt, ". . .worked to our very certain detriment in
the last campaign."[9]

The 1934 election results were immensely pleasing to
the Democratic party. Even though 1934 was a non-presi-
dential election year, Farley had audaciously predicted a
few gains for his party in the Senate and a stand-off in
the House. He was correct about the Senate, but the administration gained an unprecedented nine seats in the

---

[9]Roosevelt to Edward P. Costigan, Nov. 12, 1934,
Roosevelt Papers, PPF 1971; Schmedeman to Col. Joseph E.
Davis, August 2, 1934, Albert G. Schmedeman Papers, Box 2,
State Historical Society of Wisconsin, Madison, Wisconsin;
Samuel I. Rosenman (ed.), The Public Papers and Addresses of
Franklin D. Roosevelt (13 vols., New York, 1938-1950), III,
370-74; Duffy to Roosevelt, Feb. 1, 1935, Roosevelt Papers,
PPF 443.

House. Senate Minority Leader McNary wrote to Couzens that
"the avalanche was a little larger than either of us suspected." Because Roosevelt had forced his party into the
background during much of the campaign, the electorate
really registered its overwhelming approval of his performance as President. The London Morning Post concluded
that the American people followed "Mr. Roosevelt. . .as the
Israelites had followed Moses." The Insurgents chose to
regard the election as a tremendous victory for liberalism.
Hiram Johnson noted that even two "hard-boiled reactionaries,"
Senator Arthur H. Vandenberg of Michigan and Senator David
Reed of Pennsylvania, had pleaded with their constituents to
elect them because they were Progressives. "I said to both
of them," Johnson remarked, "that I was delighted with their
position, for not only were they demonstrating that it was
respectable to be a Progressive, but now that it was fashionable." Bob LaFollette thought the election returns
demanded new reforms from the New Deal. Roosevelt was also
convinced of this, and he wrote to Vice President John N.
Garner that the voters still wanted action.[10]

When the new Congress convened, in January, 1935,
however, the President's initial actions appeared to be
anything but progressive. In fact, one of his first moves

---

[10]Charles L. McNary to Couzens, Nov. 24, 1934, Charles
L. McNary Papers, Box 5, Library of Congress, Washington,
D. C.; Time, XXIV (Nov. 19, 1934), 11; Johnson to John Francis
Neylan, Feb. 25, 1934, Johnson Papers, Part III, Box 16; Bob
and Phil LaFollette to Roosevelt, Sept. 30, 1934, Roosevelt
Papers, PPF 1201; Roosevelt to Garner, Roosevelt Papers, PPF
1416.

proved to be a direct insult to the Insurgents: he permitted Dennis Chavez, the defeated Democratic Senatorial candidate from New Mexico, to institute a contest for Bronson Cutting's seat. Cutting was the only Progressive Republican who had bolted his national ticket in 1932 but failed to win an endorsement from Roosevelt in 1934. This, apparently, was a calculated omission on Roosevelt's part. When Norris had written the President in January, 1934, that New Mexico Democrats were "laying the foundation to defeat Senator Cutting for reelection," Roosevelt had replied, "I wish you would speak to me someday about Bronson Cutting. I do not want to do anything to hurt him, but a lot of Bronson's retainers in New Mexico are not especially fine citizens." The President subsequently remained silent while Farley engineered a conservative Democratic-Republican coalition against the New Mexico Senator. "I have never seen such a combination of the representatives of the big financial interests as there is against me today," Cutting wrote a fellow Insurgent. "I should not ordinarily be alarmed about this. . .but when combined with the Roosevelt popularity. . . it may make a plausible appeal for votes."[11] Cutting, in the end, won a narrow victory, only to face the administration's attempt to take his seat away from him.

---

[11]Norris to Roosevelt, Jan. 19, 1934, Roosevelt Papers, PPF 1201; Roosevelt to Norris, Jan. 24, 1934, Roosevelt Papers, PPF 1201; Harold L. Ickes to Roosevelt, Sept. 30, 1934, Roosevelt Papers, OF 300 (New Mexico Politics); Cutting to Hiram Johnson, Oct. 22, 1934, Bronson M. Cutting Papers, Box 26, Library of Congress, Washington, D. C.

It is difficult to explain the President's motives
in dealing with Cutting, but Raymond Moley has speculated
that perhaps Roosevelt never forgave the New Mexico Senator
for having charged the President with "a want of humanity"
during the debates for veterans compensation. At any
rate, in May, 1935, Cutting was killed in a plane crash
while returning from New Mexico with affidavits relating
to his contested election. When the news of Cutting's death
reached Washington, the Insurgents were distraught, and some
of them wept openly; they believed Cutting to have been the
victim, in effect, of a political assassination. When
Chavez, who had been appointed by New Mexico's Democratic
Governor to replace Cutting, appeared to take his seat,
Johnson, LaFollette, Norris, Nye, and Shipstead stormed out
of the Senate in protest. Norris told waiting newsmen that
it was "the greatest case of ingratitude in history," and
"a blot on the record of the administration."[12]

With relations already strained, the President pro-
ceeded to alienate the Insurgents further. In January,
1935, Roosevelt asked the Senate to approve American ad-
herence to the World Court. At first, observers predicted
an easy administration victory, but they did not take into

---

[12] Johnson to Hiram Johnson, Jr., Dec. 24, 1934, Johnson
Papers, Part IV, Box 4; Raymond Moley, After Seven Years (New
York, 1939), pp. 193, 195; Time, XXV (May 20, 1935), 14-15.
Borah, who was absent from the Senate at the time Chavez took
his seat, told reporters that he had walked out "in spirit."
New York Times, May 21, 1935, p. 1. Arthur Schlesinger has
speculated that the similar backgrounds of Roosevelt and
Cutting (both were of old established families, and both at-
tended Groton and Harvard) and their rivalry to wear the man-
tle of liberalism made estrangement inevitable. Schlesinger,
The Politics of Upheaval (Boston, 1960), pp. 139-41.

consideration the opposition tactics of Hiram Johnson and
William Borah. Johnson told the Senate that Roosevelt had
been talked into this venture by Secretary of State Cordell
Hull, and Borah denounced the plan as an effort to sneak
into the League of Nations through the back door. The
hysterical rhetoric of Father Coughlin and the Hearst press
stimulated additional opposition to the proposal. Frightened
Senators took the path of least resistance with the result
that approval of American membership in the World Court
fell seven votes short of the required two-thirds majority.
Among the Insurgents, only Capper, Costigan, Couzens, and
Cutting cast their vote with the administration.[13]

The defeat of the World Court proposal stunned Roosevelt. Especially upset by the rabid Insurgent opposition
to the measure, he questioned why Senators "with virtuous
emotions so often /were_7 somewhat lacking in brains." For
their part, the Insurgents believed that the President had
enough problems at home without "sighing for new worlds to
conquer." Even prominent Cabinet members thought that
Roosevelt's advocacy of the World Court had been "a major
political blunder." Later, Roosevelt himself concluded
that he had made a mistake. "There is. . .no question that
the rest of this session will be a madhouse—every Senator
a law unto himself and everyone seeking the spotlight,"

---

[13]Johnson to Charles K. McClatchy, March 11, 1934,
Part III, Box 16; Congressional Record, 74th Cong., 1st Sess.,
p. 1147.

he confided to Colonel House.[14]   As predicted, on the issues
of work relief, labor legislation, extension of the NIRA,
and payment of veterans compensation, the Senate continued
to assert its independence of the President.

The administration's $4.8 billion work relief bill
occupied the attention of the Senate from January through
March. Conservatives fought to cut the appropriation in
half by substituting the dole; some Senators sought to
transform the request into a pork-barrel measure; and the
Insurgents, along with some liberal Democrats, worked to
increase the sum allocated and to boost the standard for
work relief pay to prevailing wage rates. The economizers,
led by Virginia's Harry F. Byrd and North Carolina's Josiah
W. Bailey, tried to intimidate their colleagues into
thriftiness. "The pay day will come," Bailey warned. "The
bottom of your Uncle Sam's barrel will be reached." Most
Senators refused to heed this dire admonition, however, and
voted down two amendments to the bill that would have reduced funds substantially. The Senate was also unwilling
to appropriate a greater sum than the President had requested, and it similarly rejected LaFollette's amendment
calling for increased expenditures for public works.[15]

---

[14]Norman Hapgood to Roosevelt, Aug. 22, 1935, Roosevelt
Papers, PPF 2278; Johnson to Charles K. McClatchy, March 11,
1934, Johnson Papers, Part III, Box 16; Harold L. Ickes, The
Secret Diary of Harold L. Ickes, I (New York, 1953), 290;
Roosevelt to House, Feb. 16, 1935, Roosevelt Papers, PPF 222.

[15]Josiah W. Bailey, "Vested Interest in Public Spending,"
Saturday Evening Post, CCVII (Feb. 2, 1935), 5; Congressional
Record, 74th Cong. 1st Sess., p. 2559. Summarizing the con-
flict in Congress over the relief bill, George Norris wrote:
"There seems to be quite a following of the idea that we

Once the issue of funds had been resolved, controversy regarding the work-relief bill centered on the McCarran prevailing wage-rate amendment. The Insurgents supported the President's emphasis on work relief, but they thought it imperative for the unemployed to receive a wage corresponding to that paid by private employers in each locality. In accordance with these views the Senate incorporated into the bill a prevailing wage-rate proviso that had been introduced by Nevada's Pat McCarran. Roosevelt, on the other hand, insisted on a "security wage" of approximately $50 a month and informed the Senate that he would not accept a relief bill with McCarran's amendment attached to it. Ridiculing the "childishness" and "peevishness" that obviously existed at the other end of Pennsylvania Avenue, Wheeler retorted that he would "not vote for the proposed legislation under the crack of the whip." With his relief bill at an impasse and convinced that the Senate was nothing but a "big headache" anyway, the President unexpectedly embarked on an ocean cruise. "The entire incident," Hiram Johnson concluded, "rather confirms my idea that Roosevelt is not quite sure of himself and that his plans for the future are wholly nebulous and inchoate." Realizing the dangerous consequences of withholding relief any further, the Senate reversed its stand on the McCarran amendment and adopted a compromise plan that gave the President discretionary control over all relief

---

should discontinue public works projects and, in effect, go back to the dole system. I am opposed to the dole. I would rather spend more money and give jobs than to feed the starving from appropriations." Norris to E. Glenn Callen, Feb. 7, 1935, George W. Norris Papers, Tray 13, Box 5, Library of Congress, Washington, D. C.

wages, except those on public building projects. LaFollette,
who was among the Insurgents voting for this compromise, was
convinced that many Senators had favored the prevailing-wage
amendment not because they believed in the principle involved but because they saw in it an opportunity to block
the passage of the entire relief bill.[16]

Although all the Insurgents voted for the Emergency
Relief Appropriation Act, many of them did so with a degree
of apprehension. To the Insurgents, the most irritating
feature of the measure was that it allowed Roosevelt complete autonomy in the disbursement of funds. In January,
1935, when the legislation was first introduced, James
Couzens had expressed concern about the President's demand
that Congress relinquish its control over relief funds.
"Should Congress abdicate these powers to the President,"
the Michigan Senator declared, "there seems to be very little
reason for our being here." Couzens joined Borah, Johnson,
and others in the Senate in an attempt to "earmark" relief
expenditures. When Norris, however, correctly pointed out
that success in that endeavor would result in "no relief but
a lot of pork," the effort to earmark quickly collapsed.[17]

The Insurgents also objected to large increases in
governmental spending without a corresponding increase in

[16]*Congressional Record*, 74th Cong., 1st Sess., p.
2564; Johnson to Hiram Johnson, Jr., March 3, 1935, Johnson
Papers, Part IV, Box 4; *Progressive*, March 23, 1935.

[17]Couzens to B. E. Begal, Jan. 30, 1935, James Couzens
Papers, Box 108, Library of Congress, Washington, D. C.;
Congressional Record, 74th Cong., 1st Sess., p. 3365.

taxes. An ominous 30 per cent of the total Insurgent vote consequently supported three amendments aimed at reducing the amount of the relief appropriation. Hiram Johnson conceded that such "a financial outlay which staggers even one as improvident and as imprudent as I am. . .gives me the Willies." Sounding very much like Hoover, William Lemke charged that the New Deal relief program had made "tramps and beggars of a once proud people." These views revealed the almost instinctive Insurgent fear of an unbalanced budget. Later, when the New Dealers decided on a program of deficit spending of indefinite duration that rural Congressmen believed benefited the cities and labor at the expense of agriculture, some of the Insurgents allied themselves with conservatives in opposition to increased appropriations.[18] A major difference between Insurgents and conservatives on relief spending, however, was that the Insurgents were willing to vote for heavier tax loads to support necessary projects whereas the conservatives were not.

In the midst of the relief controversy, Roosevelt sent a message to Congress recommending a two-year extension of the NIRA in modified form. The President indicated that he

---

[18]Johnson to Hiram Johnson, Jr., March 5, 1935, Johnson Papers, Part IV, Box 4; Progressive, Sept. 14, 1935, p. 3. In 1935, however, all of the Insurgents agreed with the views of Peter Norbeck: "I think the expenses of the government can be curtailed, but after all, I think substantial curtailments very difficult, if not impossible. I find the men who honestly disbelieve in relief are generally people who eat three square meals a day and know where the money is coming from to pay for next winter's coal bill." Norbeck to Juui Dieserud, August 24, 1935, Peter Norbeck Papers, Richardson Archives, University of South Dakota Library, Vermillion, South Dakota.

wished the extension to retain the act's labor provisions,
to exclude some small businesses from price and production
controls, and to include certain restrictions on monopolistic practices. "The fundamental purposes and principles
of the Act are sound," he declared. "To abandon them is
unthinkable. It would spell the return of industrial and
labor chaos." The Senate, however, seemed to favor a full
restoration of the antitrust laws; an amendment to this
effect, offered by Borah, had narrowly missed being attached
to the Relief Act. The Idaho Senator regarded Roosevelt's
request to extend the NIRA as condoning the malpractices of
"large business which no one except one possessing the greed
of a highwayman would employ, and no one who did not believe
in the highwayman's technique would defend." Nye responded
to the President's message by introducing a resolution
calling for a Senate Finance Committee investigation of the
administration of codes under the NIRA.[19]

The Senate hearings on the NIRA resolution brought
claims that the NIRA directly threatened the existence of
the small businessman. Believing that its investigation
justified its refusal of the President's request for a
two-year extension, the Senate Finance Committee substituted a resolution proposed by Senator Bennett Champ Clark
of Missouri that called for the extension of the NIRA only
until April 1, 1936, exempted intrastate business from its
provisions, barred price fixing except in certain "sick"

[19]Rosenman (ed.), Public Papers of FDR, IV, 82-3; Congressional Record, 74th Cong., 1st Sess., p. 4183; Ibid., pp.
2608, 3199.

industries, and allowed only thirty days for the revision of existing codes to conform with these new standards. When the Senate approved the Clark Resolution by a voice vote, Hugh S. Johnson confided that his NRA "was so dead that he could smell the faint scent of Lilies of the Valley." *Time* concurred that the Senate, in effect, "had offered an emasculated Blue Eagle less than ten months to flutter to its grave."[20] It appeared, however, for awhile at least, that the House would grant Roosevelt his desired two-year extension, but on May 27, 1935, the Supreme Court intervened to prevent a probable deadlock between the two chambers by declaring the NIRA unconstitutional.

No Insurgent tears were shed over the NRA's demise. Only LaFollette, who had announced his opposition to the Clark Resolution because it made no attempt to retain the NIRA's good features—prohibition of child labor, guarantee of collective bargaining for labor, and the establishment of minimum wages and maximum hours—, reacted with what might be vaguely called regret. Norris, who was more inclined to follow Roosevelt's lead than were other Insurgents, contended that "a fair trial of the NIRA has demonstrated that in its operation it has been injurious to small businesses and has given preference to the big fellows." Such a conclusion was not at all surprising to a jubilant Burton K. Wheeler, who long had been convinced that the legislation

---

[20]Hugh S. Johnson, *The Blue Eagle From Egg to Earth* (Garden City, N. Y., 1935), p. 386; *Time*, XXV (May 13, 1935), 14.

was conceived by the United States Chamber of Commerce, an
organization not known for its liberal views. Peter Norbeck
was delighted to see the NRA go, for he felt it had retarded
agricultural recovery by increasing the cost of everything
that the farmers had to buy. Henrik Shipstead, in a national
radio address, argued that since monopolies had caused the
depression, the opportunity now should be seized to restore
the antitrust laws and thus guarantee recovery. At the
same time, however, the Minnesota Senator urged quick Congressional approval of the Wagner bill, which would give
labor an equitable chance to bargain with capital "for a
better deal than they have had under the N.R.A." Unless
this was done, he warned, there would undoubtedly be another
crash worse than the one of 1929.[21]

About a week later the Senate acted on Shipstead's
advice and passed the National Labor Relations Act by a
substantial margin of 63 to 12. This act, which William
Leuchtenberg called "one of the most drastic innovations of
the decade," encountered surprisingly little opposition. It
set up a National Labor Relations Board to conduct elections
for determining proper bargaining agents for employees and
to restrain employers from committing unfair labor practices.
The one-time Wilsonian George Creel remarked that this New
Deal reform "gave organized labor the status of a privileged

---

[21]*Congressional Record*, 74th Cong. 1st Sess., p. 7482;
Norris to E. C. Wiggenhorn, May 14, 1935, Norris Papers,
Tray 13, Box 7; Norbeck to G. G. Harris, March 12, 1935,
Norbeck Papers, Drawer 37; Shipstead Radio Address, May 10,
1935, Henrik Shipstead Papers, Box 22, Minnesota Historical
Society, St. Paul, Minnesota.

class."[22]   In the not-too-distant future, many of the Insurgents would agree with Creel's assessment, but for the moment they regarded the Wagner Act as a long overdue reform necessary to counterbalance the dominant influence of big business.

Secretary of Labor Frances Perkins recalled that Roosevelt "never lifted a finger" for the labor bill until mid-June, 1935, when he perfunctorily urged the House to approve it. In fact, from January to May, 1935, Congress, and especially the Senate, had regained some of the legislative initiative from an indecisive President. Although he realized the necessity of Roosevelt's leadership, Peter Norbeck wrote in February that he was pleased that Congress was reasserting its prerogative as the chief legislative branch of government. Congressional action, however, eventually aroused the President from his apparent torpor. Defying precedent, he appeared in person before Congress to deliver a stinging veto of the Patman Bonus bill. Roosevelt's dramatic performance puzzled the Insurgents. Since the bill would have provided for the payment of the bonus through an expansion of the currency, the Insurgents thought it a logical way to furnish a portion of the populace with additional purchasing power. Disappointed over rumors of a probable Presidential veto of the bonus bill, an angry William Lemke suggested one way to persuade Roosevelt to be more amenable and thereby

---

[22]William E. Leuchtenberg, Franklin D. Roosevelt and the New Deal, 1932-1940 (New York, 1963), p. 151; George Creel, Rebel at Large (New York, 1947), p. 297.

revealed the strained state of Congressional-Executive relations. "When the President finishes delivering his veto
message," the North Dakota Congressman facetiously wrote a
friend, "I think we ought to close the doors and keep him
there until we do the job, to show him that the Congress of
the United States is still functioning, and is not overawed
by a chief executive who at one time was nothing short of
a deity, but who has dethroned himself, and now must stand
upon the merit of his performance, rather than on the theory
that the king can do no wrong."[23]

During the first five months of 1935 the Senate, with
virtually no prodding from the President, held up the relief
bill for an extended period before finally passing it, enacted far-reaching labor legislation, approved an inflationary bonus bill, and emasculated the NIRA. To many
Senators these accomplishments represented a proud achievement—especially in contrast to the impotence which Congress
had demonstrated during the prior session. The Insurgents
looked with favor upon this partial reassertion of legislative independence, but they recognized that the condition of
the country demanded more than the program Congress had
offered. The Insurgents were particularly critical of Congress' failure to approve legislation involving such matters
as social security, banking, and public-utility holding

[23]Leuchtenberg, Roosevelt and the New Deal, p. 150;
Norbeck to A. G. Blanchard, Feb. 21, 1935, Norbeck Papers,
Drawer 16; Lemke to James A. Bell, May 22, 1935, William
Lemke Papers, Box 12, The Orin G. Libby Manuscript Collec-
tion, University of North Dakota Library, Grand Forks, North
Dakota.

companies. On April 1, 1935, <u>Time</u> joined the Insurgents in
chastising Congress for remaining quiescent on these crucial
issues." If a drowsy member of Congress," the magazine
editorialized, "had on January 3 lain down to nap. . .and
if by some miracle he had slept until last week, he would,
on awakening, have had no reason to believe that he had
taken more than three winks. For the sum total of legislation passed by Congress during those eleven weeks was substantially nothing."[24]

For the most part, the lethargy in the Senate reflected the uncertainty of Roosevelt. One Insurgent frankly
observed that Congress had no idea where it was going. "I
don't complain so much of this, for frankly and candidly,
we avowed that we are experimenting. . . . But when the
Administration blithely says it knows nothing about what
will be done," he continued, "some of us with only a small
conception of our duty hesitate to act." Ickes also noted
that Roosevelt appeared "distinctly dispirited. . .looked
tired and seemed to lack fighting vigor. . . . I came away
not at all reassured as to his ability to fight his program
through."[25] The President, as a matter of fact, was uncertain regarding the legislative course that he should follow.
Despite the nation's liberal bent exhibited in the 1934
elections, Roosevelt still fancied himself as a coalition

[24]<u>Time</u>, XXV (April 1, 1935), 9.

[25]Johnson to Hiram Johnson, Jr., April 7, 1935,
Johnson Papers, Part IV, Box 4; Ickes, <u>Secret Diary</u>, I,
306.

leader of all interests. Faced with mounting pressure on
all sides, he was now forced to reevaluate his role as a
bipartisan leader and to decide in which direction he should
move. Before he could make these decisions, however, he
needed clearer directives from his advisors, from interest
groups in the country at large, and from members of the
Congress who represented opposing factions.

The controversy involving the "men around the President"
had been submerged by an emphasis on unity to combat the
emergency. In 1933-1934 the NIRA was the New Deal's primary
recovery measure, and the "planners" and the advocates of
business-government cooperation were clearly in the forefront. In the spring of 1934 one of the chief advocates of
business-government cooperation, Raymond Moley, was satisfied
enough to proclaim that the New Deal was nearly complete and
merely required consolidation of its accomplishments.[26]
Moley's program and attitude angered the Brandeisians,
believers in competition whose major victory during the First
New Deal had been the successful fight to regulate the stock
exchanges.

The Brandeisians, who viewed big business and high
finance as responsible for the depression, believed that to
invite these "pillagers of the people" into a governmental
partnership under the NRA seemed the height of folly. Instead, they maintained, the proper policy would be to punish
concentrated wealth by strict enforcement of the antitrust
laws and by enactment of more progressive tax legislation.

---

[26]Schlesinger, Politics of Upheaval, p. 212.

In June, 1934, Ben Cohen, a disciple of Brandeis, wrote his
mentor, Felix Frankfurter, about the existing struggle
"between Isaiah /Brandeis/ on the one side, who wants to
ride ahead hard with his full program, completely contemp-
tuous of political obstacles; and Ray /Moley/ on the other
side, who is afraid of Isaiah's belligerence, quite through
with the agony and sweat of reforming, and wearily eager to
settle down to a false security of sweet reasonableness."[27]
When the Supreme Court ruled the NIRA unconstitutional,
Brandeis himself reminded Roosevelt that "it was the eleventh
hour." At the same time Frankfurter, insisting that the
policy of cooperation had failed, urged the President to
declare war on bigness.[28] Before Roosevelt would consent
to act on Frankfurter's promptings, however, he had to be
convinced that big business was really the enemy.

---

[27]Many New Dealers (the so-called neo-Brandeisians)
preferred that a "trust busting" approach be coupled with a
program of planned governmental spending. Most of the Insurgents, except possibly LaFollette and Norris, never endorsed this emphasis on spending for recovery. Tom Corcoran
and Ben Cohen to F. F., June 18, 1934, quoted in Max Freedman (ed.), Roosevelt and Frankfurter: Their Correspondence,
1928-1945 (Boston, 1967), p. 224.

[28]Leuchtenberg, Roosevelt and the New Deal, pp. 148-
150. Frankfurter has recently indicated that the differences between the so-called "two New Deals" were not so tidy
as historians have reported. Roosevelt's policies were often
determined by the exigencies of the moment. To Arthur M.
Schlesinger, Jr., the most noted exponent of the two-New
Deal interpretation, Frankfurter wrote: "I must reject your
assumption that there was a real clash of views between
Moley-Tugwell and F. F.-Brandeis. This assumes that the
respective parties had coherent and systematic views on some
of the problems that are involved in Roosevelt's policies."
Frankfurter to Schlesinger, June 18, 1963, quoted in Freedman (ed.), Frankfurter and Roosevelt, pp. 24-26.

The view that business was indeed the culprit was urged on Roosevelt by many so-called "radical groups." In late 1934 and early 1935 the country was undergoing a process of polarization. Conservative discontent centered in the business and financial communities, while liberal discontent permeated the agricultural Northwest. Hard times and frustration produced a plethora of candidates to fill the leadership vacuum created by the President's indecisiveness. On any given day Huey Long, Father Coughlin, Frances Townsend, Floyd Olson, Phil LaFollette, or Gerald P. Nye competed for headlines. The Wisconsin Progressive, Congressman Tom Amlie, reported that most of his constituents were looking away from Roosevelt because of the inadequacy of his program. Usher Burdick, an Insurgent Congressman from North Dakota, warned the Democrats that they would soon be displaced by some other party, "some new party, which will come up from the people themselves, consecrated to the accomplishment of the great task ahead."[29] Publicly, the President appeared to be unconcerned about any threat to the Democratic party from the radical elements. "There is no question that it is all a dangerous situation," he told Colonel House, "but when it comes to a showdown, these fellows cannot lie in the same bed and will fight among themselves with almost absolute certainty. They represent every shade." Privately, however, Roosevelt was worried. He commissioned Farley to conduct a

---

[29]Amlie to Walter Morton, March 22, 1935, Thomas R. Amlie Papers, Box 15, State Historical Society of Wisconsin, Madison, Wisconsin; Progressive, Feb. 23, 1935, p. 3.

secret poll of Huey Long's electoral appeal, and he feared
that LaFollette or Nye would head up an independent Progressive party and capture the liberal vote in 1936.[30]

Roosevelt did not succumb to the pressure from the
left until he was formally repudiated by the business community. In the summer of 1934 a group of conservatives had
organized the anti-New Deal American Liberty League, but its
roster read so much like a "millionaires' Who's Who" that
no one, including the President, gave it much attention.
The real parting of ways between much of the business community and the New Deal occurred at the 1935 annual Chamber
of Commerce meeting. There, irate businessmen denounced the
entire New Deal as an attempt to "sovietize America." They
even went on record against an extension of the NIRA. In
comparing this meeting with the Chamber's annual gathering
two years earlier, a New York Times reporter pointed out
that in 1933 the annual convention had been an earnest
prayer meeting devoted to securing government aid. The
burden of the prayer was, "Please do something, and don't
waste any time about it, for we have forgotten the way out

[30]Roosevelt to House, Feb. 16, 1935, Roosevelt Papers,
PPF 222; James A. Farley, Jim Farley's Story (New York,
1948), p. 51. Thomas Amlie reported that the popular Long,
with the aid of Milo Reno's Farm Holiday Association, was
capturing the drought-stricken farmers of the Midwest. "I
was just over in the Senate Chamber this afternoon," Amlie
wrote. "Huey Long talked briefly from time to time. The
galleries were jammed and there were about a thousand people
standing outside trying to get in. The question on every
lip was 'Is Huey Long talking?' or 'What is Huey Long saying?'
or 'I wish I could hear Huey.'" Amlie to Howard Y. Williams,
April 24, 1935, Howard Y. Williams Papers, Box 25, Minnesota
Historical Society, St. Paul, Minnesota.

of this maze." What a difference two years had made! Now
the cry of business was "regimentation." "And regimentation
means anything the government does," a friend wrote Brandeis.
"The papers I have been reading. . .are pre-1929."[31]

The frontal assult by many businessmen on his program
stunned Roosevelt, but it galvanized the Insurgents into
action. LaFollette remarked that he considered the Chamber
of Commerce's attack on the President as most fortunate. In
a few days, Frankfurter arranged a White House dinner for
five Insurgent Senators: Costigan, Johnson, LaFollette,
Norris, and Wheeler. All present frankly expressed the
opinion that under no circumstances could the New Deal count
on the support of big business; and all exhorted Roosevelt
to supply the leadership the country so desperately needed
and wanted. Wheeler suggested that the road ahead would be
difficult since many Democrats were hostile toward the New
Deal, and LaFollette stated that the President would have
to go against members of his own party—just as Theodore
Roosevelt had done on occasion. After listening to their
pleas for about four hours, Roosevelt assured the Insurgents
that their "time had come."[32]

In early June Roosevelt took the initiative and insisted on the passage of five pieces of "must" legislation:

---

[31] Delbert Clark, "The President Reaches a Turning
Point," New York Times, VIII (May 26, 1935), 3; Norman Hap-
good to Louis Brandeis, May 20, 1935, Roosevelt Papers,
PPF 2278.

[32] Ickes, Secret Diary, I, 363-64; Freedman (ed.),
Frankfurter and Roosevelt, pp. 269-73.

the social security bill, the Wagner labor bill, the banking
bill, the public-utility holding company bill, and some sort
of "soak the rich" tax scheme. This reassumption of Presidential leadership occurred just in time to bring some order
out of the chaos that had developed in Congress. Key Pittman observed that the division rampant in the countryside
was mirrored in the Senate. "We are faced with an unscrupulous regular Republican representation," Pittman warned
Roosevelt, "a progressive Republican membership determined
on going further left than you will go, a Democratic representation who have more sympathy for the Republican progressive position than they have for yours. And in the midst
of this disloyalty you have a regular Democratic representation that conscientiously believe they are saving you by
destroying you."[33]

A bipartisan conservative coalition that would later
stymie the New Deal had its origins in the period just prior
to the "second hundred days."[34] This rudimentary coalition
was most active during the debate over the work relief bill
when an "economy bloc" of regular Republicans and Southern
Democrats attempted to pare the appropriation. Josephus
Daniels reserved special disdain for the southern Democrats
in this clique. "It makes my blood boil," he wrote Roosevelt, ". . .to see the legislators who were elected on the

[33]Pittman to Roosevelt, Feb. 19, 1935, Roosevelt
Papers, PPF 745.

[34]See James T. Patterson, Congressional Conservatism
and the New Deal (Lexington, Kentucky, 1967), chapter 2.

pledge to 'stand back of the President,' standing so far
back that it would require a telescope to see them." Congressional liberals also became dissatisfied with the President during this period. One Insurgent indicated that he
was about to switch his loyalties to Wisconsin's Governor
Phil LaFollette if the situation did not improve. In the
House, Progressives had abandoned the policy of cooperation
with Democrats. Led by Lemke, they formed their own steering
committee and issued an eleven-point program for social and
economic justice. David K. Niles, liberal leader of the
Ford Hall Forum and an organizer of the 1932 National Progressive League for Roosevelt, was bothered by this and
similar incidents. "Two years ago was the first time that
the liberals and progressives participated in a victory and
it is a new experience for them," he wrote in an effort to
explain the Insurgent unrest. "They are naturally impatient
and for the most part they are so emotionally constituted
that it is easier to be anti-administration than pro." To
prevent a foolish split between the Insurgents and Roosevelt,
Niles had pleaded with Frankfurter to set up the aforemen-
tioned White House meeting, at which the decision was made
to push a program of reform.[35]

One of the first legislative beneficiaries of the
White House conference was the public-utility holding company bill. The President did not require instruction from

---

[35]Daniels to Roosevelt, April 5, 1935, Roosevelt
Papers, PPF. 86; Amlie to Louis M. Howe, March 14, 1935,
Roosevelt Papers, OF 1600; Progressive, March 23, 1935, p. 1;
Niles to Frankfurter, April 22, 1935, quoted in Freedman (ed.),
Frankfurter and Roosevelt, pp. 261-62.

the Insurgents on the malpractices of the utility holding

companies. Indeed, it was primarily because Roosevelt had

earned the enmity of the power magnates while he was the

governor of New York that many of the Insurgents supported

him in 1932.

In his annual message to Congress of January, 1935,

Roosevelt, supported by the investigative findings of the

Federal Trade Commission, the National Power Policy Commit-

tee, and the House Commerce Committee, had called for aboli-

tion of the evils of holding companies. Although there was

near unanimity that something must be done in this area,

there were conflicting opinions within the administration

as to the method to be applied. The FTC favored the use of

graduated taxes on the amount of income holding companies

derived from their subsidiaries. Treasury officials pre-

ferred the taxation of intercorporate dividends. Some In-

surgents, most notably Borah, Capper, and Norris, advocated

the complete destruction of all holding companies.[36] Other

Insurgents, although sharing this point of view, believed

that legislation embodying so drastic a solution would stand

little chance of passage. They therefore sponsored various

measures designed to regulate holding companies until such

time as Congress would legislate their complete abolition.

---

[36]"I submit that there is no use for all these things
existing," George Norris declared. "Everyone of these corporations must be oiled by somebody's money. They are par-
asites, in the main. They are not only useless, but they
are harmful, and in the end, the little, humble home with
electric light is contributing to the payment for the oil
to grease all those corporations." Congressional Record,
74th Cong., 1st Sess., p. 8493.

Wheeler was among those who had drawn up one of these
regulatory measures; the day before he planned to present it
to the Senate Roosevelt called him, along with Borah and
Norris, to the White House. Much to their delight, the President insisted that Wheeler's bill include a mandatory "death
sentence" for all utility holding companies. All such net-
works were to be dissolved within a period of five years
unless the Federal Power Commission certified them as "first
degree" companies, necessary for the operation of regional
economic units. With this addition, the bill was introduced both by Wheeler in the Senate and by Texas Democrat
Sam Rayburn in the House on February 6, 1935.

Since the Senate was preoccupied with the work relief
bill, the utility company proposal was placed far down on
its legislative calendar. This gave the power companies
time to mobilize a counterattack on the bill. They maintained that the "wanton" destruction of private property
that the bill intended would bankrupt electrical operating
units, retard recovery, and wipe out the invested savings
of "poor widows and orphans." The arguments of the holding
companies prompted Roosevelt to send Congress a scathing
message denouncing the manufactured "propaganda" against
the Wheeler-Rayburn bill. Instead of fleecing the public,
the President let it be known that reorganization of holding
companies would protect the investor. "The utility holding
company with its present powers must go," his message stated.
"It is a device which does not belong to our American traditions of law or business. . . . It is time to make an effort

to reverse that process of concentration of power which has
made most American citizens, once traditionally independent
owners of their own businesses, helplessly dependent for
their daily bread upon the favor of a very few." To some it
sounded as though Justice Brandeis himself had written
Roosevelt's speech. Rexford Tugwell knew that this was
not so, but he sorrowfully claimed that "in Franklin's
Valhalla no figure loomed larger than the Old Justice."[37]

With the help of a reinvigorated Roosevelt, Wheeler
managed to get his bill out of committee and onto the Senate
floor in late May. This led to another barrage of attacks
from the ubiquitous utility lobby. Led by Wendell L. Wilkie
and Philip J. Gadsden, the power companies unleashed a horde
of lobbyists on Washington; their actual numbers were greater
than the sum total of Congressmen. Their circulars screamed
"Last Chance," by which they meant that this was the last
chance for investors to protect their savings from annihila-
tion by President Roosevelt. Gadsden urged the public to
"wire your Representatives," and this the investors did with
a vengeance. So many Congressmen began denying that they
had ever supported the bill that one pundit labeled it
another "Gadsden Purchase." Even the Democratic leaders of
the Senate became jittery and urged Wheeler to drop the
death sentence. One night at a party given by SEC Director
Joseph Kennedy, Jimmy Byrnes cornered Wheeler in the bath-
room and informed him that the President really did not

---

[37]Rosenman (ed.), _Public Papers of FDR_, IV, 98-103; Freedman (ed.), _Frankfurter and Roosevelt_, p. 288.

favor the retention of the death sentence. When rumors that
the President had retreated persisted, Wheeler rushed over
to the White House and received from Roosevelt written assurance that he was standing firmly behind the original bill.
Wheeler, satisfied that he had the President's support,
pocketed the statement for future use.[38]

As the bill neared a final vote in the Senate, Senator
William H. Dieterich of Illinois rose and introduced an
amendment intended to substitute regulation for dissolution
of holding companies. If approved, the Dieterich substitute would have killed the death sentence. Norris repri-
manded his colleague from Illinois for pretending that
regulation of holding companies could be effective. The
Federal Trade Commission "could hunt from one end of the
country to the other and never find any of them to be any
good," the Nebraska Senator exclaimed. "They would not be
in business if they were good." Wheeler responded to
Dieterich by reading Roosevelt's note, which stated that
any amendment striking "at the heart of the bill. . .is
wholly contrary to the recommendation of my message." This
show of Presidential determination kept enough Democrats in
harness to defeat the Dieterich proposal by the narrow
vote of 44 to 45. Another crippling amendment, offered by

---

[38]Time, XXVI (July 8, 1935), 10–11; Burton K. Wheeler,
Yankee From the West (Garden City, N. Y., 1962), pp. 307–
14.

Augustine Lonergan of Connecticut, was voted down 43 to 45 before the Senate finally passed the bill.[39]

In the House, however, the mandatory death sentence was replaced by a provision giving the SEC only discretionary power to order dissolution. When the two versions of the bill went into conference, deadlock resulted. Rather than compromise on the elimination of holding companies, Wheeler and Norris preferred to take the issue to the country in the next election. Roosevelt and a majority of his assistants, however, feared that the entire bill would be endangered by such a delay. The conference committee, as a result, followed Felix Frankfurter's suggestion of a modified death sentence. Under its terms, holding companies of the "third degree" were to be abolished completely, and the SEC was to move as quickly as possible after January, 1938, to integrate the others into single geographic and economic units.

Although the Public Utility Holding Company Act fell significantly short of Insurgent desires, it was a substantial, as well as symbolic, victory for the foes of economic concentration. Ignoring its shortcomings, the Insurgents displayed enthusiasm over the measure. They had stood unanimously behind the President in repelling the crippling Dieterich and Lonergan amendments. Norris could think of no better way "to drive the money changers from the temple;" and Hiram Johnson believed the act "was eternally right." Brandeis conceded that it would achieve "considerable

---

[39]*Congressional Record*, 74th Cong., 1st Sess., pp. 8524, 9042.

toward curbing bigness." In the midst of the controversy
over the act, a jubilant Wheeler stated that Roosevelt
should not limit his assault on bigness to holding companies.[40]

Another major achievement of the "second hundred days"
was the Banking Act of 1935. Although the President did not
play as decisive a role in the enactment of this measure as
in the passage of the Holding Company Act, he nevertheless
adopted it as one of his "must" bills in late May. Behind
the proposal was the desire of Marriner Eccles, Roosevelt's
nominee as chairman of the Federal Reserve Board, to lessen
the influence of large private banks and to transfer the
nation's financial capital from New York to Washington.
Theoretically, the Insurgents believed the decentralized
banking system envisioned under the original Federal Reserve
Act to be the ideal, but time had exposed the serious de-
fects of this so-called unit banking system. The depression,
for example, had revealed that many small rural banks
possessed far too limited resources to provide adequate
emergency service. Consequently, such Insurgents as Cutting, Frazier, LaFollette, Nye, Shipstead, and Wheeler
favored a nationalized banking system. Nye introduced a
central bank measure in the Senate, but it went down to
defeat by an overwhelming vote of 10 to 59.[41] Thwarted in

[40]Norris to Dan Stephans, May 20, 1935, Norris Papers,
Tray 13, Box 2; Johnson to Hiram Johnson, Jr., July 21, 1935,
Johnson Papers, Part IV, Box 4; Norman Hapgood to Roosevelt,
June 16, 1935, Roosevelt Papers, PPF 2278.

[41]Congressional Record, 74th Cong., 1st Sess., p. 11906.

this attempt, the Insurgents joined administration forces
and concentrated on effecting the passage of the Eccles
bill, which they believed would strike a blow at high
finance by ending the dominant influence of the New York City
Federal Reserve Bank.

The bill received speedy approval in the House, but
in the Senate it was forced to hurdle an obstacle course
engineered by Carter Glass. The proud Virginian regarded
any tinkering with the Federal Reserve System a personal insult. "Carter Glass," another old Wilsonian wrote Roosevelt,
"is obsessed with the idea that the Federal Reserve Act, of
which Carter thinks he is the sole author, makes no other
legislation whatever necessary." Glass's opposition to the
Eccles' bill drove him into the open arms of the New York
banking crowd, which camouflaged its fear of losing prestige
and wealth by objecting that the bill would result in the
"political control" of banking. To generate hostility to
the administration measure, Glass invited the leaders of
Eastern finance to be the first witnesses to testify before
his banking committee. While chairing these hearings, Glass
busied himself by redrafting the banking proposal into a
bill that seemingly left his beloved Federal Reserve System
intact. Soon after Glass had finished this arduous task,
Roosevelt signed the bill into law. The wily Senator
boasted, "We didn't leave enough of the Eccles' bill with
which to light a cigarette." Arthur Krock agreed and reported that "it was a triumph of reputation and a man."

Walter Lippmann, however, thought the final act was really a victory for Eccles "dressed up as a defeat."[42]

The truth probably lay somewhat closer to Lippmann's assessment, for the act gave the federal government additional control over currency and credit. The most important new tool was the establishment of the Federal Open Market Committee, which shifted control over open-market operations from the various reserve banks to the Board of Governors of the Federal Reserve System. Although approving the ultimate aim of the act, Borah worried that the vastly strengthened Board of Governors had acquired absolute and thus dangerous control over the volume of currency in the country. LaFollette, Norbeck, and Shipstead objected to the act's inclusion of private bankers on the Board of Governors. "It is like a dog. . .going back to the vomit," Shipstead proclaimed, "to allow control of national credit to bankers, who were the worst speculators of all /and/ . .who were to blame for the policies that brought us to chaos and to national disaster."[43]

To put an end to banker control of the system, Norbeck called for the creation of an independent financial board similar to the Supreme Court to oversee the banking structure.

---

[42]Daniels to Roosevelt, Oct. 11, 1934, Roosevelt Papers, PPF 86; Leuchtenberg, Roosevelt and the New Deal, p. 160; Time, XXVI (August 5, 1935), 9; Walter Lippmann, Interpretations, 1933-1935 (New York, 1936), p. 194.

[43]Congressional Record, 74th Cong., 1st Sess., pp. 11908, 11914.

The most glaring deficiencies of the act, according to the
Insurgents, were that it constituted a threat to existing
state banks and that it permitted reserve banks to do a
limited business in underwriting securities.[44] The former
danger was somewhat lessened by a subsequent extension of
the benefits of the federal deposit insurance system to
some of the state banks. As for the latter, LaFollette's
amendment to prevent the underwriting of securities by
banks failed in a close vote of 22 to 39.[45] In spite of
these weaknesses, the Insurgents favored the act because it
did lessen the control of the banking community over the
nation's economy.

Though the Insurgents' reaction to the Banking Act was
rather lukewarm, they evinced considerable enthusiasm for
Roosevelt's tax reform program. On June 19, 1935, which
was unusually late in the session, the President added tax
reform to his list of "must" legislation. In a message to
Congress Roosevelt announced that reform was necessary because

[44]The Insurgents believed that the Banking Act of 1935
constituted a threat to many state banks because it set requirements for membership in the Federal Reserve System so
high that smaller banks could not possibly meet them. This
situation was somewhat alleviated when Congress agreed to extend the coverage of the Federal Deposit Insurance Corporation to state banks outside the Federal Reserve System.
Norbeck to John Vold, April 1, 1935, Norbeck Papers, Drawer
25.

[45]Congressional Record, 74th Cong., 1st Sess., p.
11935. Even Roosevelt chided Glass for allowing banks to
underwrite securities. "If you were not of such a trusting
and unsuspicious nature, and if you had my experience with
certain elements in certain places—you would know that the
old abuses would come back again if underwriting were restored in any shape, manner or form." Roosevelt to Glass,
August 9, 1935, Roosevelt Papers, OF 230A.

"our revenue laws have operated in many ways to the unfair advantage of the few, and they have done little to prevent an unjust concentration of wealth and economic power." Specifically, he recommended the enactment of increased inheritance and gift taxes, more steeply graduated levies on "very great individual incomes," a tax on intercorporate dividends, and a tax graduated according to the amount of corporate income because "size. . .threatened small business without which our competitive economic society would cease."[46]

The President's position on tax reform had been prompted by his anger over business and conservative opposition to the New Deal and by his desire to reduce the appeal of Huey Long's "Share the Wealth" plan. But it also reflected the pressure exerted on him by the Insurgents. It was no secret that Democratic opposition to tax reform in the 73rd Congress had been a major Insurgent disappointment. The Insurgents remained convinced that large fortunes must be broken up through progressive taxation both to alleviate the depression by augmenting consumer purchasing power through a more equitable distribution of wealth and to maintain government credit by providing revenue to finance federal relief programs. George Norris believed it imperative that the administration move quickly to redistribute wealth. "If these fortunes are not broken up by law," the

---

[46]Rosenman (ed.), Public Papers of FDR, IV, 270-77.

Nebraskan warned, "the time will come when they will be broken up by the mob."[47]

When the New Deal's position on tax reform remained unknown as late as April, 1935, LaFollette delivered a national radio address criticizing Roosevelt for his failure to face the issue. The Wisconsin Senator served notice that, regardless of what the administration did, the Insurgents would again make "the best fight of which they are capable to meet the emergency by drastic increases in taxes levied upon wealth and income." Nye warned that the President's handling of the tax question would determine the amount of Insurgent activity in his behalf in 1936. If tax reform was allowed to become a campaign issue, the North Dakota Senator threatened, "many of us will lose faith and may even be found quiescent. . .or actually fighting with the Republicans."[48] Roosevelt understood such language all too well, and he feared the consequences. He remarked that "Progressive Republicans like LaFollette, Cutting, Nye, etc. are flirting with the idea of a third ticket. . .that. . . would defeat us, elect a conservative Republican and cause a complete swing to the left before 1940." More than anything else, reported Arthur Krock, the President's tax

---

[47]Norris to Lucien B. Fuller, March 6, 1935, Norris Papers, Tray 2, Box 7.

[48]Congressional Record, 74th Cong., 1st Sess., p. 7648; New York Times, June 22, 1935, p. 21.

message demonstrated his "passion" to keep "the liberal or radical forces" behind him.[49]

One week after his tax message Roosevelt still had done nothing further to effect tax reform. Democrats spread the rumor that the tax message constituted nothing more than a political move designed to retain the support of the Progressive bloc. The Insurgents thought it time to test the President's sincerity. Borah, Johnson, LaFollette, and Norris, consequently, drew up a petition stating that, since Roosevelt had espoused a "cardinal measure of their political philosophy," they were prepared to aid him by staying in session all summer to enact his tax program. This Progressive Round-Robin, as it was known, circulated through the Senate and garnered the signatures of twenty-two Senators. LaFollette further increased the pressure for action by proposing to add the tax-reform package to a pending resolution extending certain nuisance taxes that had to be approved in five days or the government would lose $1.5 million in revenue every day thereafter.[50]

Stimulated into action by the Insurgent pressure, Democratic Congressional leaders hurried over to the White House and emerged with the startling news that Roosevelt approved of LaFollette's plan. That the President demanded enactment of a major reform measure in less than a week's

---

[49]Roosevelt to House, Feb. 16, 1935, Roosevelt Papers, PPF 222; New York Times, July 17, 1935, IV, 3.

[50]New York Times, June 22, 1935, pp. 1, 2; Ibid., June 28, 1935, p. 20.

time stunned and infuriated friend and foe alike. The pro-New Deal New York Daily News reminded Roosevelt that it had taken "six days to make the world." Walter Lippmann called for a filibuster ("a miserable weapon") to prevent a deed which could only "be stigmatized as nothing less than a flagrant abuse of power." This flood of criticism induced Roosevelt to deny publicly that he had ever requested Congress to attach his tax-reform proposal to a pending resolution. Much to their chagrin, Senate Majority Leader Joseph T. Robinson and Senate Finance Committee chairman Pat Harrison were forced to retreat and acknowledge that they had misunderstood the President. To halt LaFollette from adding his amendments to the nuisance tax legislation, Harrison had to promise the Insurgents that his committee would report out a tax reform package before the session was over.[51]

Contributing to the rising tempers resulting from the tax struggle was the "jungle heat" of the Washington summer. Nothing seemed to be going right. "Even the so-called heating plant of the senate chamber has gone cock-eyed," Hiram Johnson wrote his son, "although some of us have a dirty suspicion that it was inefficiently run to put the heat on the senate." New York's Senator Royal S. Copeland, M.D., announced that he had never seen his "patients" in such sad shape and confirmed reports that hospital beds

---

[51]Time, XXVI (July 8, 1935), 10; Joseph Alsop and Robert Kintner, "Joe Robinson, The New Deal's Old Reliable," Saturday Evening Post, CCIX (Sept. 26, 1936), 6, 8.

were being rapidly filled by the exhausted legislators.
Arthur Krock also thought that the Congress "looked dead
tired," and he blamed both Roosevelt and the Insurgents
for this state of affairs. Krock reported that the pressure for tax reform so late in the session had produced
nothing but resentment among Congressmen other than the
Insurgents.[52]

After being entangled for more than a month in the
red tape of Representative Robert L. Doughton's Ways and
Means Committee, the tax reform bill emerged onto the
House floor on July 30. Although it still retained the
principle of graduated taxation, the bill was essentially
one of Doughton's own creation. His committee had deleted
the intercorporate dividend tax, lowered the graduated
corporate rates, and included an excess-profits tax.
Doughton prematurely divulged his committee's bill when he
informed reporters that Congress had "no constitutional
right to levy taxes for any other purpose than to raise
revenue." His watered-down version of tax reform passed
in the House by a vote 282 to 96.[53]

In the Senate Borah announced that he considered the
House bill unacceptable. He claimed that the measure was
devoid of all social content and was simply masquerading as
tax reform. As a bill merely to raise revenue, the Idaho

---

[52] Johnson to Hiram Johnson, Jr., July 21, 1935, Johnson
Papers, Part IV, Box 4; New York Times, July 17, 1935, p. 18;
Ibid., July 14, 1935, IV, 3.

[53] Time, XXVI (July 15, 1935), 22; Congressional Record,
74th Cong., 1st Sess., p. 12499.

Senator argued, it was deflationary because it took the money of both the rich and poor out of circulation. Borah, therefore, introduced his own "must" legislation, a $5 billion inflationary proposal designed to refinance farm mortgages and to pay the veterans bonus through expansion of the currency. Announcing that he regarded vacations a luxury, he threatened to keep Congress in session until November if his program was not adopted. Other Insurgents, however, persuaded Borah to change his mind by warning him that such action would destroy all opportunity for tax reform.[54]

When the Senate finally took up the tax-reform bill, Borah and Norris collaborated in an attempt to halt the issuance of tax-exempt federal bonds. The Senate adopted their amendment by a vote of 40 to 39, but it was later deleted by the conference committee. Also, LaFollette tried but failed to include in the bill a more steeply graduated schedule of personal income tax rates. After LaFollette's amendment was voted down, 22 to 56, Harrison skillfully guided the tax bill to passage on August 15, 1935.[55] The final bill, signed by Roosevelt on August 31, contained only moderately graduated taxes on both corporate incomes and intercorporate dividends. It also increased surtax rates on all personal incomes over $50,000, upped capital gains and estate taxes, and changed the method of determining

[54] New York Times, July 22, 1935, pp. 1, 6.

[55] Congressional Record, 74th Cong., 1st Sess., p. 13254.

the House excess profits tax by substituting graduated rates
for flat rates.

As finally passed, the Wealth Tax Act of 1935 did little
either to redistribute wealth or to raise revenue. The Insurgents recognized these facts, but they believed that the
philosophy behind Roosevelt's tax message of June 19 was
more important than the act itself. Brandeis agreed that the
tax message revealed that "F. D. appreciated the evils of
bigness." Arthur Capper placed himself "heartily with my
whole soul behind the President" because the bill intended
"to encourage the continuation of the smaller business concerns." The Progressive pointed out that Roosevelt had
"borrowed another page from the Progressive philosophy of
government" and characterized the measure as "the outstanding achievement of the present national administration."[56]

Approval of the Tax Act brought to a close the flurry
of legislative activity known as the "second hundred days."
On the day Congress adjourned, newspaper publisher Roy W.
Howard begged Roosevelt to grant business "a recess from
further experimentation." Howard reported that businessmen

---

[56]Hapgood to Roosevelt, August 3, 1935, Roosevelt
Papers, PPF 2278; New York Times, July 1, 1935, p. 2; Progressive, July 6, 1935, p. 4. Although the Insurgents were
enthusiastic over the Wealth Tax Act, it hardened many
Democrats in their opposition to the New Deal. "One of the
most interesting things in the political situation here,"
Hiram Johson wrote, "is that the leadership on the Democratic
side, generally speaking, has little more stomach for what
Roosevelt is doing than the leadership on the Republican
side. It is simply the old story of the bipartisan combination when you touch the quickened financial nerve." Johnson
to Hiram Johnson, Jr., July 21, 1935, Johnson Papers, Part
IV, Box 4. For a detailed account of the Democratic divi-
sions on the tax bill, see Patterson, Congressional Conservatism, pp. 58-76.

believed that recent administration measures had been motivated by the President's desire for "revenge on business."
Roosevelt, delighted with his accomplishments, all too
hastily assured Howard that the basic program of the New
Deal had "now reached substantial completion."[57]

The "breathing spell," promised by the President, remained in effect for the next half year. The calm was shat-
tered on March 3, 1936, when Roosevelt called for a tax on
undistributed corporate profits. His message to Congress
exhibited a continuing animus against big business, but the
bill was also intended to raise new revenue to compensate
for the funds lost by payment of veterans bonuses and by
Supreme Court invalidation of the AAA processing taxes.
In addition, the administration anticipated an increase
in consumer purchasing power if corporations were forced
to distribute their surpluses in the form of dividends.

Conservatives were outraged over the proposal. Business executives labeled it a "ruinous tax" that would limit
industrial expansion by "breaking the nest egg." The Insurgents, on the other hand, were jubilant. LaFollette
regarded the proposal a significant extension of the principle of taxation according to the ability to pay. Henrik
Shipstead remarked that it was about time that the government took something from the monopolies and gave it back
to the people who had been impoverished by exorbitant prices.
From Mexico City, Ambassador Josephus Daniels wrote Roosevelt:

---

[57]Moley, After Seven Years, pp. 317-18.

"Glory be! I have just read your tax message to the Congress and I wish I were near you long enough to tell you how
it heartened me."[58]

The House speedily approved the President's request
with only a few minor changes. Bowing to intense business
pressure, however, Senator Pat Harrison loaded the measure
with crippling amendments with the result that the Senate
Finance Committee version of the bill appeared to disregard Roosevelt's original proposal almost completely. It
imposed a negligible tax on undistributed surpluses and
increased the corporate income tax by only a flat 3 per
cent. The President was furious over Harrison's mutilation
of his proposal. In a strong letter, which aides wisely
persuaded him not to send, Roosevelt expressed his true
sentiments. "I must be frank in telling you," he wrote his
Finance Committee chairman, "that. . .the amendments increase very heavily the taxes of those who now pay full
taxes and do not prevent the avoidance by people whose
earned income ought to, but does not, pay the proportionate
share of taxes." Despite the President's objection,
Harrison's version passed the Senate on June 5, 1936, by a
vote 42 to 29. All the Insurgents voted with the majority,
but they agreed with Marriner Eccles, who said that the

[58]Progressive, May 16, 1936, p. 1; Congressional
Record, 74th Cong., 2nd Sess., p. 9053; Daniels to Roosevelt,
March 5, 1936, Roosevelt Papers, PPF 86.

bill "was better than nothing, but not very much better."[59]

Roosevelt, however, emerged with a justifiable claim to

victory when the conference committee incorporated into the

bill an undistributed profits tax graduated from 7 to 27

per cent.

Final approval of the Revenue Act of 1936 occurred

just before the end of the session. On the whole, the

record of the 74th Congress had proved extremely gratifying

to the Insurgents. Norris concluded that more social

legislation for the benefit of the common man had been

enacted during the preceding two years than during his

entire tenure in Washington. In addition to the anti-

monopolistic legislation of the "second hundred days,"

there were many other important measures enacted by the 74th

Congress. Of special interest to the Insurgents was the

establishment of the Rural Electrification Administration.

This agency provided funds for rural cooperatives to con-

struct their own electrical distribution systems, thus

making possible an easier life for a large segment of the

population whom the private power companies had earlier

refused to serve on the grounds that it was not economically

[59]Roosevelt to Pat Harrison, May 24, 1936, Roosevelt Papers, PSF 62; Ellis W. Hawley, The New Deal and the Problem of Monopoly (Princeton, 1966), p. 356; Congressional Record, 74th Cong., 2nd Sess., p. 9110.

feasible to do so.[60] The Insurgents also favored the Social
Security Act, although they had sought to provide greater
benefits for those covered by the act; and 1936 finally
witnessed the enactment of the Patman Bonus Act, which Congress easily repassed over a perfunctory Presidential veto.

On the agricultural front the 74th Congress passed a
new farm mortgage law, but the big achievement in this area
was the enactment of the Soil Conservation and Domestic
Allotment Act to replace the defunct Agricultural Adjustment Act. To evade the Supreme Court's objection to the
AAA, the new legislation was designed to control agricultural production through the increased planting of soil-
conserving crops in place of soil-depleting crops. Again
the Insurgents failed to secure a cost-of-production amendment as an alternative to crop reduction, and they called
in vain for the adoption of amendments that would have
forbidden reciprocal trade agreements to include agricultural products. The fact, however, that the new law allowed
the farmers to receive benefit payments for promoting soil
fertility and not directly for curtailing production made it
more acceptable to the Insurgents than the AAA had been.

---

[60]New York Times, July 14, 1935, VII, 3. Norris believed that electricity would relieve some of the drudgery
in rural life. "I could close my eyes," the Senator mused,
"and see the innumerable scenes of the harvest and the un-
ending punishing tasks performed by hundreds of thousands of
women. . .growing old prematurely; dying before their time;
conscious of the great gap between their lives and the lives
of those whom the accident of birth or choice placed in the
towns and cities." George W. Norris, Fighting Liberal: The
Autobiography of George W. Norris (New York, 1945), p. 314.

Historians have generally agreed that the legislation
enacted from June to August, 1935, marked a change in emphasis in the New Deal—some have gone further and concluded
that this shift constituted a Second New Deal. These same
historians, however, have not been able to agree on which
New Deal was the more "radical" or the more "conservative."
The First New Deal, the argument runs, was characterized by
joint government-business planning, with big business emerg-
ing as the dominant partner. Under the NIRA, in fact, the
antitrust laws had been suspended thus increasing monopolistic practices and leading to the further decline of
small business. The Second New Deal supposedly deempha-
sized governmental planning, moved against bigness and
large personal fortunes, and attempted to restore competition among business units.[61]

Although the Insurgents would have pointed to exceptions to the two-New Deals distinction, they believed that
Roosevelt in 1935 had finally recognized the combination
of big business and high finance as the enemy. The Insurgents responded by casting 96.8 per cent of their total vote
in favor of the major legislation of the Second New Deal.[62]

---

[61]For a good analysis of this historical controversy,
see Otis L. Graham, Jr., "Historians and the New Deals,"
Social Studies, LIV (April, 1963), 133-40.

[62]These measures included the National Labor Relations
Act, the Banking Act of 1935, the Social Security Act, the
Public Utility Holding Company Act, the Wealth Tax Act,
and the Revenue Act of 1936. The only Insurgent defections
were Capper and Couzens on the undistributed-corporate-
profits tax.

In the midst of the "second hundred days" Frankfurter reported to Brandeis that "the Progressives—Ickes, Norris,
Hi Johnson, Gruening, Bob LaF.—feel much better about F. D.
than they did three or four months ago." Norbeck admitted
that he found "himself today more disposed to support
Roosevelt than. . .at any time during the whole Administration."[63]

The Progressive confirmed that "great progress had
been made" in not only domestic legislation but also in
foreign policy. To be sure, many observers felt that
Roosevelt had given the Insurgents almost complete freedom
in the area of foreign policy. By default, the President
allowed Senator Nye to head a Senate investigation, the
findings of which held bankers, munitions makers, and, to
a degree, former President Woodrow Wilson responsible for
American entry into World War I. Acting on these findings
and prompted by the Italo-Ethiopian crisis of May, 1935,
the Congress passed so-called neutrality legislation that
was intended both to prevent United States involvement in
any future war and to curtail discretionary presidential
decision-making in foreign affairs. Roosevelt remained
practically silent while Congress established limits on
presidential authority in matters of foreign policy. Nye
enthusiastically remarked that the President "had come

---

[63]Quoted in Leuchtenberg, Roosevelt and the New Deal,
p. 191; Norbeck to Herman D. Eilers, July 15, 1935, Norbeck
Papers, Drawer 18.

around entirely to the ideas of Mr. Bryan" on the matter of
neutrality legislation.[64]

Norman Hapgood concluded that the legislative program
of the "second hundred days" had absorbed the Insurgents
into the New Deal. "The true division today between liberals
and their opposites," he suggested to Borah, "is between
those who have favored the Holding Company Act, the T.V.A.,
and the acts regulating the issues of securities, on the
one side, and those opposing those measures on the other."
In the summer of 1935 it looked as though this assessment
might have been correct, but under the surface irreconcilable
differences between Roosevelt and the Insurgents remained.
"With monopolies," Roosevelt admitted, "Brandeis is one
thousand per cent right in principle, but in certain fields
there must be a guiding or restraining hand of Government
because of the very nature of the specific field."[65] The
Insurgents agreed that there were certain "natural monopolies" that could best be operated by government, but they
were concerned about the New Deal's expansion of governmental power into so many areas of American life.

Insurgent uneasiness with the New Deal's centralizing
and bureaucratic tendencies had surfaced as early as 1933,
especially in the debates preceding the enactment of the
Economy Act, the Agricultural Adjustment Act, and the

---

[64]_Progressive_, Sept. 7, 1935, p. 4; Wayne S. Cole,
Senator Gerald P. Nye and American Foreign Relations
(Minneapolis, 1962), p. 99.

[65]Hapgood to Roosevelt, May 30, 1936, Roosevelt Papers,
PPF 2278; Roosevelt to Hapgood, Feb. 24, 1936, Roosevelt
Papers, PPF 2278.

National Industrial Recovery Act. The Insurgents believed
that too great a concentration of governmental power at the
top constituted a grave threat to individual liberty. This
distrust of governmental power was an inherent part of their
"grass-roots" liberalism, a brand of liberalism that resembled that of Jefferson, Jackson, and Bryan more than it
did Franklin D. Roosevelt's New Deal. The Insurgents, to be
sure, advocated government intervention to rectify obvious
inequities in American life and to guarantee equality of
opportunity for competing individuals and groups, but many
of them believed that the New Deal had departed from this
ideal and had assumed for the federal government the
dominant role in the country's social, economic, and
political life.

Borah charged that the New Deal's continuous involvement in the economy would destroy "our form of government."
The New Dealers, however, did not share this deeply rooted
Insurgent concern for limited government. They argued that
the highly organized society of the United States could be
controlled only by a very powerful state. Their major interest was in erecting a government sufficiently powerful
to guarantee the necessities of life for each individual.
Unlike most Insurgents, the New Dealers wanted the government to provide for the security of each individual rather
than simply helping the individual to help himself. Like
the Insurgents, New Dealers sought to remove the most
glaring inequities in American life, but generally they
tried to create new privileges to balance old ones rather

than seeking to liquidate existing privileges in an effort
to equalize the opportunities in life. Thus, the New Deal
tried to give farmers and labor unions power to equal that
already enjoyed by industry rather than attempting to strip
industry of much of the power it already enjoyed.

Perhaps the Public Utility Holding Company Act more
than any other single piece of legislation revealed the
nature and limits of the Insurgents' liberalism. Wheeler
made it perfectly clear that the philosophy behind the measure was that there was an inherent evil in size itself.
Borah pointed out that great combinations of capital endangered the liberty of each American. "It therefore
becomes the duty of the Congress of the United States,"
the Idaho Senator exclaimed, "to exercise whatever power it
has to break down the concentration of economic wealth."
Wheeler conceded that the power of the national government
had to be utilized to destroy inflated economic power, but
he believed that a proper use of governmental power would
result not only in the decentralization of the economy but
also in the decentralization of government as well. If the
federal government by legislation like the public utility
holding company measure succeeded, for example, in destroying big business units, the resulting smaller units could
be successfully regulated by state and local governments.
"Excessive centralization in whatever form it may exist
negated American ideals," Wheeler proclaimed. "Unless we
stop the present trend toward monopoly and get back to
economic democracy," he warned, "we are going to build up

greater and greater bureaucracies until finally the Nation
itself will go down."[66] Ironically, at the same time that
the New Deal pleased the Insurgents by striking against
economic monopoly, it disturbed them by the big government
that its reforms produced. During Roosevelt's second term,
the Insurgents' primary endeavor would be to combat the
increasing influence and power of the national government.

---

[66]*Congressional Record*, 74th Cong., 1st Sess., pp.
2199-2208, 9050. Wheeler sponsored a tax on bigness to replace the inoperative antitrust laws. "In theory our antitrust legislation may have been an attempt to avoid undue
concentration of economic power," the Montana Senator explained, "but it has largely failed in practice to achieve
such an end, because the vague criterion of monopoly rather
than the more concrete criterion of corporate size was
adopted." Interview with Burton K. Wheeler, Nov. 22, 1968.

CHAPTER IV

INSURGENCY AND THE 1936 PRESIDENTIAL ELECTION

By the end of the 74th Congress political observers
predicted that most of the Insurgents, for one reason or
another, would support Roosevelt for President in 1936.
These predictions were generally accepted without question,
for the program of the "second hundred days" was regarded
as a fulfillment of many progressive dreams. Many Insurgents seemed to agree with journalist Raymond Clapper, who
concluded that the Second New Deal was "best understood as
reviving the progressive movement which developed early in
the century under the elder LaFollette."[1]

Although some of the Insurgents continued to express
reservations about the New Deal despite the administration's
program of 1935-1936, most of them still held Roosevelt in
high esteem. George Norris, who frankly admitted that no
other President had acted so courageously in an attempt
"to limit the power of organized monopoly and human greed,"
believed that Roosevelt's defeat would be "a national
calamity." Furthermore, after the Republican national convention, it was evident that the Insurgents had no choice
but to support Roosevelt as an alternative to a return of

---

[1]Progressive, Nov. 28, 1936, p. 8.

Hooverism. Since the Wisconsin Progressives and the Minnesota
Farmer-Laborites enthusiastically advocated the President's
reelection, there was no possibility of fielding an appealing
third-party ticket in the Northwest. Tom Amlie concluded
that all "radicals" must endorse Roosevelt in 1936 and "wait
for the real showdown until 1940."[2]

Although liberals had no better alternative in 1936
than to support Roosevelt, some Insurgents refused to endorse the President, and others did so only at the last
possible moment. It was party affiliation in many instances
that prevented several Insurgents from endorsing Roosevelt
or caused them to delay their decision to do so. Although
there were Insurgents in all parties, the group consisted
mainly of dissident Republicans. Usually party lines
meant less than nothing to these men, who had earned a
reputation for being pugnaciously independent. Presidential
elections, however, rekindled in some of them a dormant
loyalty to the Republican party. This was especially true
of William Borah and to a lesser extent of Lynn Frazier,
Gerald Nye, Peter Norbeck, James Couzens, and Arthur Capper.

It has been said that Borah became an ardent Republican every fourth year, and the record substantiates this
generalization. The only time he rebelled against his
party's nominee for president was in 1896, when he joined
the Silver Republicans in opposition to William McKinley.

[2] New York Times, June 15, 1936, pp. 1, 3; Amlie to
Vernon Lawrence, Jan. 23, 1936, Thomas R. Amlie Papers,
Box 13, State Historical Society of Wisconsin, Madison,
Wisconsin.

Astonishingly, the Idaho Senator refused to follow his hero
Theodore Roosevelt into the Bull Moose party in 1912. Although he despised the policies of Harding and Coolidge,
Borah enthusiastically backed Hoover in the 1928 campaign.
And even after the "Great Engineer" had betrayed the Insurgents on agricultural legislation and tariff policy, Borah
"silently" endorsed the Republican President's bid for reelection in 1932. It was not so much that the Senator
revered the Republican party as that he had such a poor
opinion of the Democratic party. He acknowledged that
there were some good individual Democrats, but he adhered
to the traditional belief that the party of Jefferson and
Jackson consisted of a coalition between corrupt Tammany
Halls and an unscrupulous Solid South. Although his party's
national leadership was conservative, Borah did not feel
compelled to step down from his position as leader of the
progressive Republican party in Idaho.[3]

Borah's displeasure with the centralizing tendencies
of the New Deal probably precluded his formal endorsement
of Roosevelt in 1936. An equally decisive factor in the
Senator's withholding support from the President was Borah's
hope that the Republican party could be purged of its reactionary leadership by the time of the 1936 election. "I
do not propose to accept the line of least resistance and
go into the Democratic Party," the Idaho Senator said. "I

---

[3]For a brief summary of Borah's political activities,
see William E. Leuchtenberg, "William Edgar Borah," Dictionary of American Biography, XI (Supplement 2), 49-52.

propose to accept the line of most resistance and hope to
make the Republican Party what it ought to be." He believed
that the debacle of the 1934 Congressional elections had
eliminated Old Guard resistance to party reform. Proclaiming that the country would no longer tolerate "an old conservative party," Borah cautioned fellow Republicans that
their party must be liberalized or, like the Whig party,
die "of sheer cowardice." Hiram Johnson and James Couzens
retorted that the party was already dead and that nothing
remained to be reorganized, but Gerald Nye, supporting
Borah, stated that there might be a future for the party
if it adopted the "liberalism which some Republicans have
been voicing for years, only to have their voices drowned
by the jeers of Republican leaders, who cried: 'Red,'
'Insurgents,' 'Traitors.'" At the same time, however, Nye
declared that the reactionary leadership of the party
would not "permit any material liberality if it can help
it." Nye's fears were soon justified by national party
chairman Charles Hilles, who resolutely announced that the
party would not "stagger to the left."[4]

Responding to Hilles, Borah declared, "We are not
going to stagger to the left, but. . .we are going to the
left as sure as I am alive." To accelerate this process,
the Idaho Senator recommended in April, 1935, that dissatisfied Republicans hold their own convention in Chicago

---

[4]William E. Borah, "Reorganization of the Republican
Party," Vital Speeches, I (Dec. 31, 1934), 201; New York
Times, Nov. 9, 1934, p. 2; Time XXIV (Dec. 24, 1934) 11;
Progressive, May 11, 1935, p. 1.

to adopt a progressive declaration of principles. He sug-
guested that such a statement include the following four-
point program: avoidance of foreign entanglements, elimination of all forms of monopoly, maintenance of tariff protection for agriculture, and abandonment of the New Deal
policy of economic scarcity. Fearing that the proposed
convention might lead to the formation of a rival organization, Charles Hilles intervened and extinguished yet another
reform scheme by ordering Republicans to disassociate themselves from any movement that would result in factionalism.[5]

Since the party had rebuffed his intial efforts for
reform, Borah announced that he would take his cause directly
to the people by seeking the Republican presidential nomination for himself. He stated that this course of action was
necessary to insure a convention of liberal delegates who
would write a liberal platform and name a liberal candidate.
"To that end I shall devote my efforts," he declared. "If
in any state or district the liberal forces think it will
help the liberal cause to pledge their delegates to me, I
shall cooperate fully with that plan." Among the Insurgents
Frazier and Norbeck immediately pledged their support for
Borah, and it was rumored that Johnson and Nye would soon
do the same. Norbeck wrote that Borah was the only nominee

---

[5]Arthur M. Schlesinger, Jr., The Politics of Upheaval
(Boston, 1960), pp. 524-25; Marian C. McKenna, Borah (Ann
Arbor, Michigan, 1961), pp. 319-20.

who could regain the farm vote lost to Roosevelt in 1932 and
thus guarantee a Republican victory in 1936.[6]

Skeptics belittled Borah's candidacy as nothing more
than a calculated attempt to enhance his prestige with his
Idaho constituency prior to a tough Senatorial reelection
campaign against three-term Democratic Governor, C. Ben
Ross.[7] Sincere in his intentions, however, the Idaho Senator
allowed friends to enter his name on December 20, 1935, in
the Wisconsin presidential primary, in which he easily captured all but two of the State's twenty-four delegates.
Unperturbed, Eastern Republicans ridiculed the Insurgent's
triumph. "Senator Borah's victory in Wisconsin," the Old
Guard press reported, "will be as much help in winning the
Republican nomination as Hitler's endorsement would be to

[6]Time, XXVI (Dec. 30, 1935), 9; Progressive, Oct. 26,
1935, pp. 1, 3; Peter Norbeck to the Republican National
Committee, Jan. 25, 1936, Peter Norbeck Papers, Borah For
President File (1936), Richardson Archives, University of
South Dakota Library, Vermillion, South Dakota.

[7]Richard L. Neuberger, "Behind the Borah Boom" Current History, XLIII (Feb., 1936), 463. Neuberger recalled
that one Idaho supporter of Borah confessed: "Well, Bill
Borah's Presidential bee is a-goin' to hurt Ben Ross about
forty times more than it's a-goin' to harm old Franklin D."
Hiram Johnson suggested an even more bizarre reason for
Borah's candidacy—it was the result of a "cunning pact"
between the Idaho Senator and Roosevelt! "I see two none
too scrupulous politicians, each endeavoring to out-fox the
other," Johnson wrote his son. "Roosevelt fondly imagines
that Borah's prating of 'liberalism' and. . .denouncing
other candidates in the Republican primary will so disrupt
the Republican Party as to make it an even weaker weapon
against him; Mr. Borah, believing the President can render
him tremendous aid in his primary fights, looks forward to
a victory in the /Republican/ primary, and then tearing the
hide off. . .Roosevelt in the finals." Johnson to Hiram
Johnson, Jr., March 15, 1936, Hiram W. Johnson Papers, Part
IV, Box 4, Bancroft Library, University of California,
Berkeley.

a candidate in The Bronx." Conservative party leaders decided, nevertheless, that they could not allow Borah to run
unopposed in other primaries. At a secret conference in New
York the national committee accordingly drew up a list of
favorite-son candidates to run against the Senator. In addition to its obvious intent of reducing the number of
delegates committed to Borah, this stategy was designed to
prevent a confrontation between the Idaho Senator and the
hand-picked GOP candidate, Governor Alfred M. Landon of
Kansas.[8]

So successful were the party professionals in dividing
the delegate strength of the contenders that Landon clinched
the nomination without venturing outside his Kansas baili-
wick. By the time Borah arrived at the Cleveland convention
site in early June, he knew that his chances to head the
ticket were nonexistent. He informed the Idaho delegation
that his main interest was now in the content of the platform. Borah wished to see two planks adopted—a strong
antimonopoly plank and an isolationist foreign policy plank.
He also stipulated that the platform should make no reference
to the gold standard. Largely through the determined support of Landon and William Allen White, Borah achieved his
platform objectives. Although the final platform contained
many compromises, it was essentially moderate in substance.
Borah, nevertheless, enigmatically left Cleveland for
Washington without declaring for Landon. Nye's explanation

---

[8]_Progressive_, April 18, 1936, p. 8; McKenna, Borah, p.
326.

for Borah's hasty departure was that the proceedings at the
convention were "more likely to attract reactionary support
in the East. . .than to regain for the party its Progressive
backing in the Prairie States."[9]

The _Progressive_ editorialized that Landon was the
nominee of the "standpat bosses of the G.O.P." because he
was "the man most like Hoover in political and economic
philosophy and who still hasn't Hoover's onus of unpopularity." Although it was unfair to equate Landon with Hoover,
there is no doubt that the convention that nominated the
Kansas Governor was definitely Hooverish in outlook. The
Cleveland gathering was marked by an atmosphere of bored
solemnity until the former President made his appearance.
After the emotionally overwrought delegates cheered him for
a full fifteen minutes, Hoover chastised the New Deal by
labeling it an un-American threat to fundamental liberties.
The _New York Times_ related that the speech ignited the
audience into "a wild and uncontrollable burst of frenzy,"
demonstrating that Herbert Hoover was still the dominant
personality in the Republican party.[10]

This outburst for Hoover proved unfortunate for Landon.
The Kansas Governor was a moderate progressive, who had
backed Theodore Roosevelt in 1912 and Robert LaFollette,
Sr., in 1924, and he earnestly desired to rally Insurgent
support for his campaign. The Cleveland convention's

---

[9] _New York Times_, June 13, 1936, p. 9.

[10] _Progressive_, Oct. 19, 1935, p. 4; _New York Times_,
June 11, 1936.

adulation of Hoover, however, appalled the Republican liberals. George Norris believed that the delegates had revealed their preference for "Hoover and Hoover principles of
government." If the delegates had carried out their "true
sentiments," the Nebraska Senator reasoned, they would have
nominated Hoover for President; but "they knew that the
Hoover lesson of despair" was still "too fresh in the minds
of the American people for them to succeed in any such
reactionary program."[11]

Deprived of Insurgent support, Landon was forced to
rely completely on the reactionary leaders who had formally
sponsored his nomination. Landon's choice of John D. M.
Hamilton for national chairman reflected this dependency,
and it drove the few remaining liberals from his camp. To
Landon's assertion that Hamilton was a progressive, fellow
Kansan William Allen White retorted that "if this were true,
then Wally Simpson was a nun!" Even though White remained both Landon's chief supporter and leading critic,
he later reminisced that three minutes after the convention closed, he sent the new GOP nominee a telegram "in
which I congratulated him, gave him my love, and declared
'from now on you walk alone.'"[12]

[11]Interview with Alfred M. Landon, July 11, 1969;
George W. Norris, "Behind the Political Smokescreen," June
14, 1936, reprinted in the Congressional Record, 74th Cong.,
2nd Sess., pp. 9320-22.

[12]Milton Plesur, "The Republican Congressional Come-
back of 1938," Review of Politics, XXIV (Oct., 1962), 530-
31; William Allen White to Marion Ellet, quoted in Walter
Johnson (ed.), Selected Letters of William Allen White,
1899-1943 (New York, 1945), p. 369.

The real tragedy for Landon was that he did not walk
alone. Early in the campaign the Governor was a model of
moderation. "None of my campaign speeches will be merely
an attack on the opposition," he wrote Borah in August.
". . .I cannot criticize everything that has been done in
the past three years and do it sincerely. Neither do I
believe such an attack is good politics." Landon admitted
that for him any other type of campaign would be "too much
out of character." As election day approached, however, he
discarded his self-imposed rules of restraint and spread
the Hoover message that the issue at stake was New Dealism
versus Americanism. William Allen White claimed that
Hamilton "turned over what ought to have been a good
middle-of-the-road campaign to the hard-boiled political
reactionaries." Landon complained that he did not have
"enough help on the Liberal or Progressive side to pick up
the ball and emphasize my really liberal stand on many
issues." Both men were correct, for by early October most
of the Insurgents had decided it was either "Roosevelt or
Ruin."[13]

The Democrats met in Philadelphia with a single purpose in mind: the renomination of Franklin D. Roosevelt.
Only one other issue, the repeal of the anachronistic rule
requiring that a candidate receive a two-thirds vote for
nomination, competed for the delegates' attention. After
repealing the two-thirds rule, the delegates accepted a

---

[13]Schlesinger, Politics of Upheaval, pp. 613-14; interview with Alfred M. Landon, July 11, 1969.

platform that lauded the accomplishments of the New Deal,
and then they perfunctorily nominated Roosevelt. The President, as in 1932, appeared in person to deliver his acceptance speech. Before a capacity crowd at Franklin Field,
he defended the New Deal as the foe of economic tyranny and
thanked the people for their patience and understanding. "I
come not only as a leader of a party. . .but to salute those
of other parties, especially those in the Congress of the
United States who on so many occasions have put partisanship aside." Roosevelt asked for continued bipartisan support "for the duration of the war."[14]

A new third party appeared on the scene after the Democratic convention and momentarily contested Roosevelt for
liberal support. The Union party, spawned from a common
hatred of the President by Father Charles E. Coughlin,
Francis Townsend, and Gerald L. K. Smith (the self-appointed
successor of Huey Long), chose as its presidential nominee
North Dakota Congressman William Lemke. Candidate Lemke did
not belong to the "lunatic fringe" as his three sponsors
did, but he did share their hatred for Roosevelt. The North
Dakotan possessed the typical Insurgent dislike of centralization under the New Deal, but what irritated him most was
the administration's farm program. "In regard to the allotment, the whole program to my mind is make-believe," he
wrote his brother. "I think the farmers should go on a
strike and kick it out of the window." Instead of crop

---

[14]Samuel I. Rosenman (ed.), The Public Papers and Addresses of Franklin D. Roosevelt (13 vols., New York, 1938-
50), V, 230-36.

restriction, Lemke supported the refinancing of farm mortgages by government issuance of fiat money, and he joined
with Senator Lynn J. Frazier in introducing several measures
of this sort in Congress. Roosevelt specified that Lemke's
panacea was completely unrealistic. "If this type of wild
legislation passes," he informed Vice President Garner, "the
responsibility for wrecking recovery will be squarely on the
Congress, and I will not hesitate to say so to the nation in
plain language." When the House, on May 13, 1936, voted down
the last of the so-called Frazier-Lemke refinancing bills,
Lemke blamed his defeat upon the President and charged that
he had sent "bureaucratic lobbyists" to Congress to work
against the measure. Roosevelt now had acquired another
bitter enemy, and in his frustration and anger Lemke joined
the only allies available to him to challenge the President.[15]

Although most liberals doubted Lemke's claim that his
refinancing bill would solve the crisis in agriculture,
they could not forget the persistency with which he had
fought for the farmers' welfare. Lemke's participation in
the Union party raised perplexing questions for the progressives. Although rejecting the new party, Tom Amlie admitted
that "many of the elements that have been united in this
movement have deep roots in the American tradition." Lemke

[15]Lemke to B. W. Lemke, Feb. 26, 1934, William Lemke
Papers, Box 11, Orin G. Libby Manuscript Collection, Univer-
sity of North Dakota Library, Grand Forks, North Dakota;
Franklin D. Roosevelt to Marvin H. McIntyre, April 10, 1934,
Franklin D. Roosevelt Papers, OF 1038, Franklin D. Roosevelt
Library, Hyde Park, New York; Lemke to H. A. Bone, May 21,
1936, Lemke Papers, Box 12.

himself believed that he was leading a "new Progressive party," and he thought that he could attract Insurgent support. Since the entire Congressional delegation of the Wisconsin Progressive party and the Minnesota Farmer-Labor party had voted unanimously for the Frazier-Lemke bills, Lemke had reason to hope that these two organizations would support him. Robert and Philip LaFollette, along with Minnesota Governor Floyd Olson, stated, however, that they had an informal agreement with other liberals not to endorse a presidential candidate until they could confer to decide on a united course of action. The progressives held their conference in Chicago on September 11, 1936, and they formed the Progressive National Committee Supporting Franklin D. Roosevelt for President (PNC). The PNC demanded a coalition of liberal forces "to prevent the self-seeking, reactionary groups backing Landon from turning back the hands of the clock of progress and returning us to the condition that existed at the end of the Hoover administration." The Committee warned that any endorsement of Lemke would only split the liberal vote and thus lend "direct support for reaction." In the end, Frazier was the only Insurgent to declare for Lemke.[16]

The PNC actually grew out of the skeleton organization surviving from the National Progressive League to Support

---

[16]Thomas R. Amlie, "How Radical is the New Deal?" Common Sense, IV (August, 1936), 21-24; Lemke to B. W. Lemke, May 25, 1936, Lemke Papers, Box 12; Leo T. Crowley to Marvin H. McIntyre, Sept. 8, 1936, Roosevelt Papers, PPF 6659; New York Times, Sept. 28, 1936, p. 10; New York Times, Oct. 4, 1936, p. 1; Edward C. Blackorby, Prairie Rebel: The Public Life William Lemke (Lincoln, Nebraska, 1963), pp. 217-57.

Franklin D. Roosevelt for President in 1932 (NPL). As early
as September, 1934, Melvin D. Hildreth of the NPL's executive
committee volunteered his organization's services to Roosevelt for the 1936 election. Nothing more was done until
early 1936, when the President urged Secretary of the Interior Harold L. Ickes to contact Norris and Johnson about
revamping the NPL. After the Democratic convention, Roosevelt himself asked Robert LaFollette to establish and to
become chairman of what was to become the PNC.[17]

LaFollette busied himself in seeking to persuade
leading progressives to sponsor the Chicago conference.
Surprisingly, he had a great deal of difficulty in obtaining the participation of Norris. The Nebraska Senator,
who had already endorsed Roosevelt, stated that he was ill
and would not be able to work actively for the President.
LaFollette replied that the conference's lack of approval
from Norris would be misunderstood by other liberals, who
regarded him as their leader. "Frankly," Edward Keating,
the editor of Labor, wrote the Nebraska Senator, "I am afraid
that this will give Landon's propaganda agents an opportunity
to spread the report that you are no longer earnestly supporting Roosevelt for reelection." After the President himself interceded, Norris finally agreed to join with LaFollette
to sponsor the conference.[18]

---

[17]Hildreth to Louis Mc H. Howe, Sept. 4, 1934, Roosevelt Papers, PPF 3933; Harold L. Ickes, The Secret Diary of
Harold L. Ickes (New York, 1953), I, 532, 655.

[18]LaFollette to Norris, August 17, 1936, George W.
Norris Papers, Tray 8, Box 5, Library of Congress, Washington,

The keynote speech, written by Norris, urged the conference to "take a firm stand in favor of the reelection of
President Roosevelt." The conference acted on Norris' advice, but, at Tom Amlie's request, it announced that endorsement of the President did not include endorsement of
the Democratic party. By separating Roosevelt from the
Democratic party the conferees left the way open for the
establishment of a progressive third party in 1940. The
conference then approved a Declaration of Principles whose
preamble called for "a fair distribution of wealth" and
"equality of opportunity." Senator LaFollette was formally
named the Committee's chairman, Norris was designated the
honorary chairman, and Senator Edward P. Costigan and Grace
Abbot were appointed as vice-chairmen.[19]

An executive committee, headed by Presidential ad-
viser Frank P. Walsh and with headquarters in the Hotel
Roosevelt in New York City, coordinated the Committee's
activities. All PNC activities were first cleared by
Stanley High and Thomas Corcoran, who served as liaison
between Roosevelt and the Committee. The PNC's Correspondence Division distributed nearly a million pamphlets and

D. C.; Keating to Norris, August 19, 1936, Norris Papers,
Tray 8, Box 5; Roosevelt to Norris, August 22, 1936, Norris
Papers, Tray 8, Box 5; Donald R. McCoy, "The Progressive
National Committee of 1936," Western Political Quarterly,
IX (June, 1956), 459.

[19]Norris to The Conference of Progressives, Sept. 11,
1936, Norris Papers, Tray 8, Box 5; New York Times, Sept.
12, 1936, p. 1; Progressive National Committee Supporting
Franklin D. Roosevelt for President, Declaration of Principles (New York, 1936), PNC Papers, Box 2, Library of
Congress, Washington, D. C.

copies of pro-Roosevelt speeches. The most important work
of the Committee was performed by the Speakers' Bureau,
which sponsored numerous speeches by well-known liberals
in support of the President. All Committee speakers emphasized that "A PROGRESSIVE VOTE CAST FOR ANY OTHER CANDIDATE
THAN ROOSEVELT WILL DIVIDE LIBERAL STRENGTH AND WILL CON-
STITUTE A VOTE FOR LANDON!"[20]

Roosevelt conducted precisely the type of campaign
advocated by the PNC—a liberal crusade that largely ignored
party lines. The President relegated Farley and the Democratic party to the background and directed a "non-political"
campaign in which he ostensibly worked through independent
organizations like the PNC, the Good Neighbor League, and
Labor's Non-Partisan League. He mentioned the Democratic
party only three times during the entire campaign, and, as
in the 1934 Congressional elections, he called for the election of the "right kind of people regardless of party."
Consistent with this approach, he engineered an alliance
between Farmer-Laborites and Democrats in Minnesota, and he
worked with the LaFollette Progressives in Wisconsin and
the American Labor party in New York. After James Couzens
was defeated in the Michigan Republican primary, Roosevelt
sought to induce the Senator to be the candidate for the
Democratic party. Finally, the President repudiated his
party's nominee in Nebraska and urged the reelection of

[20]Progressive National Committee Supporting Franklin
D. Roosevelt for President, Speakers Manual (New York, 1936),
PNC Papers, Box 3; McCoy, "Progressive National Committee of
1936," pp. 454-69.

149

George Norris, "one of the major prophets of America /whose/
candidacy transcends State and party lines."[21]

At the beginning of the campaign only four Insurgents,
LaFollette, Norris, Costigan, and Wheeler, openly supported
Roosevelt. Especially hard to explain were the positions
taken at this time by Johnson and Nye. When Nye had been
mentioned as a probable third-party presidential candidate
for 1936, he had claimed disinterest, adding that his candidacy "would draw the extreme liberals away from Mr. Roosevelt." In August, 1935, the North Dakota Senator indicated
that "unless the Republicans nominate a real liberal I
imagine I'll support Roosevelt in 1936, providing he re-
mains Liberal." Ickes maintained that Nye's endorsement of
Roosevelt was vital, for the Senator was a Republican and
the country's outstanding leader of the "peace faction."
Although the Secretary of the Interior believed that Roosevelt had "badly fumbled the Progressive situation" by not
insisting that Nye be appointed chairman of the PNC, Ickes
still felt that Roosevelt could win the Senator's support
if he would make an unequivocal statement "that so long as
he is President he will leave nothing undone to keep us from
becoming embroiled in another European war." After delivering such an address at Chautauqua, New York, on August 14,

---

[21]Raymond Moley, After Seven Years (New York, 1939),
p. 343; Stanley High, "Whose Party Is It?" Saturday Evening
Post, CCIX (Feb. 6, 1937), 317; James MacGregor Burns, Roose-
velt: The Lion and the Fox (New York, 1956), Chapter 14;
Harry Barnard, Independent Man: The Life of Senator James
Couzens (New York, 1958), pp. 309-10; Rosenman (ed.), Public
Papers of FDR, V, 430-32.

1936, the President invited Nye to Hyde Park, where Ickes
hoped the Senator would issue a statement endorsing the
President for reelection on the basis of his peace record
and his peace talk. The meeting failed to produce this result, however, and a few days later Nye declared that he
would remain neutral in the presidential race.[22]

Nye's vigorous opposition to the NRA and the AAA
partly explains his failure to support Roosevelt, but it
was also reported that he distrusted the President's commitment to isolationism.[23] There was speculation, in addition, that the North Dakota Senator harbored an ambition to
head a new progressive party in 1940 and feared an endorsement of Roosevelt in 1936 might hamper this undertaking.
Other reasons for Nye's neutral position in 1936 were probably his innate Republicanism and the complicated political
situation in North Dakota. He firmly believed that when
the Roosevelt presidency ended, the old Democratic conservatives, submerged for the time being by the New Deal, would
resume party leadership, and then the Republican party would

[22]Wayne S. Cole, Senator Gerald P. Nye and American
Foreign Relations (Minneapolis, 1962), p. 136; Ickes, Secret
Diary, I, 655-56, 661, 663; Roosevelt to Nye, August 17,
1936, Roosevelt Papers, PPF 1614; New York Times, Oct. 2,
1936, p. 9.

[23]Cole, Gerald P. Nye, p. 137. In his Chautauqua address, Roosevelt lauded the neutrality legislation and Nye's
contribution to the munitions investigation. But he also
warned that "no matter how well we are supported by neutrality legislation, we must remember that no laws can be
provided to cover every contingency, for it is impossible to
imagine how every future event may shape itself." This com-
ment might have dissuaded Nye from endorsing the President
on the basis of his "peace record." Rosenman (ed.), Public
Papers of FDR, V, 285-92.

emerge as the "party of constructive liberalism." Also, the Republican party in North Dakota was controlled by the liberal Nonpartisan League, and Nye feared that his backing of the Democratic presidential candidate would cost him League support when he ran for reelection in 1938. Finally, there was the annoying candidacy of William Lemke. On one occasion, the North Dakota Senator thus announced that he was following a "hands-off" policy in the presidential campaign "as a matter of courtesy to the Presidential candidate from my own state."[24]

Hiram Johnson also sat silently on the sidelines during the 1936 campaign. Apparently the Senator was piqued by the administration's refusal to appoint his chosen candidate to a federal judgeship in California, a favor that he assumed he deserved from Roosevelt.[25] In addition, the California Senator's wife lobbied actively against the President. Johnson admitted to his son that "your mother has conceived a tremendous prejudice against Roosevelt, which, in many instances, I do not share. The result is, I am in a quandary here."[26] The Senator's failure to endorse Roosevelt in

---

[24] Cole, Gerald P. Nye, p. 137; New York Times, Dec. 14, 1934, p. 2; ibid., Oct. 2, 1936, p. 9.

[25] Johnson to William Gibbs McAdoo, Oct. 14, 1935, Roosevelt Papers, OF 300 (California Politics); Chester H. McCall to Marguerite LeHand, Feb. 5, 1936, Roosevelt Papers, OF 126; Ickes to Roosevelt, Nov. 21, 1934, Roosevelt Papers, PPF 1134.

[26] Johnson to Hiram Johnson, Jr. August 26, 1936, Johnson Papers, Part IV, Box 4. Actually, Mrs. Johnson ("The Boss") thought Roosevelt's reelection would be a national disaster. "There is still a chance to save our country," she wrote a friend. "While I am convinced that

1936, however, reflected more than displeasure over patronage or pressure from a domineering wife. Although Johnson
conceded that Roosevelt was "fundamentally right on great
national policies," he disliked the immense power that had
accrued to the presidency under the New Deal. By mid-1936
the Senator indicated that he also was beginning to distrust
the President, especially his "desire to monkey with the
situation abroad." "This restless mentality of his that
drives him in all directions just to do something," he wrote
of Roosevelt, "may at any moment raise hell with him." To
guard the nation against precipitous Presidential action,
Johnson was convinced that he must retain his own "singular
independence."[27]

All efforts to involve Johnson in the Roosevelt campaign met with failure. The California Senator spurned
Ickes' invitation to sponsor the call for the PNC; and
although he regarded the Republican nominee to be an utterly
unacceptable candidate, he refused the plea of Josephus
Daniels to make a speech "in our common devotion to liberalism to point out to the country that Landon's repudiation
of his attitude in 1912 is assurance of his sorrow for one

Mr. Landon does not know what it is all about, I would pre-
fer to have him puttering around, if a few things be saved,
than to have the plans of the other fellow all ready to be
executed." Mrs. Hiram Johnson to Mrs. Edward G. Lowery,
Sept. 15, 1936, Johnson Papers, Part III, Box 17.

[27]Johnson to Hiram Johnson, Jr., Jan. 26, 1935, June
16, 1935, Feb. 16, 1936, March 1, 1936, Johnson Papers,
Part IV, Box 4.

time following the gleam."[28] Personal appeals by the President and Farley also failed to move Johnson. The Senator
replied that he was too ill to make a statement. "I know
it is perfectly useless to tell these people anything of
this sort," he fumed. "They are utterly ruthless, and the
fact that one is disabled does not appeal to them at all,
in fact, they don't believe it. Well, to hell with them!"
In the end, Johnson surreptitiously voted for Roosevelt,
"although with many misgivings."[29]

Three Insurgents, Shipstead, Norbeck, and Couzens,
publicly endorsed Roosevelt without much White House pressure
being put on them. In February, 1936, despite the fact that
Governor Floyd Olson and the Farmer-Labor party had already
agreed to support Roosevelt, LaFollette advised the President that Shipstead's personal endorsement was still vital
since he had "a greater hold on the people of Minnesota
than anyone else in the State." Acting on LaFollette's
advice, Roosevelt invited Shipstead to lunch to talk about
the upcoming election; and in a radio broadcast from Minneapolis, on October 30, 1936, the Senator thanked the administration for its sympathetic treatment of the Northwestern

---

[28]Daniels to Johnson, August 1, 1936, Roosevelt Papers,
OF 300 (1936 Political Trends). Of Landon, Johnson wrote
that the Kansan "is a very nice fellow, but he is utterly
unable to put his thoughts, if he has any, in an attractive
or sequential form." Johnson to Hiram Johnson, Jr., Oct. 24,
1936, Johnson Papers, Part IV, Box 4.

[29]Ickes, Secret Diary, I, 693, 697-98; Roosevelt to
Mr. and Mrs. Hiram W. Johnson, Oct. 26, 1936, Roosevelt
Papers, PSF 62; Johnson to Hiram Johnson, Jr., August 26,
1936, Oct. 24, 1936, Johnson Papers, Part IV, Box 4.

154

states and announced that he would vote for the President
"no matter on what ticket his name appeared."[30]

Peter Norbeck was another Insurgent who hoped in vain
that the Republican party would reform itself. He believed
that this reform would materialize only if the Insurgents
were invited "into the Party" and given "a voice in Party
affairs." Accordingly, the South Dakota Senator initially
backed Borah "as the nearest of any of the candidates meeting the requirements of our peculiar situation." After the
Republican convention, Norbeck declared that the party obviously was still controlled by "the large industrial interests and money scalpers." For the next three months the
Senator wavered between following his liberal convictions
or his party, and it appeared that he would take no active
part in the campaign. He did, however, attack Landon's
stand on agricultural problems and accused the Kansan of
having "but little grasp of the problems of agriculture,
while we have made some gains under Roosevelt. With nothing
else to depend on but agriculture, we have too much at
stake to let anything interfere." On October 14, 1936,
Norbeck and former Republican national committeeman from

---

[30]LaFollette to Roosevelt, Feb. 6, 1936, Roosevelt
Papers, PSF 55; _Progressive_, August 22, 1936, p. 1; Sister
Mary Rene Lorentz, "Henrik Shipstead: Minnesota Indepen-
dent, 1923-1946" (Ph.D. thesis, The Catholic University of
America, 1963), p. 44; copy of Shipstead's speech in Roose-
velt Papers, PPF 2863.

South Dakota, S. X. Way, issued a joint statement: "We are
going to vote for one Democrat, Franklin D. Roosevelt."[31]

In the spring of 1936 James Couzens announced that he
favored "a new deal" and that the country could not withstand a return to "the old order"; but he stopped short of
endorsing Roosevelt. Couzens' comments antagonized the
Michigan Republican party leaders, who were busy laying plans
to replace him in the Senate. When the state Republican
convention endorsed the conservative Wilbur J. Brucker for
Couzens' seat, prominent Michigan Democrats urged Couzens
to run on their ticket. The Michigan Senator refused the
offer, stating that such action would merit his being called
"a turncoat" and that he "could not tolerate that." Subsequently, Couzens ran against Brucker in the Republican
primary, but the Senator ran as a supporter of the President. This, of course, clinched his defeat. "I could have
cried at your sacrifice," wrote Hiram Johnson. "I doubt
if it was worth it." Roosevelt praised Couzens' action as
"a feat unprecedented in American politics" and urged him
to accept the chairmanship of the new Maritime Commission.
"Irrespective of party affiliations the country needs you
in public service," the President declared. Before he was

---

[31]*New York Times*, August 11, 1935, IV, 8; Peter Norbeck to B. K. Bettelheim, Feb. 3, 1936, Norbeck Papers,
Borah for President File (1936); Norbeck to Andrew Marvick,
Oct. 30, 1936, Norbeck Papers, Drawer 31; Gilbert Courtland
Fite, *Peter Norbeck: Prairie Statesman* (Columbia, Mo., 1948),
pp. 199-204. Norbeck's secretary concluded that the Senator's
endorsement of Roosevelt caused "a last minute switch" in
South Dakota from Landon to the President. Chet H. Johnson
to W. J. Funk, Nov. 7, 1936, Norbeck Papers, Drawer 31.

able to make a final decision on Roosevelt's offer, the
Senator become acutely ill, and he died on October 22,
1936.[32]

Even Borah came perilously close to jumping on the
Roosevelt bandwagon. After the Cleveland convention, the
Idaho Senator let it be known that he was angry over the
strong-arm tactics used to nominate Landon. Later he fumed
over Landon's failure to live up to his promise not to mention the gold standard during the campaign. One of Borah's
advisors reported that the Senator was now ready to support
Roosevelt: "He entertains a very high regard and warm
friendliness for the President, and seems to feel that there
is no essential difference in the things they desire and
the beliefs they hold"[33]

Mutual friends of Borah and Roosevelt told Farley that
if he could persuade Borah's Democratic opponent to withdraw
from the Idaho Senatorial contest, Borah would reciprocate
by endorsing Roosevelt. This proposed deal was backed by
a dissident faction of the state Democratic party, and

---

[32]Couzens to George R. Averill, Feb. 21, 1936, James
Couzens Papers, Box 118, Library of Congress, Washington,
D. C.; Barnard, Couzens, pp. 303-21; Johnson to James Couzens,
Sept. 30, 1936, Johnson Papers, Part III, Box 17; New York
Times, August 23, 1936, p. 1; Roosevelt to James Couzens,
Oct. 7, 1936, Roosevelt Papers, PSF 62.

[33]Orr Chapman to Harlee Branch, July 1, 1936, Roosevelt Papers, PPF 2358. Hiram Johnson discounted any and
all reports that Borah would support Roosevelt. "Just
exactly as Borah has been found for the past thirty years
growling each four years and yet before the end of the
campaign being a most enthusiastic supporter of those at
whom he growled." Johnson to Hiram Johnson, Jr., March 29,
1936, Johnson Papers, Part IV, Box 4.

157

Burton K. Wheeler personally talked to the President about
it. After contacting Ross, however, Farley concluded that
he could not persuade the Idaho Democrat to withdraw from
the race. Despite this Farley bet Roosevelt that Borah
would, in the end, support him. In late October newsmen
still reported Borah as saying that if reactionary Republicans did not stop trying to force him to declare for
Landon, he would "blast them with a pro-Roosevelt pronouncement." Such a pronouncement was not made, however. "I
shall confine myself entirely to the issues," the Idaho
Senator announced on October 10, 1936, "and I shall not
make a speech for any candidate."[34]

As the campaign drew to a close, Raymond Clapper believed that the real choice to be made on election day was
between "the existing system to which President Roosevelt
is committed or. . .the system as it was under Harding,
Coolidge and Hoover." Recognition of this fact seemed to
have a sobering effect on the staunch Republican Insurgent,
Arthur Capper. Like the other Insurgents, the Kansas
Senator disliked the centralizing and financial policies
of the Roosevelt administration. "No country can con-
tinually go into the hole at the rate of 4,000 million
dollars a year. . .without facing ultimate bankruptcy,"
he exclaimed. Quite apart from his loyality to a fellow
Kansan, Capper explained that he was supporting Landon

---

[34]Will Durant to Marvin McIntyre, June 26, 1936,
Roosevelt Papers, PPF 2358; James A. Farley to Will Durant,
July 24, 1936, Roosevelt Papers, PPF 2358; Progressive,
Oct. 10, 1936, p. 1; New York Times, Oct 10, 1936, p. 1.

because as President he would retain the "good things" and
abolish the "bad things" of the New Deal. Republican Congressman Clifford R. Hope warned Capper that his support of
Landon would probably cost the Senator many votes in his
bid for reelection. Capper stayed with Landon until the
end, but he amazed everyone when, in a speech on the evening
before the election, he reminded his radio listeners that
they were free to split their tickets.[35]

The election of 1936 was a landslide victory for
Roosevelt, who carried every state except Maine and Vermont.
Roosevelt's plurality of more than eleven million votes
over Landon would not be surpassed until 1964, and his 523
to 8 margin in the electoral college was the biggest since
1820. In addition, the President's popularity resulted in
impressive Congressional gains for the Democratic party.
In the House there would be 334 Democrats and a modern low
of 89 Republicans; in the Senate there would be 75 Democrats
and only 17 Republicans. George Norris commented that the
empty seats on the Republican side of the Senate chamber
reminded him of a "plucked chicken." Young Everett McKinley
Dirksen of Illinois, one of the few Republican Congressmen
to be reelected, lamented the fact that his party "did not

---

[35]Raymond B. Clapper, "Looking Forward to November,"
Current History, 44 (April, 1936), 8; Arthur Capper to Will
Morton, August 19, 1936, Arthur Capper Papers, General Cor-
respondence New-OPA, Kansas State Historical Society, Topeka,
Kansas; New York Times, April 27, 1936, p. 4; New York Times,
Oct. 18, 1936, p. 40; Homer E. Socolofsky, Arthur Capper:
Publisher, Politician and Philanthropist (Lawrence, Kansas,
1962), Chapter XV; copy of radio broadcast, Nov. 3, 1936,
Capper Papers, General Correspondence, Landon-Mac.

have even enough members of Congress to force a roll call."
William Allen White assured his readers that "it was not an
election the country had just undergone but a political
Johnstown flood."[36]

In the four most urbanized and industrialized Insurgent states (California, Michigan, Minnesota, and Wisconsin)
and in the two Mountain states of Idaho and Montana, Roosevelt collected a larger percentage of the total popular vote
in 1936 than he had in 1932. Also, in these six states,
the pro or anti-Roosevelt position assumed by each Insurgent in 1936 involved little individual political risk.
Since the Minnesota Farmer-Labor party and the Wisconsin
Progressive party functioned almost as New Deal adjuncts
during the 1936 campaign, Shipstead and LaFollette counted
only political gain from their support of President. Had
he chosen to do so in 1936, California's Hiram Johnson could
have duplicated his enthusiastic 1932 endorsement of Roosevelt without endangering his political career. James Couzens
faced a considerably more difficult situation in Michigan,
but he probably would have been defeated in the state Republican Senatorial primary even if he had not courageously
announced for Roosevelt beforehand. Since Wheeler was a
Democrat anyway, Borah was the only Insurgent in the Mountain states "forced" to make a political decision in 1936.
The Idaho Senator was a fixture in Idaho politics, however,

---

[36]Time, XXVIII (Dec. 28, 1936), 11; ibid., XXVIII
(Nov. 16, 1936), 23.

and he probably could have endorsed the President without fear of political reprisal.[37]

In the four primarily agricultural Insurgent states (Kansas, Nebraska, North Dakota, and South Dakota), Roosevelt's 1936 majority was about 10 per cent less than it had been in 1932, except for Kansas. Since the Nonpartisan League dominated the GOP in North Dakota, Frazier and Nye did not support Roosevelt. In Kansas, Arthur Capper remained loyal to the Republican party and to his friend, Alfred M. Landon. George Norris and Peter Norbeck were the two Insurgents in these states who had to make difficult political decisions in 1936. Norris, however, was not in a quandary about whether or not to support Roosevelt but rather whether or not to run for reelection himself. The Nebraska Senator ultimately won reelection by running as an Independent and as a supporter of the President. Among the Insurgents, only Peter Norbeck's 1936 announcement for the President involved a real political risk. Had he lived, the South Dakota Senator probably would have been ignored by the state Republican party had he sought reelection in 1938.[38]

---

[37] Edgar Eugene Robinson, They Voted For Roosevelt: The Presidential Vote, 1932-1944 (Stanford University, Calif., 1947), pp. 41-46.

[38] Ibid., pp. 41-46. The voters of Kansas actually gave Roosevelt a slightly higher percentage of the total vote in 1936 than they had in 1932, 53.8 per cent and 56.6 per cent, respectively. This increase in the Roosevelt vote is largely explained by the popularity of the AAA among Kansas farmers. See Wilta Maxine Smith, "Reactions of the Kansas Farmers to the New Deal Farm Program" (Ph.D. Thesis, University of Illinois, 1960).

In addition to being a triumph for the Democratic
party and a personal victory for Roosevelt, the 1936 election demonstrated the immense popularity of the New Deal.
What Roosevelt and many other astute political observers
did not sense, however, was that the New Deal programs,
especially the relief agencies and the labor legislation,
had begun to create rising expectations among people who
had long accepted their low social and economic positions
without question. Most of these people were among the
"forgotten elements" of society: relief workers, union
members, Negroes, slum dwellers, and the poorer farmers.
Their political consciousness now awakened, these previously
downtrodden segments of the population embraced the New Deal
and formed the core of Roosevelt's majority in 1936. Their
vote also represented a shift in the power base of the
Democratic party from the rural Solid South to the urban
North.[39] During the President's second term, this new
Democratic coalition would make strong demands upon the
administration. More often than not, the satisfaction of
these demands would require the augmentation of the federal
bureaucracy, large increases in federal spending, and more

---

[39]See Samuel Lubell, The Future of American Politics
(2nd. rev. ed., New York, 1956), pp. 1-60; and Samuel J.
Eldersveld, "The Influence of Metropolitan Party Pluralities
in Presidential Elections Since 1920," American Political
Review, XLIII (Dec., 1949), 1189-1206.

governmental intervention into the daily lives of the people—
all of which would contribute to Insurgent opposition to the
New Deal.[40]

Among the Insurgents, only LaFollette and Norris were
enthusiastic about Roosevelt's "smashing victory." Both
agreed that the election represented a "victory for Progressive principles. . ./and/ a mandate to carry on the
battle for economic freedom."[41] The President's enormous
margin of victory frightened most of the other Insurgents,
however. They were worried that Roosevelt would use the
election as a mandate to increase the power of the presidency and thus endanger "Progressive principles." With
abject Democratic majorities in both Houses, Hiram Johnson
believed that Congress would offer no resistance to the
President's desires. The California Senator also discounted
the possibility that the Insurgents had any remaining influence on Roosevelt. "With his power and the vote he has

---

[40]Hiram Johnson indicated what was to come. He complained that the New Deal's relief policies had really bought
the 1936 presidential election for Roosevelt: "He will win
because there will be nobody really against him, first, and
secondly because of the class war which has been engendered;
and the have-nots in the voting are in the vast majority."
The California Senator also resented the "special privileges" the New Deal had given to the various interest
groups—especially to the labor movement. "It is the sort
of thing which makes me feel uncertain about Roosevelt,"
Johnson wrote his son. "Besides, there are too damned many
Bridges, John L. Lewises, Dubinskys, and Zaritskys and others
in this fight." Johnson to Hiram Johnson, Jr., Sept. 22,
1936, Nov. 2, 1936, Johnson Papers, Part IV, Box 4.

[41]Progressive, Nov. 7, 1936, p. 1.

received, the views of men like myself will receive scant attention," Johnson grieved.[42]

To preserve the doctrine of separation of powers, Nye called for the instant reorganization of the Republican party so that it could become an effective voice of opposition in Congress. Hiram Johnson responded that party reform was out of the question, for many of the so-called Progressive Republicans had gone over to Roosevelt. "When you think that of the Senators, the leader of the Republican party, McNary, was in secret conferences with him /Roosevelt/ whenever necessary in the past, and that Borah started a campaign for the Presidency under agreement with him, and that Norris is so infatuated with his TVA and Electrification of homes that he regards Roosevelt as god, you will see," the California Senator lamented, "there is mighty little left to stop anything that he wishes to do." Johnson hoped that the President would recognize the dangers inherent in his powerful position and would act with caution. The Senator, however, did not really believe that this would happen; he predicted that Roosevelt's "love of the dramatic" would lead to numerous experiments, "some of which will give us the cold shivers." In the end, Johnson and most of the other Insurgents did the only thing they could do: they promised to preserve their "self-respect

---

[42] Johnson to Hiram Johnson, Jr., Nov. 10, 1936, Nov. 15, 1936, Johnson Papers, Part IV, Box 4.

and independence," which would enable them to choose between the President and what they thought was best "for the future of the Republic."[43]

---

  [43]_Progressive_, Dec. 5, 1936, p. 1; Johnson to Hiram Johnson, Jr., Nov. 10, 1936, Johnson Papers, Part IV, Box 4; Johnson to H. L. Carnahan, April 23, 1937, Johnson Papers, Part III, Box 17.

CHAPTER V

TURNING POINT: INSURGENCY AND THE COURT FIGHT

Hiram Johnson did not have to wait long for Roosevelt
to exhibit his "love of the dramatic." On February 5, 1937,
the President sent Congress his proposal to "pack" the
Supreme Court. To all but Attorney General Homer S. Cummings and a few intimate White House assistants, Roosevelt's
Court plan came as a complete surprise. In his message to
Congress on judicial reform, the President indicated that
the federal courts were overworked and were unable to keep
up with their case loads. He suggested that these delays
were in part due to "aged or infirm judges—a subject of
delicacy and yet one which requires frank discussion." To
remedy this situation, Roosevelt asked the Congress to grant
him the authority to appoint a new judge whenever a federal
magistrate with ten or more years of service refused to
retire within six months after his seventieth birthday. If
adopted, the plan would have permitted Roosevelt to appoint
a maximum of six new judges to the Supreme Court and forty-
four new "coadjutors" to lower federal tribunals. In essence,
the President requested power to "vitalize the court" with
younger men in the interest of efficiency.[1]

---

[1]Samuel I. Rosenman (ed.), The Public Papers and Addresses of Franklin D. Roosevelt (13 vols., New York, 1938-
1950), VI, 51-66.

Roosevelt's Court message revealed an animosity that had existed for quite some time between the executive and judicial branches of the national government. Although informed observers did not predict a warm reception for New Deal legislation by the Court, the judiciary's devastating attack completely surprised both liberals and conservatives. In 1930 Felix Frankfurter had predicted that the Court would make "a general shift over to the left from its general vortex of Harding-Coolidge 'prosperity.'" For awhile it appeared as though Frankfurter's prophecy would be realized. In the 1934 "Minnesota Moratorium" and "Nebbia" cases the Court's decisions seemed to concede that an "emergency may furnish the occasion for the exercise of power." New Dealers rejoiced that the Court had at last discarded its laissez-faire orientation. This conclusion proved premature, however, for by early 1935 Supreme Court decisions were threatening the very existence of the New Deal. The verdict striking down the NIRA was followed by the invalidation of the AAA, the Guffey Coal Act of 1935, and a New York price-fixing law. Waiting on the docket, presumably for similar treatment, were the National Labor Relations Act and the Social Security Act. "At no time in the country's history," reported the Harvard Law Review, "was there a more voluminous outpouring of judicial rulings in restraint of acts of Congress. . . ."[2]

---

[2]Gerald Garvey, "Scholar in Politics: Edward S. Corwin and the 1937 Court-packing Battle," Princeton University Library Chronicle, XXXI (Autumn, 1969), 2; Home Building and Loan Association v. Blaisdell, 290 U. S. 398 (1934); Felix Frankfurter and Adrian S. Fisher, "The Business of the

Roosevelt's assessment that the problem lay with the
Court's personnel was, in part, correct. It was not, however,
as the President announced, that the justices were too old
and too slow but rather that some of them opposed the New
Deal ideology. Many of the Court's decisions against
the administration had been by the narrow margin of 5 to 4.
The inveterate opponents of New Deal legislation on the
Court were Justices James McReynolds, Pierce Butler, Willis
VanDevanter, and George Sutherland. They were called the
"Four Horsemen," and their decisions reflected a rigid ad-
herence to the nineteenth-century philosophy of laissez
faire. "The guiding faith of the four justices was that
civilization and progress depended on the massive and un-
ending protection of property from government," Arthur
Schlesinger, Jr., has written. "From these Tories," Homer
Cummings complained, "the Administration could not expect
a favorable vote if the Angel Gabriel made the argument."[3]
This bloc of four "unmovables" was able to out-vote the
three liberal justices—Benjamin Cardozo, Louis Brandeis,
and Harlan Stone. This left Chief Justice Charles Evans
Hughes and Associate Justice Owen Roberts, neither of whom
could be considered a zealous defender of the New Deal, in
the center and holding the balance of power.

Although his Court message surprised and shocked Congressmen, Roosevelt, for almost two years, had been exploring

---

Supreme Court at the October term, 1935 and 1936," Harvard
Law Review, LI (Feb., 1938), 577-637.

[3] Arthur M. Schlesinger, Jr., The Politics of Upheaval
(Boston, 1960), p. 458; quoted in Joseph Alsop and Turner
Catledge, The 168 Days (Garden City, N. Y., 1938), p. 18.

various methods to force the Court to be more amenable toward New Deal legislation. Ever since May 27, 1935, "Black
Monday," when the Court, in three unanimous decisions, in-
validated the NIRA and the Frazier-Lemke Act and ruled, in the
Humphrey case, that the President could not remove members
of independent regulatory commissions unless Congress consented, Roosevelt had sought to curb the judiciary's power.
First, he favored a Constitutional amendment narrowing the
Court's jurisdiction and, at the same time, expanding Congress' power under the interstate commerce clause. Roosevelt,
however, soon concluded that the amendment process would
take too much time and might easily be obstructed. "Ten
million dollars," the President informed Ickes, "can prevent
any amendment to the Constitution from being ratified in
the necessary number of states."[4] Roosevelt, moreover,
believed that the situation did not require a change in
the Constitution but a change in the membership of the Supreme
Court. He vaguely remembered that Herbert Asquith had
threatened in pre-World War I Britain to pack the House of
Lords by creating new peers, but he initially dismissed the
packing of the Court with liberal justices as a "distasteful idea." Roosevelt changed his mind, however, when Cummings

---

[4]Harold L. Ickes, The Secret Diary of Harold L. Ickes
(3 vols., New York, 1954), I, 467; ibid., II, 18. Later,
Roosevelt wrote Ickes that his original estimate of
$10,000,000 was incorrect. ". . .$5,000,000 properly placed
could easily prevent any kind of vote or a referendum on an
amendment for at least four years. First I said it would
take $10,000,000, but on mature reconsideration I have cut
that figure in half." Roosevelt to Ickes, March 17, 1937,
Franklin D. Roosevelt Papers, PPF 3650, Franklin D. Roosevelt
Library, Hyde Park, New York.

uncovered a memorandum, written by none other than Justice
McReynolds when he had been Woodrow Wilson's Attorney
General, recommending that if a federal judge in the lower
courts failed to retire at an age provided by law, the
President should appoint another judge who would have as
much authority as the older one. Roosevelt, describing this
plan as "the answer to a maiden's prayer," believed that he
could apply it to the Supreme Court. In addition to being
a quick and simple solution to the problem, the President
was delighted that the plan had been conceived by McReynolds,
now the most stalwart of the Court's conservatives.[5]

Roosevelt decided to keep the ingenious plan a secret
for the time being. Armed with the popular mandate of the
previous November, the President apparently did not expect
that there would be substantial opposition to his plan, even
though it attacked an institution considered sacred by most
Americans. When Chief Justice Hughes administered the oath
of office on Inauguration Day, Roosevelt could hardly restrain himself from divulging his scheme. Hughes spoke
about protecting and defending the Constitution; and the
President later related to an assistant, "I felt like saying:

---

[5]Ickes, Secret Diary, I, 496; interview with Alfred M.
Landon, July 11, 1969; Alsop and Catledge, 168 Days, pp. 32-
37. For an excellent discussion of the origins of the Court
plan, see William E. Leuchtenberg, "The Origins of Franklin
D. Roosevelt's Court-Packing Plan," in Philip B. Kurland (ed.),
The Supreme Court Review (Chicago, 1966), pp. 347-400.
Josephus Daniels painted a tragic portrait of McReynolds.
"I like him and believe he is honest," Daniels wrote, "but
his mind has been closed so long that he does not know the
world revolves and that courts are set up for the protection
of people. He acts as if he believed upholding 'res ad-
judicata' is the beginning and end of judicial duty." Daniels
to Roosevelt, January, 1935, Roosevelt Papers, PPF 86.

'Yes, but it is the Constitution as I understand it, flexible
enough to meet any new problems of democracy—not the kind
of Constitution your Court has raised up as a barrier to
democracy.'" In early January, when Roosevelt appeared
before a joint session of Congress to deliver his State of
the Union message, he criticized the Supreme Court for its
anti-New Deal decisions, but he failed to reveal his remedy.
"The message was well received," reported New York Times
correspondent Turner Catledge. "The Democrats cheered every
remark which they could interpret as aimed against the
Court." Two weeks before he announced his intention to
pack the Court, Roosevelt invited the Justices and their
wives to a White House dinner. "That reminded me of the
Roman Emperor who looked around his dinner table and began
to laugh when he thought how many of those heads would be
rolling on the morrow," William Borah later remarked.[6]
Finally, just moments before he sent his message to Congress, Roosevelt revealed its contents to his cabinet members and a few Congressional leaders. When the President
finished reading his message, he immediately left the
hastily called cabinet meeting to give the same message to
members of the news media. There was no discussion, and
Ickes recorded that all reacted with "pokerish" silence.[7]

Silence, however, did not mean approval of the President's plan, and most of the Democratic Congressional

---

[6]Rosenman (ed.), Public Papers of FDR, VI, 144; New
York Times, Jan. 7, 1937, p. 1; Time, XXIX (March 1, 1937),
15.

[7]Ickes, Secret Diary, II, 64-67.

leaders never forgave Roosevelt for not having taken them
into his confidence at an earlier time. On the return trip
to the Hill, House Judiciary Committee Chairman Hatton
Sumners announced, "Boys, here's where I cash in my chips."
Later, in an off-the-record news conference, he gave the
proposal "Hell, specifically and generally." Senate Judiciary Committee Chairman Henry F. Ashurst of Arizona announced that he supported the bill, but only after he had
performed an about-face by quoting Emerson to the effect
that "a foolish consistency is the hobgoblin of little minds,
adored by little statesmen." Only two weeks prior to
Roosevelt's court message, Ashurst had announced that he
would regard any attempt to enlarge the Supreme Court as
"a prelude to tyranny." He had urged the President to be
patient and to wait for age, either through retirement or
death, to take its natural toll. "It will fall to your
lot," he predicted to Roosevelt, "to nominate more Justices
of the Supreme Court than any other President since General
Washington. Father Time with his scythe, is on your side.
Anno Domini is your invincible ally."[8] Majority Leader
Robinson, who would try to pilot the bill through the Senate,
wrote a friend that "the President would have done well to

---

[8]Alsop and Catledge, 168 Days, pp. 67-68; Stephen Early
to Roosevelt, Feb. 8, 1937, Roosevelt Papers, PSF 61; George
F. Sparks (ed.), A Many-Colored Toga: The Diary of Henry
Fountain Ashurst (Tuscon, Arizona, 1962), pp. 368-70; Alva
Johnston, "The Dean of Inconsistency," Saturday Evening Post,
CCX (Dec. 25, 1937), 33; Marvin McIntyre to Henry F. Ashurst,
April 24, 1937, Roosevelt Papers, PPF 195.

have advised more frankly with his friends before precipita-
ting this issue. In the failure to do so, some believe that
he made a mistake."[9]

Roosevelt did not seek advice from any of the Insurgents about his Court plan. If he had, he would have found
that most of them were more interested in restricting the
power of the presidency than the power of the Supreme Court.
"At present the legislative functions have been largely
usurped by the President," one Insurgent informed his constituents. "I do not believe the Supreme Court is endowed
with divine wisdom. . . ./but/ I believe that any person who
honestly approaches this subject will find that the President has violated the constitution oftener /sic_7 than the
Supreme Court."[10] To be sure, no group of men in public
office realized the necessity of judicial reform more than
the Insurgents did. Some of them had stood at Armageddon
with Theodore Roosevelt in 1912 when the Rough Rider advocated the recall of certain state judicial decisions;
others had supported Robert LaFollette in 1924 on a

---

[9]Quoted in Nevin E. Neal, "A Biography of Joseph T.
Robinson" (Ph.D. Thesis, University of Oklahoma,
1958), p. 456. Alben Barkley, Robinson's successor as
Senate Majority Leader, also criticized Roosevelt for his
secrecy. "I have always regretted that he dropped the measure on us. . .with hardly any advance consultation to work
out a strategic plan for piloting the measure through the
Senate. . . . In retrospect, had F.D.R., as the Quarterback,
given us the signals in advance of the play, not after he
tossed us the ball and told us to run with it, we might have
covered more ground." Alben W. Barkley, That Reminds Me
(Garden City, N. Y., 1954), p. 153.

[10]William Lemke Newsletter, Feb. 24, 1937, William
Lemke Papers, Box 28, Orin G. Libby Historical Manuscripts
Collection, University of North Dakota Library, Grand Forks,
North Dakota.

Progressive party platform demanding that Congress be granted
the right to override Supreme Court decisions. Throughout
the 1920's the Insurgents denounced the Supreme Court as the
calloused defender of big business. Borah went so far as
to call it an "economic dictator."[11]

In the 1930's most Insurgents continued to voice the
opinion that the Court was "out of touch with the people,"
but their major quarrel was with the lower federal courts
for delaying the enforcement of New Deal legislation though
the use of injunctions. Norris denounced this government
by injunction. "I think the greatest evil of all comes from
the inferior courts," the Nebraska Senator declared. "The
injunctions which have been issued in the past—the injunctions which are now standing waiting for a decision by the
higher courts, make it impossible for the country to advance." To remedy this deplorable state of affairs, the
Insurgents urged Congress to pass a statute limiting the
jurisdiction of the lower courts and speeding up the process
of appeal to the Supreme Court. This proposal did not get
beyond the calendar of the Senate Judiciary Committee.[12]

If Roosevelt's manner of introducing the plan offended
the Senate's Democratic leaders, the Insurgents initially
were more disturbed by the deviousness of the proposal.
Hiram Johnson accused the President of "cunningly hiding
the issue in a hypocritical pretense." The California

[11]Schlesinger, Politics of Upheaval, p. 485.

[12]George W. Norris to J.B.C. Hardman, March 5, 1937,
George W. Norris Papers, Tray 27, Box 2, Library of Congress, Washington, D.C.

Senator explained to newsmen that Roosevelt really "seeks
the reversal of the decisions of the Supreme Court by the
short-cut method of naming new judges." Johnson, of course,
was correct, but the President, for calculated and near-
sighted reasons, had chosen to base his plea for judicial
reform on the alleged inefficiency of the Court rather than
on its need for a greater number of liberal judges to sus-
tain New Deal legislation. His oblique approach, the Insurgents believed, was an unwarranted attack on Justice
Louis D. Brandeis, who at eighty-one was the Court's foremost liberal. No one could honestly charge Brandeis, or the
entire Court for that matter, with being inefficient, for
the most recent Attorney-General's report indicated that
the Court was fully up-to-date in its work. "Cleverness
and adroitness in dealing with the Supreme Court," editorialized the New York Times, "are not qualities which
sober-minded citizens will approve."[13]

Initial Congressional reaction was about what Roosevelt had anticipated. Rabid New Dealers, like Indiana's
Sherman Minton and Pennsylvania's Joseph Guffey, publicly
lauded the plan, and "irreconcilable" Democrats like Carter
Glass and Josiah Bailey strongly opposed it. To Glass,
especially, the plan was despicable. "Of course I shall
oppose it," he responded to the query of a reporter. "I
shall oppose it with all the strength that runs to me."
Moderate Democrats, however, and most of the Insurgents,

---

[13] Johnson to Hiram Johnson, Jr., Feb. 14, 1937, Hiram
W. Johnson Papers, Part IV, Box 4, Bancroft Library, University of California, Berkeley; New York Times, Feb. 6, 1937,
p. 1.

two groups on whose support the President was counting, remained noncommittal or silently hostile. Among the Insurgents, only LaFollette announced his support.[14] Strangely,
all of the Republican Senators maintained total silence.

Before the Court fight Senate Republicans were still
badly divided. During Roosevelt's first term Eastern and
Midwestern conservatives remained the party's chief spokesmen in Congress, and their narrowly partisan attacks on the
New Deal played directly into the hands of the administration. Not only did they sound like the "economic royalists"
whom the President denounced so effectively, but they also
widened the rift between themselves and the Republican progressives. In 1937, after Roosevelt's reelection, only ten
regular Republicans and five progressives remained in the
Senate, and the continued existence of the party depended on
the merging of these two wings.[15] Such a union, however,
seemed improbable. William Allen White indicated forlornly
that only Roosevelt could rescue the Republicans. "I don't
see how we can get enough cohesion to stand for another
victory unless the President hands us the issue. He might
do it on the Supreme Court," White accurately predicted,

---

[14]Alsop and Catledge, 168 Days, p. 71 New York Times,
Feb. 14, 1937, p. 28.

[15]By 1937 LaFollette and Norris had left the Republican
party and for all practical purposes were Roosevelt Democrats,
even though they were Progressive and Independent, respectively; Cutting, Couzens, and Norbeck had died; and because
of illness, Costigan was forced to retire. As the 75th Congress opened, Borah, Capper, Frazier, Johnson, and Nye were
the only Republican Insurgents in the Senate. Farmer-
Laborite Henrik Shipstead and the Democratic Burton Wheeler
completed the Insurgent ranks.

"but nothing that we can do is going to help that much."[16]
Roosevelt's attack on the Supreme Court did what GOP strategy could not have done—it united the Senate Republicans
for the first time in nearly three decades.

Although all Senate Republicans opposed the Court
plan, it was essential that party leaders devise a strategy
to maintain this new and fragile unity. The Republican Insurgents let it be known that they would not tolerate a
partisan attack on the plan by their conservative colleagues.
Borah indicated that he was willing to play a leading role
in the fight "if it is not trademarked in advance a 'Hoover
fight' or a 'Republican fight.'" Sensing this, McNary met
with Borah and Michigan's conservative Republican Senator
Arthur Vandenberg and persuaded both Senators to do what
he had been doing since 1933, namely, keeping quiet. "Let
the boys across the aisle do the talking," the Senate
Minority Leader said. "We'll do the voting." Directions
to maintain a "conspiracy of silence" were sent out to national Republican leaders and party members in the House.
Kansas Representative Clifford Hope thought it a brilliant
tactic. "There is no question in my mind," he wrote, "about
the wisdom of this strategy. If we can just keep the Liberty
League and the United States Chamber of Commerce, as well

---

[16]Quoted in James T. Patterson, Congressional Conservatism and the New Deal (Lexington, Ky., 1967), p. 101.

as the old guard Republican leaders out of the picture, the
President is licked."[17]

Even with unanimous Republican Senatorial opposition,
however, Roosevelt could have won the Court fight if the
GOP had been able to win support only among conservative
Democrats. It was mandatory if the plan was to be defeated
that the opposition forces be led by a Democrat who was a
recognized liberal. Only a liberal Democrat could attract
enough support from Democratic moderates to insure the Court
plan's defeat. "The President need have no fear of opposition from the right," wrote William Allen White, "but opposition on the left he cannot overcome so easily. In the first
place, he doesn't know the tactics, and in the second place,
that group loves martyrdom and thrives on it, and the more
he lambasts it, the bigger it gets." Congressional conservatives found an unlikely leader and willing martyr in the
Insurgent Burton K. Wheeler. The Court fight would pit the

---

[17]Vandenberg Notes, Feb. 6, 1937, in Scrapbook 1937,
Arthur H. Vandenberg Papers, Clements Library, University of
Michigan, Ann Arbor, Michigan; Joseph Alsop and Robert Kin-
ter, "Let Them Do the Talking," Saturday Evening Post, XXCIII
(Sept. 28, 1940), 18; Karl Lamb, "The Opposition Party as
Secret Agent: Republicans and the Court Fight," Papers of the
Michigan Academy of Arts and Letters, XLVI (1961), 539-50;
Walter K. Roberts, "The Political Career of Charles L. McNary,
1924-1944" (Ph.D. Thesis, University of North Carolina, 1954),
pp. 221-31; Hope to H. H. Heaps, March 2, 1937, Clifford R.
Hope Papers, Legislative Correspondence, 1936-1937, Religious-
S, Kansas State Historical Society, Topeka, Kansas. The Republican silence infuriated the administration. "The Republicans are as meek as skimmed milk," Ickes fumed. "None of
them raises his voice. The strategy is to let the Democrats
tear each other to pieces and then for the Republicans to
move in and enjoy the fruits of victory. . .without suffering
any casualties themselves." Ickes, Secret Diary, II, 93.

178

liberal Franklin D. Roosevelt against the liberal Burton K. Wheeler.[18]

Wheeler was formally recognized as leader of the anti-Court packing forces at a dinner at the home of Senator Millard Tydings of Maryland. Other dinner guests included Vandenberg, Harry Byrd of Virginia, Edward Burke of Nebraska, Bennett Champ Clark of Missouri, Tom Connally of Texas, Royal Copeland of New York, Peter Gerry of Rhode Island, Walter George of Georgia, Kenneth McKeller of Tennessee, and Frederick Van Nuys of Indiana. The dissident Senators selected a steering committee to coordinate their activities and to put pressure on their uncommitted colleagues. At first, Wheeler felt uneasy among his former enemies, but as the gathering was about to disband the Montana Senator warmed to the occasion and confidently told his cohorts that "a small army that believes in a principle can lick a bunch of mercenaries, and we'll lick them."[19]

---

[18]Quoted in Patterson, _Congressional Conservatism_, p. 117. Hiram Johnson exhibited the love of martydom described by William Allen White. "I have grown too old to have any other consideration than the future of my country control my action," the California Senator wrote to his son imme- iately after Roosevelt's Court message. ". . .No one can prevent what is happening, but at least, an official as old as I am, with little in the future for him, can stand on his feet and make clear the situation. I am under no il- lusions about the puny power one man in opposition wields, but it is better to die fighting a fight like this." Johnson to Hiram Johnson, Jr., Feb. 6, 1937, Johnson Papers, Part IV, Box 4.

[19]Burton K. Wheeler, _Yankee From the West_ (Garden City, N. Y., 1962), pp. 322-23; Alsop and Catledge, _168 Days_, p. 104.

Wheeler's opposition to President Roosevelt left seasoned political observers incredulous. Wheeler had been the
first prominent party member outside of New York to endorse
Roosevelt's 1932 nomination as the Democratic standard
bearer. In addition, the Montana Senator had worked hard
to convince Republican progressives that the New York
governor was a liberal candidate worthy of their support.
During Roosevelt's first term it appeared as though Wheeler
and he had worked together intimately to expand the New
Deal. In the "second hundred days" especially, the Montana
Senator's persistent and deft handling of the utilities
bill earned the praise of the President and the enmity of
conservatives. The year 1936 found Wheeler campaigning for
Roosevelt once again. The Senator assured the President
that he would carry every Western state "because the people
believe you are on their side against the overlords of
finance." Roosevelt cordially responded: "My dear Burt,
it is good to know in these days that I have fine friends
like you."[20]

Also, Wheeler was no worshipper of the Supreme Court.
He had been Robert LaFollette's progressive running mate
in 1924, and he continued to criticize the Court as the
bulwark of the big industrial interests. In invalidating
the AAA, the Court, Wheeler believed, had overstepped its
bounds; and he thought that Congress should intervene to
limit the Court's power. "I suggest that constitutions are

---

[20]Wheeler to Roosevelt, Oct. 24, 1936, Roosevelt
Papers, PPF 723; Roosevelt to Wheeler, Oct. 23, 1936,
Roosevelt Papers, PPF 723.

made for men not men for constitutions," he said angrily. "I am not one of those who believe in the principle of curtailing production, but now I feel if we are going to help the farmers we may have to change the Constitution to do it." After the 1936 election, Wheeler urged Norris to chair a conference to draft a Constitutional amendment to curb the Court's power. "I would not want to go as far as some people do," he wrote his fellow Insurgent, ". . .but I am willing and I think perhaps the people would go as far as to amend the Constitution to permit Congress to fix the hours of labor and minimum wages and let competition proceed from that point."[21]

When he was informed of Roosevelt's Court plan, however, Wheeler was "flabbergasted," and he accused the President of being "drunk with power." Wheeler had both personal and ideological reasons for opposing Roosevelt's Court-packing scheme. Beneath the thin veneer of public cordiality, the Senator and the President were not really compatible; there had been friction between the two men from the start of the Roosevelt presidency. After Roosevelt's Attorney-General designate, Senator Thomas J. Walsh, who was Wheeler's fellow Montana Insurgent, died on the eve of the inauguration, the President selected Homer S. Cummings in Walsh's place. To Wheeler this was a poor appointment, for Cummings was not a liberal but a "John W. Davis Democrat"

---

[21]New York Times, Jan. 17, 1936, p. 13; Wheeler to Norris, Nov. 25, 1936, Norris Papers, Tray 27, Box 3; interview with Burton K. Wheeler, Nov. 22, 1968.

and a "cheap politician." To make matters worse, the new
Attorney General channeled Justice Department patronage to
Montana through National Committeeman J. Bruce Kremer, a
lobbyist for the Anaconda Copper Company and Wheeler's bitter enemy.[22]

The Montana Senator also complained that Roosevelt
never gave him an audience at the White House, and he resented the fact that LaFollette and Norris were the Insurgents on whom the President relied for liberal advice. In
addition, Wheeler felt that he had been treated rather
cavalierly on the silver issue, for when Roosevelt finally
decided "to do something for silver," he overlooked the
Montana Senator and chose Key Pittman as his spokesman.
Finally, Wheeler regarded himself as a better liberal than
Franklin D. Roosevelt, and he was envious of all the adulation liberals showered upon the President. The Montana Insurgent was quick to point out that in the 1920's he was
fighting for the "liberal cause" in the West while Roosevelt
was "hobnobbing with reactionaries in New York" and supporting the Morgan lawyer, John W. Davis, for President. Wheeler
was always suspicious of Roosevelt's commitment to liberalism; even in the midst of the fight over the holding-

---

[22]Wheeler, Yankee From the West, pp. 298-305; Ickes,
Secret Diary, I, 363-64; Max Freedman (ed.) Roosevelt and
Frankfurter: Their Correspondence, 1928-1945 (Boston, 1967),
p. 271; Hubert Kay, "Boss Isolationist: Burton K. Wheeler,"
Life, X (May 19, 1941), 117; interview with Burton K.
Wheeler, Nov. 22, 1968.

company bill the Senator was confident that the President
was "sweet-talking" the utility magnates behind Wheeler's
back.[23]

   Wheeler's antagonism to the Court plan was not solely
the result of his personal animosity toward Roosevelt, however; much of his opposition must be attributed to the
ideological differences between Insurgent progressivism and
New Deal liberalism. Like most other Insurgents, Wheeler
based his liberalism on opposition to centralized power.
At first, his antimonopolistic wrath was directed primarily
against concentrated corporate and financial wealth. An
attack on "the Company," Anaconda Copper of Montana, had
preceded his election to the United States Senate. Once
in Washington the Montana Senator continued his assault on
concentrated economic power, with railroads, Wall Street
bankers, and holding companies serving as his favorite tar-
gets. His opposition to the NIRA had been mainly on the
grounds that it condoned and strengthened economic monopolies. Wheeler was just as opposed to government power
as to corporate power if it threatened to submerge the individual, and he was consequently concerned about the large
amount of power that had accrued to the President as the

---

   [23]Potomacus, "Wheeler of Montana," New Republic, CIX
(Sept. 20, 1943), 391; James MacGregor Burns, Roosevelt: The
Lion and the Fox (New York, 1956), p. 341; Wheeler, Yankee
From the West, p. 311. Wheeler believed that Roosevelt
could not be a true liberal given his aristocratic background. The Montana Insurgent called the President a "Tory
liberal"—one who paternalistically bestows gifts on the
masses rather than seeking to remove the inequities from the
system so that the masses could help themselves. Interview
with Burton K. Wheeler, Nov. 22, 1968.

result of the New Deal. To Wheeler, the Court plan was evidence that New Dealers desired to place all political power
in the hands of Roosevelt.[24]

In Wheeler, the opposition Senators had a determined
leader who was probably as skilled a politician as Roosevelt
himself. The Montana Senator did not wait long to reveal
his political cunning and his intense aversion for the
President's Court plan. Roosevelt had counted on automatic
and enthusiastic support from Wheeler and the other Insurgents. When Wheeler did not immediately endorse the plan,
the President sent Tommy Corcoran to discuss the issue with
the Montana Senator. During the course of the conversation,
Corcoran learned that the Senator wanted a liberal Court
but that he did not approve of the method Roosevelt had
chosen to accomplish that end. When Wheeler indicated his
preference for a Constitutional amendment or a Congressional
statute restricting the Court's power, Corcoran replied that
the President's plan was the only certain and speedy way to
reduce the Court's influence. The White House emissary then
added that it would be futile to oppose Roosevelt since his
Court plan would gain Senate approval. "Well, Tommy, he
isn't going to get it!" Wheeler angrily retorted. Amazed
at this response, Corcoran switched tactics and pleaded
with the Senator not to announce his opposition to the plan
until he had talked to the President. At first Wheeler
agreed, but realizing that Corcoran's visit was just the

---

[24]Interview with Burton K. Wheeler, Nov. 22, 1968;
Robert S. Allen, "Wheeler and the Liberals," Current History, LI (March, 1940), 25-27.

beginning of White House pressure, the Montana Senator decided to take drastic action to protect himself from future
Presidential persuasion. He placed himself on record
against the Court plan by releasing a statement to reporters
denouncing the proposal as "fundamentally unsound, morally
wrong, and an attempt to set up a dictatorship in this
country." A few moments later Charles Michelson, publicity
director for the Democratic party, telephoned and invited
the Senator to the White House for dinner. Wheeler informed
Michelson that the President should "save the plate for
someone who persuaded more easily."[25]

The effect of Wheeler's opposition was felt immediately
at the White House. Roosevelt was compelled to rely on
Robert LaFollette, rather than on the Montana Senator, to
rally Insurgent support for the Court plan. Unfortunately
for the President, however, the Wisconsin Progressive no
longer held the respect of most of his fellow Insurgents.
Wheeler claimed that LaFollette was too "radical," and Hiram
Johnson stated that "young La Follette. . .has become one
of the first Vice-Presidents of A. K., Inc., and shows just
what he has probably always been. He will raise the standard aloft for the LaFollette family at any time and in their
behalf will lead a gallant charge; but on any other subject,

[25]Wheeler, Yankee From the West, pp. 321-22; Alsop and
Catledge, 168 Days, pp. 100-101; New York Times, Feb. 14,
1937, p. 28. Wheeler has claimed that Corcoran went so far
as to promise him a voice in naming new justices if he went
along with the President's plan. Interview with Burton K.
Wheeler, Nov. 22, 1968.

he is a broken reed."[26] LaFollette, moreover, could not
match Wheeler in political skill, a fact that was quickly
demonstrated when Wheeler outmaneuvered the Wisconsin Senator
in winning Nye and Frazier to the opposition. To insure
Nye's commitment, Wheeler persuaded the North Dakota Senator
to make the first nationwide radio address against the Court
plan. Although Roosevelt threatened to withhold a large
amount of federal assistance from North Dakota, Nye delivered
the speech. Later, Wheeler gained another convert in Henrik
Shipstead. Working closely with Borah, the Montana Senator
saw to it that only Norris and LaFollette among the Insurgents supported the plan.[27]

Although Wheeler fully appreciated the necessity of
keeping liberals in the forefront of the "crusade against
dictatorship," he realized that he must depend on conservatives for financial support. Once again, he was able to
capitalize on his close friendship with Borah. The Idaho
Senator introduced his friend to newspaper publisher Frank
Gannett, who had financed Borah's attempt to secure the 1936
Republican presidential nomination. After hearing Roosevelt's

---

[26]Interview with Burton K. Wheeler, Nov. 22, 1968;
Johnson to Hiram Johnson, Jr., April 2, 1938, Johnson Papers,
Part IV Box 4.

[27]Alsop and Catledge, 168 Days p. 103; Wayne S. Cole,
Gerald P. Nye and American Foreign Policy (Minneapolis, 1962),
pp. 140-42. Just before he was to give his address against
the Court plan, Nye received a visit from President William
Thatcher of the Farmers' Union. Thatcher had just come from
the White House, and he suggested that Nye could get out of
making the speech by pretending to sprain an ankle and enter-
ing a naval hospital for a few days. Gerald P. Nye Lecture
Series, "North Dakota and the New Deal," (University of North
Dakota, Nov. 15, 1967), Tape MR 69-3(1), Roosevelt Papers;
Marian C. McKenna, Borah (Ann Arbor, Michigan, 1961), p. 316.

Court message, Gannett had successfully solicited funds from
prominent conservatives to establish a "nonpartisan" committee to work against passage of the Court plan. Gannett offered his services to Wheeler, and during the next half year
Gannett's National Committee to Uphold Constitutional Government distributed more than ten million pieces of literature
in opposition to the plan. The Republican National Committee also participated, as it helped finance national radio
speeches against the plan and paid the traveling expenses
of opposition witnesses testifying before the Senate Judiciary Committee.[28]

By the end of February, 1937, the Court plan faced opposition from a smooth-functioning and well-financed bipartisan coalition of United States Senators. Roosevelt
intended to surmount this hurdle by first introducing the
bill in the House. Since many Democrats owed their seats
to his landslide victory in November, the President assumed
that he could expect quick approval from the Lower Chamber.
He believed that positive House action would then force
the Senate to accept the proposal. House Democratic leaders
informed Roosevelt, however, that they opposed this procedure, and they expressed concern that approval of the
controversial measure might cost the Democrats control of
the House in the 1938 elections. Because of this worry and

[28]Patterson, Congressional Conservatism, pp. 118-19;
Harry W. Morris, "The Republicans in a Minority Role, 1933-
1938." (Ph.D. Thesis, University of Iowa, 1960), p. 229;
George Wolfskill, The Revolt of the Conservatives: A History
of the American Liberty League, 1934-1936 (Boston, 1962),
p. 252; interview with Burton K. Wheeler, Nov. 22, 1968.

Hatton Summers' lukewarm attitude toward the plan, Speaker William B. Bankhead and Majority Leader Sam Rayburn advised the President to have the bill introduced in the Senate. Roosevelt reluctantly consented, and hearings on the bill were scheduled to start before the Senate Judiciary Committee on March 10, 1937.[29]

It was soon obvious that Roosevelt had simply chosen the lesser of two evils, for Senate Judiciary Committee chairman Henry F. Ashurst was just as opposed to the plan as was Sumners, his counterpart in the House. Although he announced that he favored the President's proprosal, Ashurst spent the month of February working for Sumners' bill to allow Supreme Court justices to retire with full pay at age seventy. Ashurst secretly hoped that Congressional adoption of Sumners' bill would make enactment of the President's proposal unnecessary, for it was rumored that Justices VanDevanter and Sutherland would retire if guaranteed their full salary. Roosevelt, although favoring the judicial retirement bill, indicated to Ashurst that he did not regard the measure as a substitute for his own plan, and he soon accused the Arizona Senator of postponing his committee's hearings. Ashurst responded that he was going to give opponents of the measure "ample time and opportunity to explore all its implications." Having failed to convince Ashurst of the urgency of the matter, Roosevelt dispatched Corcoran to persuade the Judiciary Committee chairman

---

[29]William Bankhead to Roosevelt, Feb. 8, 1937, Roosevelt Papers, PSF 61; Time, XXIX (Feb. 22, 1937), 11.

188

to agree to a Senatorial resolution limiting the hearings
to two weeks. "No, no, I can't get a motion like that
through," Ashurst told Corcoran. "No haste, no hurry, no
waste, no worry—that is the motto of this committee."[30]
Henry Ashurst was using the only tactic at his disposal—
delay.

Since a month had passed without any Congressional
action on his recommendations for judicial reform, the President decided that it was time to exert more pressure on
recalcitrant Democrats. On March 4, 1937, Roosevelt delivered his hard-line "one third of the Nation" speech to
a Democratic victory gathering at Washington's Mayflower
Hotel. He warned fellow party members that if they did not
act on his Court message, they would not be present for a
1938 victory dinner. "We gave warning last November that
we had just begun to fight," he declared. ". . .if we
would keep faith with those who had faith in us, if we
would make democracy succeed, I say we must act—NOW!" Five
days later, on the eve of the Senate Judiciary Committee
hearings, the President appealed directly to the people in
one of his fireside chats. He asked his fellow citizens to
trust him as their leader and assured them that he wanted
to "make American democracy work." Wheeler immediately
went on nationwide radio to rebut the President's speeches.
He called Roosevelt's Mayflower Hotel address "the most
demagogic I have even heard" and warned that the Court plan

---

[30]Sparks (ed.), _Diary of Ashurst_, pp. 366-71; Alsop and
Catledge, _168 Days_, pp. 122-23.

would "create a political court" that would be a threat to each individual's liberties. As for the argument that they should trust the President, the Montana Senator implored the people to put their trust in laws rather than in men.[31]

When the Senate Judiciary Committee finally opened hearings on the bill, Cummings was the first administration witness to appear. The Attorney General's testimony attempted to corroborate the President's initial charge that the major problem was the Court's inefficiency. Assistant Attorney General Robert H. Jackson, the second administration witness, told the Senators forthrightly that the real issue was the liberalization of the Court. Jackson's candor, however, was unavailing. Seizing upon Cumming's testimony, Wheeler implored Chief Justice Hughes to testify that the Court actually was abreast of its work, thus refuting the premise on which the President had based his call for reform.

At first, Wheeler wanted Hughes to appear in person before the committee, but the Chief Justice refused to consent to this request. The Montana Senator then acted on a rumor that Justice Brandeis might offer some help. Through his daughter's friendship with Mrs. Brandeis, Wheeler had learned that the Justice was opposed to Roosevelt's plan. The Montana Senator telephoned Brandeis and received an appointment to see him. The old Justice refused to testify himself, but he indicated that another meeting with the Chief

---

[31]Rosenman (ed.), Public Papers of FDR, VI, 113-133; Wheeler, Yankee From the West, pp. 325-26; interview with Burton K. Wheeler, Nov. 22, 1968.

Justice might be to Wheeler's advantage. Brandeis arranged
the meeting, and this time Hughes agreed to compose a letter
stating that the Court was not behind in its work. Handing
Wheeler the letter, Hughes said that he hoped its contents
would receive wide publicity. The Montana Senator assured
the Chief Justice that he need not worry on that score. "I
almost laughed at his remark," Wheeler recalled later.[32]

On March 22, 1937, Wheeler, as the opposition's first
witness, read Hughes' letter before the Senate Judiciary
Committee. Hughes refuted Roosevelt's accusation of judicial inefficiency and insisted that the addition of six new
judges would slow down rather than speed up the work of
the Court; there would simply be "more judges to hear,
more judges to confer, more judges to discuss, more judges
to be convinced and to decide." Hughes charged that the
President had been forced to devise the Court-packing
scheme because most New Deal legislation had been poorly
drafted, briefs had been carelessly prepared, and arguments
before the Court had been badly presented. "We've had to
be not only the Court, but we've had to do the work that
should have been done by the Attorney General," the Chief
Justice concluded. Wheeler was jubilant. He proclaimed
that it was absurd to conclude that the nation needed "a
packing" of the Supreme Court; what it did need was a new
Attorney General.[33]

---

[32]Wheeler, Yankee From the West, pp. 327-32; Alsop and
Catledge, 168 Days, pp. 125-27; interview with Burton K.
Wheeler, Nov. 22, 1968.

[33]Wheeler, Yankee From the West, pp. 329-30; New York
Times, March 28, 1937, p. 21; Senate Report 711, 75th Cong.,
(Washington, D. C., 1937), pp. 38-40.

Both friends and enemies of the Court plan agreed that
Hughes' letter was a great setback for Roosevelt. Hiram
Johnson rejoiced that the "disingenuous plan" had finally
been exposed. Ickes secretly complimented Hughes on "good
tactics" and regretted that the President had insisted on
"going to court with a weak case."[34] Hughes' letter might
in itself have caused the Senate to reject the President's
bill, but a week later a series of favorable New Deal decisions by the Court destroyed all hope for passage for the
six-judge proposal. On March 29, 1937, with Justice Roberts
reversing himself, the Supreme Court upheld a Washington
state minimum-wage law by a 5-4 vote. To prove that this
was no accident the Court, on April 12, sustained the Wagner
Labor Relations Act, also by a 5-4 vote. To many, this
"switch in time that saved nine" was sufficient evidence
that the Court had "reformed."

Some of Roosevelt's most trusted legislative lieutenants now advised him to withdraw his original bill and seek
a compromise. "Why run for a train after you've already
caught it," quipped Jimmy Byrnes. "If the President wants
to compromise, I can get him a couple of extra judges
tomorrow," Robinson told a White House assistant. Roosevelt,
however, was not in a compromising mood. The rebellious
Congress and the vacillating Court infuriated him. Assured
by Robert Jackson that the Court would refuse to validate
the Social Security Act, the President informed his

---

[34]Johnson to John Francis Neylan, March 26, 1937,
Johnson Papers, Part III, Box 17; Ickes, Secret Diary, II,
99-100.

Senatorial leaders that he was standing resolutely behind
his original proposal. LaFollette lauded Roosevelt's decision because "the fate of democratic institutions cannot be
placed in jeopardy on such a precarious and changing factor
as Justice Roberts has demonstrated himself to be." The
Wisconsin Senator volunteered to make a speaking tour to
explain the President's Court plan and to rally support for
him.[35]

Had Roosevelt decided to seek a compromise Court plan,
many Senators would still have opposed him. Borah, for
example, in reacting to the suggestion that the number of
additional judges be reduced to two, maintained that "two
are as bad in principle as six." It was becoming evident
that the Court plan itself was not the major reason why
Senators were refusing to accede to Roosevelt's wishes.
Many Senators had long been apprehensive about the New Deal's
reform program, but because of the economic crisis and the
President's popularity with the electorate, they had not
dared to reveal their true sentiments. The unpopular Court
plan gave these men the occasion to announce their opposition to the administration's social and economic policies.
Representative Fred Vinson of Kentucky thus informed

---

[35]Alsop and Catledge, 168 Days, pp. 152-53; New York
Times, April 20, 1937, p. 17. LaFollette and Senator Hugo
Black of Alabama, under the sponsorship of Labor's Non-
Partisan League, held a series of meetings throughout the
country on the Court plan. This infuriated Hiram Johnson,
who was helpless to do anything about it. "Both of them are
men who will do anything the Administration wants, and both
are blatherskites," the California Senator wrote his son.
". . .If I were only myself I would follow them along as I
did Wilson in 1919 and 1920." Johnson to Hiram Johnson, Jr.,
April 16, 1937, Johnson Papers, Part IV, Box 4.

Cummings that Congressional resistance to the Court plan was
pronounced because many legislators did not favor the proposed extension of the New Deal. On the administration's
side, Ickes astutely sensed that defeat of the Court bill
could jeopardize the entire New Deal. "Unless the President
wins on it," the Secretary of the Interior wrote, "we will
lose everything that we have gained for the last four years
and a good deal besides. We will be set back at least ten
years, with the fight to make all over again."[36]

With both sides adamantly refusing to compromise, the
Court fight was stalemated for about a month. While Roosevelt went fishing in the Gulf of Mexico, the Senate waited
for its committee's report on the Court bill. On May 18,
1937, Willis Van Devanter announced that he was retiring as
an Associate Justice of the Supreme Court. The timing of
this decision had been cleverly planned by Borah and Wheeler
to coincide with the release of the Senate Judiciary Committee's report on the Court bill. At first Hiram Johnson,
who was a confidant of neither Borah nor Wheeler, accused
VanDevanter of cowardice. "Had I been in his place," the
California Senator proclaimed, "I am sure I would have died
on the Supreme Court or have been kicked off before I would
have yielded." Johnson, however, soon changed his mind, for
he recognized that VanDevanter's retirement meant that one

---

[36]William E. Leuchtenberg, Franklin D. Roosevelt and
the New Deal, 1932-1940 (New York, 1963), p. 237; Vinson to
Homer Cummings, July 26, 1937, Roosevelt Papers, PSF 24;
Ickes, Secret Diary, II, 89; Time, XXIX (May 17, 1937),
15.

of the reasons for the President's desire to pack the Court
no longer existed. Wheeler made certain that this fact was
also understood by the members of the Senate Judiciary Committee before they voted 10 to 8 not to recommend the Court
bill for passage.[37]

The Judiciary Committee report denounced the Court
plan as a measure that should have never been "presented to
the free representatives of the free people of America."
The Committee was also highly critical of Roosevelt's motives for suggesting the proposal. It rejected the assertion that the plan's purpose was to infuse new blood into
the Court and reported, instead, that the bill's major purpose was to force into retirement justices then over seventy
years of age. "The ultimate result," the report concluded,
"would be to make this government one of men rather than one
of law. . .and to make the Constitution what the executive
or legislative branches. . .choose to say it is—an interpretation to be changed with each change of administration."[38]

---

[37]_Time_, XXIX (May 31, 1937), 17-18; Johnson to Garrett
W. McEnery, May 19, 1937, Johnson Papers, Part III, Box 17.
When the judicial retirement bill was before the Senate,
Johnson spoke of it as "a lure and a bait" and said he would
not respect any man who retired under its provisions. Congressional Record, 75th Cong., 1st Sess., p. 1644. At one
time during the Court fight Senator Nye claimed that "Justice
Brandeis is going to resign and give the President Hell for
his bill and then, if that does not defeat the bill, and Congress goes ahead with it, the whole crowd is going to resign—the whole darn crowd!" Memorandum from Marvin McIntyre,
April 19, 1937, Roosevelt Papers, OF 41.

[38]Reprinted in New York _Herald Tribune_, June 15, 1937,
p. 1. Borah wrote a large part of the committee report.
"Borah has given a great account of himself the past few
months," a friend of the Idaho Senator wrote. "He has not
been written up, especially as to the collapsed court-packing

"This ought not to end the contest," declared Hiram
Johnson. "It is fundamental in character and goes to the
very existence of the Republic." Indeed, the contest was
far from finished, although the adverse Judiciary Committee
report, the resignation of VanDevanter, and the Court's
acceptance of the Social Security Act a week later ended
any possibility that Roosevelt's original proposal would win
Senatorial approval. "It's time for the President to withdraw it," Wheeler told reporters, "but I don't think he will
because he wants to make the Supreme Court entirely subservient." The Montana Senator was partially correct, for
Roosevelt refused to withdraw his Court bill. The President,
however, was by this time not so concerned about obtaining
an obedient Supreme Court as he was about avoiding a humilia-
ting defeat at the hands of the Congress. He badly needed
a victory, at least in principle.[39] VanDevanter's retirement, moreover, had created more problems than it had solved.
Roosevelt, of course, wanted to appoint a liberal to fill
the vacated seat, but it was public knowledge that he had
promised the post to Robinson, and fellow Senators already
were calling the Majority Leader "Mr. Justice." The naming
of sixty-five year old Robinson to the Court struck Ickes as

scheme of the President, but he was the power behind the
senatorial throne. I have forgotten whether I told you in
Boston what he confided to me in confidence, namely that he
and O'Mahoney wrote the judiciary report. Besides that he
cashed in on his long independent and constitutional career
with the opposition democrats and notably their leaders."
Salmon O. Levinson to Raymond Robins, August 5, 1937, Raymond
Robins Papers, Box 28, State Historical Society of Wisconsin,
Madison, Wisconsin.

[39]New York Times, May 19, 1937, p. 18.

absurd. "It is really an occasion for sardonic laughter and I don't relish the position the President is in," Ickes recorded in his diary. "He /Robinson/ isn't anything but a conservative at heart, and now it is proposed that he go on the Supreme Court as 'new blood' and as exemplifying a 'more liberal mind' than the irreconcilables on that Court."[40]

To extricate himself from his dilemma, Roosevelt invited Robinson to the White House and belatedly indicated a desire to compromise. Without mentioning the seat vacated by VanDevanter, the President explained that he would settle for the so-called Hatch bill. This measure retained the principle of the original plan since it would have enabled Roosevelt to appoint two new justices—Robinson and a liberal.[41] As far as most of the Insurgents were concerned, however, there was no reason to compromise. "There is no logic in it," fumed Hiram Johnson, "and it is simply the difference between petty larceny and grand larceny." The President's hopes for a compromise, however, did not depend on the Insurgents but rather on the Democratic Senators. At a political picnic on Jefferson Island in late June, Roosevelt used beer and patronage in an attempt to heal the rift

---

[40]Alsop and Catledge, 168 Days, pp. 208-28; William E. Borah to Franklin D. Roosevelt, May 19, 1937, Roosevelt Papers, PPF 2358; Ickes, Secret Diary, II, 145.

[41]The Hatch compromise would have permitted Roosevelt to name a "coadjutor" for any Supreme Court justice who had passed the age of seventy-five (instead of seventy) and who refused to retire. Although the bill's provisions would have limited the President to one such appointment per year, its passage would immediately have allowed him two new appointments since he had not yet filled the seat vacated by VanDevanter.

in his party. Robinson thought that this "harmony gathering" was effective, and he wrote Garner that there were now enough votes to pass the compromise bill. "If it were not for Bert /sic/ Wheeler," the Majority Leader added, "the opposition could be pretty well pacified but Wheeler is irreconcilable. I think this is due to his personal antagonism to the President." At Robinson's suggestion, Roosevelt himself tried to persuade Wheeler not to oppose the Hatch bill, but the Montana Senator could not be moved. "Only if I were your greatest enemy would I help you get this bill through," Wheeler told the President as he left the White House to lead the anti-compromise forces in the Senate.[42]

As the floor fight began on the Hatch bill, Robinson somberly warned Wheeler that it would be "dog eat dog." Encouraged by the prospect of attaining a seat on the Supreme Court, the Majority Leader recklessly led the fight for the compromise Court bill. "Through my medical eyes," recalled Dr. Royal S. Copeland, "I saw that he should slow down." But before Copeland could warn Robinson, the Majority Leader died of a heart attack on July 14, 1937. "Had it not been for the Court plan he would have been alive today," Wheeler said on the day after the Majority Leader's death. "I beseech the President to drop the fight lest he appear to

---

[42] Johnson to John Francis Neylan, May 4, 1937, Johnson Papers, Part III, Box 17; Neal, Robinson, p. 456; New York Times, July 7, 1937, p. 1. For an excellent sketch of Robinson and the New Deal, see Alsop and Catledge, "Joe Robinson, The New Deal's Old Reliable," Saturday Evening Post, CCIX (Sept. 26, 1936).

fight against God."[43] At this point, Roosevelt would sooner
have fought a celestial being than a hostile Senate, for with
Robinson's death the supposed majority for the compromise
proposal had evaporated.

To pay their final respects to their fallen leader,
Senators postponed the debate and boarded a train to Arkansas
for Robinson's funeral. The funeral train turned into a
"caucus on wheels" when Vice-President Garner joined the
mourners for the return trip to Washington. Since mid-June
Garner had been on a fishing trip at his home in Uvalde,
Texas, as a protest against the Court plan and other pending New Deal legislation. He had seen his beloved Democratic
party torn by division, and now he had come to Little Rock
to help restore party unity. He quickly learned that the
price of party harmony was the President's surrender on the
Court bill. Upon arriving in Washington, Garner bluntly informed Roosevelt that his Court measure simply did not have
enough votes to pass. The President repeated, "The people
are with me. I know it." Roosevelt knew, however, that he
faced certain defeat in the Senate, and he therefore authorized the Vice-President to dispose of the Court bill as
painlessly as possible. Following this conversation, Garner
went directly to Wheeler's office and told the Senator,
"Burt, you can write your own ticket."[41]

---

[43]Congressional Record, 75th Cong., 1st Sess., p. 6796;
Time, XXX (July 26, 1937), 11; New York Times, July 15, 1937,
p. 13.

[44]Alsop and Catledge, 168 Days, pp. 279-80, 283.

After conferring with some of his allies, Wheeler decided that the best way to dispose of the Court bill was to recommit it to the Senate Judiciary Committee. The administration also favored recommittal but not the type of recommittal envisioned by Wheeler. Roosevelt preferred to have the bill languish on the Senate calendar and simply not be called up for a vote. Although this really meant that he had failed in his endeavor to reform the Court, the President could justly claim that the Senate had never defeated the bill but rather had postponed action on it. Wheeler, however, was not disposed to be that magnanimous, even in victory. He wanted the bill to be recommitted with instructions that it be redrafted to exclude any reference to enlarging the Supreme Court. This emasculated bill would then be resubmitted to the Senate, and its passage would clearly indicate that Roosevelt had been defeated. Garner had no choice but to agree with Wheeler. The Vice-President did, however, secure a pledge from the Montana Insurgent that the motion to recommit would be done without a record vote and that the words "Supreme Court" would not be mentioned on the Senate floor.[45]

On the afternoon of July 22, 1937, both pledges were broken. Senator Marvel M. Logan of Kentucky asked for unanimous consent to a motion returning the Court bill to the Judiciary Committee. The Senator added, "by way of explanation," that the Judiciary Committee had authorized him to make this request "with the understanding that it

---

[45]Ibid., pp. 279-90.

200

would be instructed to report a bill for the reform of the
judiciary within ten days." Before the Senate could grant
Logan's request, Charles McNary broke the long Republican
silence on the Court bill by insisting that a record vote
be taken on the motion. Although the motion carried by a
vote of 70 to 20, which was an overwhelming defeat for the
President, Hiram Johnson was not satisfied and sought to
humiliate Roosevelt even more. "I desire to know," he asked,
"what the judicial reform refers to . Does it refer to the
Supreme Court or the inferior courts?" An embarrassed Logan
replied that the Supreme Court was not to have been mentioned.
Undaunted, Johnson continued his questioning. "Is the
Supreme Court out of the way?" he insisted on knowing.
Finally, Logan acknowledged defeat and admitted: "The Supreme Court is out of the way." Hiram Johnson raised his
arms and declared, "Glory be to God!"[46]

With the defeat of the Hatch compromise bill, the Court
fight was finished for all practical purposes. There were,
however, two episodes connected with the Court-packing plan
that revealed the strained state of Congressional-Executive
relations. One of these was the President's famous "Dear
Alben" letter, and the other was his nomination of Senator
Hugo Black of Alabama to the vacant Supreme Court seat.
When Robinson died, the post of Senate leader automatically
went to his dependable assistant, Senator Alben Barkley of
Kentucky. Most Democratic Senators looked upon Barkley as

[46]Congressional Record, 75th Cong., 1st Sess., pp.
7375-82.

an interim leader, for their personal choice for the position was Mississippi's Pat Harrison. But that was before
Roosevelt sent an open letter to Barkley, ostensibly urging
him to continue the fight for Court reform. Most Senators
were quick to infer that the President's letter suggested
his preference for Barkley as Senate leader, and they resented Executive meddling in their family affairs. "I cannot believe the President wrote such a letter," exclaimed
Wheeler. "It would not be in character for. . .the President of our country and the man other liberals and I triumphed with in 1932 and 1936." "He is losing his balance,"
wrote Hiram Johnson. "If he continues thus we may be saved
a dictatorship in this country." Roosevelt denied that he
had intended to influence the outcome of the contest for
majority leader, but this was not true. "Ostensibly, the
President has kept his hands off," Ickes recorded, "but men
like Corcoran were doing everything they could for Barkley,
realizing that the election of Harrison would be disastrous
to the President's program."[47] With White House help,
Barkley won the leadership contest by one vote. The price
was hardly worth it, however, for Roosevelt had further
antagonized an already irritable Senate.

The second episode, also caused by Robinson's death,
involved the filling of the Court vacancy previously promised to the Arkansas Senator. Roosevelt ultimately nominated

[47]New York Times, July 16, 1937, p. 2; Johnson to Hiram
Johnson, Jr., July 17, 1937, Johnson Papers, Part IV, Box 4;
Ickes, Secret Diary, 170. For a copy of the "Dear Alben"
Letter, see Roosevelt to Barkley, July 15, 1937, Roosevelt
Papers, PSF 62.

Hugo Black for the position. Since Black was a zealous liberal and a loyal New Dealer, he was an obvious choice, but the Alabama Senator was not popular with many of his colleagues for these very reasons. Hiram Johnson called him "unfit to be a Supreme Court Justice." The President knew of Black's unpopularity, but he also realized that the Senate was unlikely to violate one of its most hallowed traditions by failing to confirm the appointment of one of its own members. "They'll have to take him," he confidently informed Farley.[48]

The Senate eventually confirmed Black but not without a show of resistance. Senator Cotton Ed Smith of South Carolina "'God-damned' the nomination all over the place when it was first announced." Hiram Johnson and Edward Burke abrogated the Senate's "courtesy rule" by calling for a Judiciary Committee investigation of Black's credentials for the appointment—this was the first time there had been such a request with regard to a Supreme Court nominee since Senator L.Q.C. Lamar of Mississippi had been nominated to the Court in 1888. To make matters worse, it was discovered that Black had once been a member of the Alabama Ku Klux Klan. Six days after Black's nomination, however, the Senate confirmed the appointment by a vote of 69 to 13. "When Franklin Roosevelt is dead and buried and all his bones are rotted," concluded an unusually unhappy William Allen White, "he will be remembered in the history of this day and time

---

[48] Johnson to Frank P. Doherty, August 23, 1937, Johnson Papers, Part III, Box 17; James A. Farley, *Jim Farley's Story* (New York, 1948), p. 98.

by the fact that he was not above dishonoring the Supreme
Court by putting a Klansman there."[49]

Roosevelt's attempt to pack the Supreme Court thus
ended in an ignominious personal defeat for the President.
To be sure, Congress ultimately passed the McCarran Judicial Procedure Reform Act; but this measure, which permitted no change in federal court membership and provided
certain procedural reforms in the lower courts, was a mere
shadow of the President's original Court bill. It was such
an innocuous proposal that Garner was able to force the
bill through the Senate in only fifty-nine minutes. "The
bill passed by the Senate is a tiny step in the right
direction," Roosevelt emphasized to a friend, "and when
you get a chance to read it, I think you will agree with
me that it is a very small step."[50] A very small step,
however, was all a vindictive Senate was willing to grant
the President.

Roosevelt himself was largely responsible for the
strong opposition to the Court plan in the Senate, especially
among the Insurgents. In the first place, the scheme was
"too damned clever" for the Insurgents. "Bottomless seems
the President's bag of surprises," said Gerald P. Nye. "And
so long as the effort is one to accomplish by indirection
what ought to be gained only by direct action, it is well
that there is a storm raised by the proposal." Furthermore,

---

[49]Ickes, _Secret Diary_, II, 196; _New York Times_, August
13, 1937, p. 1; _ibid._, Sept. 15, 1937, p. 3.

[50]_Time_, XXX (August 16, 1937), 8; Roosevelt to J.
Warren Davis, August 11, 1937, Roosevelt Papers, PSF 61.

204

the manner in which Roosevelt sprang his plan on Congress
and on the country irritated the Insurgents. They had urged
the President to educate the voters on the necessity for
judicial reform by making the Court a prominent issue in
the 1936 campaign. "I have no doubt," George Norris had
written in May, 1936, "but that the people would rally to
the support of any party or any man who advocated the taking
away of much of the jurisdiction of the lower courts or in
modifying the jurisdiction of the Supreme Court." Roosevelt, however, spurned all such entreaties. He preferred
that he himself, not the "nine old men," be the major
election issue.[51]

More significant in explaining Insurgent opposition
to the President's proposal was the fact that the Insurgents regarded the plan itself as unsatisfactory because it
did not promise "fundamental" reform. For years the Insurgents had been advocating some kind of Constitutional amendment to curb the power of the Court.[52]   Roosevelt's plan,

[51]Burns, Roosevelt, p. 297; New York Times, Feb. 22,
1937, pp. 1, 4; Norris to Francis J. Heney, May 6, 1936,
Norris Papers, Tray 27, Box 2. William Allen White claimed
that Norris was insulted because Roosevelt's "sudden" decision to pack the Court had sabotaged the Nebraska Senator's
plan to chair a conference on curbing judicial power through
the adoption of a Constitutional amendment. "I know that
George Norris was in hopes to present his plan when the President jumped in with his plan," White wrote. "Norris and
his kind were well worth respecting. They had been in the
fight when he Roosevelt was a young man. To break their
heart and drive them away from his leadership was a real
tragedy." White to Felix Frankfurter, Oct. 11, 1937, quoted
in Freedman (ed.), Roosevelt and Frankfurter, pp. 16-17.

[52]The plans suggested included Constitutional amendments denying the Court review power over certain kinds of
social and economic legislation, requiring more than a mere

however, did not concern itself with reducing the prerogatives of the Court but only with the immediate situation.
"The greatest fallacy of the plan," explained Nye, "is in
its trying to deal in 'personalities' rather than 'basic
principles.'" Although Norris ultimately supported the
Court plan "as a last resort," he originally announced that
he was "not in sympathy with any scheme to enlarge the Supreme Court." "I do not like the President's proposal,"
the Nebraska Insurgent complained, "not because it is unconstitutional, but because I doubt the wisdom of proceeding
in that way and because it is not, in my judgment, fundamental and will be only a temporary remedy."[53]

The Insurgents also objected to the Court plan because
they believed it to be a threat to civil liberties. "Create
now a political Court to echo the ideas of the Executive and
you have created a weapon," warned Wheeler, "a weapon which
in the hands of another President will be an instrument. . .

---

majority of Supreme Court justices to override Congressional
statutes, or allowing Congress to veto Court decisions.

[53]*New York Times*, Feb. 22, 1937, p. 4; Norris to Lewis
C. Westwood, May 14, 1937, Norris Papers, Tray 27, Box 1; *New
York Times*, Feb. 6, 1937, p. 11; Norris to Jerome F. Heyn,
April 3, 1937, Norris Papers, Tray 27, Box 1. Both Hiram
Johnson and Wheeler were highly critical of Norris for his
eventual support of the President's Court plan. "Norris had
been a man who wanted to go to the stake, and who took a
real pleasure in being burned alive," lamented Johnson, "but
now in his old age, while senile, because of Roosevelt's
gift to him of the TVA. . .and because of his fanaticism
with respect to that project, anything that Roosevelt does,
or anything that he says, Norris will defend, although at
variance with all his former principles. He is truly a pa-
thetic figure now." Johnson to Hiram Johnson, Jr., April 2,
1938, Johnson Papers, Part IV, Box 4. Wheeler also believed
that Roosevelt "hypnotized Norris with the TVA." Interview
with Burton K. Wheeler, Nov. 22, 1968.

that can extinguish your right of liberty, of speech, of
thought, of action and of religion; a weapon whose use is
only dictated by the conscience of the wielder." Henrik
Shipstead agreed that approval of Roosevelt's plan would
establish a dangerous precedent. "What you can do today
for a good purpose," the Minnesota Insurgent reminded his
constituents, "some one else can do for a bad purpose
tomorrow." George Norris asked himself how he would have
reacted had "Harding. . .offered this bill."[54]

The major reason for Insurgent opposition to the Court
plan was that it granted the President even greater power
than he already wielded. "Roosevelt has won practically
all of his objectives," complained Hiram Johnson. "In the
Supreme Court fight, there is left only the shell of principle, but the shell is worth fighting for, so that if there
be a hereafter to this nation, we'll preserve. . .the
Republic." Johnson feared, however, that the plan would
win speedy approval, for Congress, in his opinion, was worse

---

[54]New York Times, March 11, 1937, p. 8; Henrik Shipstead News Conference, May 11, 1937, Henrik Shipstead Papers,
Box 23, Minnesota Historical Society, St. Paul, Minnesota;
Norris to J.B.S. Hardman, March 5, 1937, Norris Papers, Tray
27, Box 2; Alsop and Catledge, 168 Days, pp. 94-96. Wheeler,
who had been a United States Attorney in Montana during
World War I, declared that he led the fight against the
Court plan "because I recalled how the local state judges,
elected to office, were carried away by the World War I
hysteria in their own communities when rendering justice.
It was the federal courts—particularly the Supreme Court—
which in most instances upheld the right to freedom of
speech guaranteed by the Constitution of the United States."
Wheeler, Yankee From the West, p. 150; interview with Burton
K. Wheeler, Nov. 22, 1968. Melvyn Dubofsky, We Shall Be
All: A History of the Industrial Workers of the World
(Chicago, 1969), p. 403, reveals that Wheeler himself succumbed
to the war-time hysteria.

than subservient. Congress, however, surprised Johnson. By
1937 most Congressmen were convinced that Roosevelt's domi-
nance over the legislative branch of government had gone far
enough. The Senate was especially resentful of this fact,
and many Senators believed that the Court plan presented
the perfect issue, as well as the perfect occasion, for the
Upper House to reestablish itself as a check on the executive branch. "We have retreated from one battle to another
during the last four years," one Senator explained, "but
this is Gettysburg."[55]

The Insurgents were more than willing to assume a
leading role in this Congressional-executive struggle.
Holding the Whig view of the primacy of the legislative
branch of government, they lamented the fact that, during
the "emergency of 1933," the Congress had surrendered many
of its most treasured prerogatives to the President. To
be sure, the Insurgents realized that Roosevelt required
additional authority to combat the depression, but they had
consistently demanded that these grants of power from the
Congress to the executive be carefully circumscribed and
of limited duration. The President, on the other hand,
often insisted upon and received a large amount of discretionary authority; and, although two-year limitations were
written into most bills, the transfer of power was usually
not affected by these time limits. In addition, Roosevelt's
White House staff assumed many of the routine Congressional

---

[55]Johnson to Hiram Johnson, Jr., May 29, 1937, Johnson
Papers, Part IV, Box 4; New York Times, March 14, 1937,
VIII, 16.

duties. The "brains trusts" or "White House lobbyists" drafted bills, prepared material for debates, arranged hearings, and distributed patronage. "The legislative branch of the American government has ceased to function as an independent political institution," lamented William Allen White. "It is a sort of hereditary appurtenance appending to the Executive."[56]

Not only did the Insurgents believe this concentration of power in the hands of the President to be dangerous, but they also resented the fact that it detracted from the prestige of being a member of the United States Senate. In the 1920's the Insurgents had used the forum provided by the Senate to earn personal fame. They had exposed fraud in high government circles and had been among the few Congressmen advocating progressive legislation. "Most of the Senators from Northwest," Wheeler was fond of pointing out, ". . .were fighting the liberal cause long before the Postmaster General was known as a great liberal, or the Attorney General or many others were known as great liberals."[57]

By refusing to consult legislative leaders and friends before divulging his Court plan, Roosevelt had thus aroused a Congress which was already super-sensitive about its loss of power and prestige. "The breach between the President and the Progressives /arises/ . . .from two different philosophies," Arthur Krock reported. "The Johnson-Borah-Norris

---

[56]New York Times, April 25, 1937, VIII, 23.

[57]Ibid., July 8, 1937, p. 2.

position is against extensions of Presidential power and for
Congressional extensions." Midway through the Court strug-
gle, it became obvious, moreover, that the "reactionary"
Supreme Court was no longer the primary issue. With
VanDevanter's retirement and the Court's validation of the
Wagner and Social Security Acts the struggle became a "fight
to the finish" between Roosevelt and the Senate. This was
made clear by Wheeler, who refused to compromise even after
it became obvious that the President's Court plan was dead.
"Nothing doing," the Montana Insurgent replied to a White
House plea that he support the Hatch compromise bill. "We
must teach that man in the White House a lesson. We must
show him that the United States Senate has to be consulted
and is going to have something to say about how this Government is run."[58]

To his chagrin, Roosevelt would be reminded repeatedly
during the remainder of his second term that the Senate
played a role in the governing process—largely the negative
role of obstructing the New Deal. Not since the administration of Woodrow Wilson had a President been so humiliated
by the Senate, and in both instances the Insurgents formed
the vanguard of the opposition. To Hiram Johnson this was
an immense source of personal satisfaction. "Nothing has
so greatly interested me since the League of Nations fight,"

---

[58]Ibid., Feb. 10, 1937, p. 22; Ickes, Secret Diary,
II, 172.

Johnson exclaimed of the Court battle, "and to nothing have I devoted myself so since that historic contest."[59]

The rabid Insurgent opposition to the Court proposal shocked Harold Ickes. "For the Progressives, in such numbers as they seem to be, to oppose this reform," the Secretary of the Interior recorded in his diary, ". . .passes my understanding." The Insurgents, however, believed that the devious plan was so dangerous in its implications that it had to be rejected in toto. In an era that had witnessed the rise of Hitler and Mussolini, many Insurgents believed that the Court plan represented Roosevelt's initial move for dictatorial power. "The President," wrote an incredulous William Lemke, "is still determined to unite the Legislative, Executive and Judicial branches of our government all in one—in Franklin D. Roosevelt." Nye concurred with Lemke's assessment and warned that the Court plan could lead to a purely personal government—"a trait upon which Europe's dicatators have built their power."[60]

Although the Insurgents had originally believed that Roosevelt's charismatic personality and New Deal legislation might hasten recovery, they remained uneasy over the President's failure or inability to formulate a specific plan for reform. As the New Deal unfolded, they watched with increasing concern the centralization of authority in

---

[59] Johnson to John Francis Neylan, July 24, 1937, Johnson Papers, Part III, Box 17.

[60] Ickes, Secret Diary, II, 71; Lemke Newsletter, March 17, 1937, Lemke Papers, Box 28; New York Times, Feb. 22, 1937, p. 4.

Washington and the augmentation of the power of the presidency. "He is feeling on top of the world," Hiram Johnson
wrote of Roosevelt in 1934. "His restless personality might
lead to a sinister grasp for power." The announcement of the
Court plan, following so closely after the President's unprecedented electoral victory in November, 1936, convinced
most Insurgents that Roosevelt was determined to use his
exalted position to secure personal power and political
aggrandizement. "I fear for the existence of the Republic,"
exclaimed Johnson. "With this reaching into the Supreme
Court by his thinly disguised message, he will make himself
an absolute dictator in fact."[61]

Because of Roosevelt's attempt to pack the Supreme
Court, the Insurgents were sincerely convinced that, in the
words of Gerald P. Nye, "to preserve our form of government it was and is essential to limit strictly the power
of the Executive." Never again would the Insurgents, ex-
cepting LaFollette and Norris, trust the President. In the
future, they would summarily reject most administration
proposals which even remotely increased the powers of the
presidency. Hiram Johnson even suspected that Roosevelt
would resurrect the Court scheme. "I rather think," the
California Senator wrote to Republican Minority Leader
McNary, "we are going to have the fight all over again
unless in the next couple of months our master cools off

---

[61]Johnson to Hiram Johnson, Jr., Feb. 14, 1934; Feb. 6,
1937, Johnson Papers, Part IV, Box 4.

perceptibly and forgets his dreams of grandeur."[62]

Roosevelt was bewildered by the fanatic Insurgent opposition to the Court proposal. "He can understand the
Tories being against it, but he can't understand you being
against it," Tommy Corcoran informed Wheeler. In his dis-
gust with these so-called liberals, the President decided
to adopt the advice once given to him by Woodrow Wilson—to
rely upon "machine politicians" rather than "Progressives"
for support of reform legislation. "If you can get them
committed to your program," Roosevelt recalled Wilson as
having said, "I'd rather have the regulars, who were not
at heart with us at first, to fight for a cause than our
progressives who are so enamored with their own particular
plan that they break out of the traces when victory for the
cause cannot be won by their methods."[63]

The Court fight left a wall of suspicion and hostility
between Roosevelt and the Insurgents, and it revealed for
all to see that Insurgent fear of concentrated power, in
whatever form, was the basic difference between Insurgent
progressivism and New Deal liberalism. The nearly unanimous
support of the Insurgents for the "radical" legislation of
the Second New Deal, especially the antimonopolistic measures of 1935, had made them appear as dependable allies of
the New Deal, but the legislation of the "second hundred

---

[62] New York Times, Feb. 22, 1937, p. 1; Johnson to
Charles L. McNary, Sept. 10, 1937, Johnson Papers, Part III,
Box 17.

[63] Wheeler, Yankee From the West, p. 322; Josephus
Daniels to Franklin D. Roosevelt, March 8, 1937, Roosevelt
Papers, PPF 86.

days" encompassed the full extent of their progressivism. Like their more conservative colleagues, most of the Insurgents detested the increasing centralization, regimentation, and bureaucracy engendered by the New Deal, and during Roosevelt's second term the voting records of the Insurgents, other than LaFollette and Norris, resembled those of the anti-New Deal conservatives in Congress. The Insurgents claimed, however, that they never became Tories, and the protestations throughout the 1930's that they were remaining true to their progressive creed must be taken seriously. Their progressive creed simply did not permit them to embrace the powerful welfare state fostered by the New Deal to combat the depression.

CHAPTER VI

INSURGENT PROGRESSIVISM AND THE WELFARE STATE, 1937

The Court fight damaged Roosevelt's prestige, but, of
greater importance, it lessened his ability to secure the
enactment of additional New Deal reforms. In later years
the President claimed that he had lost the battle but had
won the war in the Court fight, and, in a sense, he was
correct. For despite the defeat of his Court bill, Roosevelt
finally did succeed in fashioning a Supreme Court that would
approve New Deal legislation. By contrast, however, the
75th Congress, which had convened in January, 1937, with
the largest Democratic majority in the nation's history,
adjourned in August with very few new reform measures having
been placed on the statute books. Arthur Krock accurately
reported that "those who wanted the President opposed should
be very happy with this session," and he noted that the
Senate had finally reestablished itself as a legislative
power.[1] Not only was the Court fight largely responsible
for the strained state of Congressional-executive relations,
but it also weakened the unity of the Democratic party,
transformed the strategy of the Republican party, alienated
liberal Congressmen, and greatly strengthened an anti-New

---

[1]New York Times, August 2, 1937, p. 1.

Deal coalition of conservative Congressmen. In the end,
the President might well have preferred an unfriendly Supreme Court to a hostile and non-cooperative Congress.

Although the Court fight seemed to monopolize the
country's attention in the early months of 1937, it was not
the only issue before the 75th Congress. In February,
Roosevelt urged legislative approval for a series of reform
proposals designed to aid the "one-third of a Nation ill-
nourished, ill-clad, and ill-housed." Specifically, he
recommended a wages-and-hours bill, more relief funds, and
a federal housing program. "There is undoubtedly work to
be done here, and serious work," said Hiram Johnson in response to the President's plea.[2] By 1937, however, the
Insurgents had become so concerned about the New Deal's
welfare-state liberalism that they were to prove reluctant
to grant Roosevelt's request for additional relief expenditures and new labor-and urban-oriented legislation.

Even before the President announced his plan to pack
the Supreme Court, the country had been beset by a number
of violent labor disputes. In their bid for national power
American labor unions, particularly those affiliated with
John L. Lewis' fledgling Committee for Industrial Organization (CIO), struck some of the country's most powerful corporations. In themselves these work stoppages were not so
surprising, but what was totally unexpected was the type of
strike conducted by the industrial unionists. For example,

---

[2]Johnson to Hiram Johnson, Jr., Feb. 6, 1937, Hiram W.
Johnson Papers, Part IV, Box 4, Bancroft Library, University
of California, Berkeley.

in late December, 1936, instead of merely withholding their services, auto workers at General Motors' Fisher Body No. 1 and No. 2 plants in Flint, Michigan, occupied their factories. After sitting down on the job for nearly a month and a half, the workers forced the GM management to recognize their union. Emboldened by the success of this sit-down strike, militant unionists elsewhere adopted the tactics of the Flint strikers.

Predictably, most middle-class Americans deplored labor's use of the sit-down strike, and the property-minded citizenry held Roosevelt at least partially responsible for what had occurred. To a constituent's plea that the federal government intervene before "the CIO militants succeed in sovietizing America," Kansas Representative Clifford Hope replied, "The present administration is so well tied up with John L. Lewis that we cannot expect much help from that quarter." Vice-President Garner regarded the "sit-downs as mass lawlessness" and urged the President to use troops to evict the strikers from the factories. Realizing that, in most instances, the workers harbored legitimate grievances against their employers and hoping that the antagonists would settle their disputes without outside intervention, Roosevelt steadfastly refused to take sides. In June, however, the President broke his public silence on the sit-down issue and during the Little-Steel strike,

he criticized both labor and management with his famous "a
plague o' both your houses" statement.[3]

Although Roosevelt was sympathetic to the aspirations
of underprivileged union members, he never considered himself a champion of organized labor. In fact, only at the
last moment had he endorsed the 1935 Wagner bill, which
effectively guaranteed labor the right of collective bargaining free from employer interference. But if the President himself had not been especially partial to organized
labor, the New Deal reform programs had encouraged the formation of strong unions. In 1933 John L. Lewis had shrewdly
capitalized on New Deal sympathy toward labor by recruiting
new members for his United Mine Workers with the cry, "The
President wants you to join the union." By 1936 organized
labor and particularly the CIO had come to recognize the
New Deal as its staunch ally and consequently had established Labor's Non-Partisan League to channel electoral
and financial support to Roosevelt. All this led Hiram

---

[3]Hope to Mrs. J. H. Shidler, July 7, 1937, Clifford R.
Hope Papers, Legislative Correspondence, 1936-37, I-Money,
Kansas State Historical Society, Topeka, Kansas; James A.
Farley, *Jim Farley's Story*, (New York, 1948), p. 85; William
E. Leuchtenberg, *Franklin D. Roosevelt and the New Deal,
1932-1940* (New York, 1963), p. 243. In a letter to Garner,
Roosevelt explained the reason for his long public silence
on the sit-down strikes. "The point is," he wrote, "that
if the Administration had made pronouncements last winter
and during the last month, the great mass of the people
would not have had certain examples before their eyes which
have taught them to take a very sound view of the situation.
For instance, they have been just as horrified about the
action of the Chicago police against the strikers as they
have been by the proposed march by coal miners on Johnstown."
Roosevelt to Garner, July 7, 1937, Roosevelt Papers, PSF
62, Franklin D. Roosevelt Library, Hyde Park, New York.

Johnson to conclude that the President was Lewis' accomplice
in the sit-down strikes. "John L. Lewis, who contributed
to the President's campaign to the amount of $600,000, de-
mands his quid pro quo, and that is the reason Roosevelt
has remained silent during all the trouble respecting sit-
down strikes."[4] The CIO, of course, approved of the President's silence, but there was no White House complicity in
the sit-down strikes. The CIO had employed the tactic because it was effective not because the organization had
been guaranteed immunity from punishment by Roosevelt.

On March 17, 1937, the issue of the sit-down strikes
was finally raised on the floor of the United States Senate.
Hiram Johnson, who had become almost paranoid on the matter
of dictatorship in America, rose and delivered the shortest
speech of his Senatorial career. The California Insurgent,
declaring that the sit-down strike had the White House's
blessing, warned that "dictatorship lurks down the road."
Johnson's statement ignited a fierce Senate debate. Knowing
that most of his colleagues detested the sit-down strikes,
Arthur Vandenberg confidently broke the Republican "conspiracy of silence" then in effect to insure the defeat of
the Court bill. "Silence gives consent," the Michigan
Senator said in reference to Roosevelt, "and that is the
trouble; there has been nothing but silence—or worse." To
everyone's amazement, none of the Senate's Democratic
leaders rose to challenge Vandenberg's remarks. In fact,

[4]Johnson to Hiram Johnson, Jr., March 26, 1937, Johnson Papers, Part IV, Box 4.

Majority Leader Robinson nodded his head in agreement, and
after Vandenberg's speech, Vice-President Garner congratulated
the Michigan Senator. "It was about time somebody said that,"
Garner declared.[5]

Encouraged by this show of Senatorial solidarity, South
Carolina's James F. Byrnes decided that the Senate should
not follow the White House precedent of maintaining silence
on the sit-down strikes. On April 1, 1937, Byrnes attached
an amendment to the Guffey coal bill that condemned the sit-
down strikes. By this method, the South Carolina Senator
hoped to force Roosevelt to take a stand on the legality
of the sit-down strikes. Byrnes chose the Guffey bill as
the measure to which to attach his amendment because the
coal industry was in dire need of governmental aid, and he
therefore reasoned that the President would have to sign
the bill even with the anti-sit-down strike rider attached
to it.

Byrnes' maneuver naturally caused concern at the White
House, and so Roosevelt requested Robinson to extricate him
from the potentially embarrassing situation of having to
condemn the sit-down strikers in order to obtain a coal
bill. Although he was in complete sympathy with the Byrnes'
proposal, the Majority Leader loyally came to the President's rescue by introducing a substitute resolution that
declared sit-down strikes, industrial spy systems, company
unions, and unfair collective bargaining "contrary to public

[5]Congressional Record, 75th Cong., 1st Sess., pp.
2337-3023; James T. Patterson, Congressional Conservatism
and the New Deal (Lexington, Ky., 1967), p. 137.

policy." After the Senate defeated the Byrnes amendment
by the relatively close vote of 48 to 36, Robinson's all-
inclusive proposal passed overwhelmingly, 75 to 3. "The
/Robinson/ resolution was so diluted," complained Hiram
Johnson, "that it was of no real value, and can be taken as
approval by the Senate of the strikers."[6]

During the Senate debate on the sit-down strikes,
LaFollette was the only Insurgent to give an unqualified
endorsement of the strikers' activities. "The sit-down
strike," said the Wisconsin Senator, "was the answer of
working men. . .to the sit-down of the Liberty Leaguers and
the National Manufacturers' Association, and the 'sit-down
strike' of a majority of the members of the Supreme Court. . .
against the whole New Deal program of social legislation."[7]
Conversely, only Hiram Johnson among the Insurgents voted
for the Byrnes amendment. The other Insurgents deplored
the CIO's use of the sit-down tactic, but they did not wish
to condemn the workers lest it appear that they were em-
bracing their traditional enemies, the captains of industry.

Although they represented districts that were primarily rural, the Insurgents, rhetorically at least, had
generally championed the rights of urban laborers against
the monopolistic corporations. It was not easy for them
to abandon this sympathy for the underprivileged by voting

---

[6] Congressional Record, 75th Cong., 1st Sess., pp. 3136,
3248; Johnson to Albert Lasker, June 26, 1937, Johnson Papers,
Part III, Box 17.

[7] New York Times, March 25, 1937, p. 21.

for an anti-sit-down strike resolution that was critical
only of organized labor. Even the outspoken Hiram Johnson
did not enjoy being placed in that position. "As a friend
of union labor I am opposed to the sit-down strike," he was
careful to explain. "I do not want in anyway to lend aid
to the shirt-front industrialists if they are unjust in their
dealings." Borah denounced the sit-down strike as a "form
of violence which a government of law and order cannot
recognize," but the Idaho Senator also advised his colleagues that there would be no "lawful action on the part
of /employees/. . .until monopolistic /employers/ are destroyed." Both Frazier and Norris, hoping to avoid taking
a stand on the legality of sit-downs, suggested that Congress should leave the entire matter to the courts. "While
I am not a lawyer," Frazier declared, "I have always been
led to believe that it was the function of the courts instead of the function of the Congress to say what is illegal
or unlawful."[8]

Although the Insurgents were reluctant to condemn the
sit-down strikers, they were highly critical of the New
Deal's labor policies. As they saw it, the violence between
labor and management was the best example of the New Deal's
tendency to incite class against class. Class warfare, the

---

[8]Johnson to Hiram Johnson, Jr., April 9, 1937, Johnson
Papers, Part IV, Box 4; Congressional Record, 75th Cong.,
1st Sess., pp. 1937, 3247. "I have never agreed with it and
often said the 'sit-down' could not be defended," George
Norris wrote in 1939. "It has been put out of existence,
I think, by the Supreme Court itself." Norris to Garlis
Finley, Nov. 28, 1939, George W. Norris Papers, Tray 33,
Box 4, Library of Congress, Washington, D. C.

Insurgents maintained, was the inevitable result of Roosevelt's broker-state politics. Instead of attempting to
harmonize competing economic interests, New Deal legislation encouraged social division by conferring favors upon
special-interest groups. "We are largely a nation of groups,
with little thought of the general welfare," complained the
former Wisconsin Insurgent, Irving Lenroot, in 1935. "Organized capital, organized labor, organized farmers, organized wets and organized drys. . .each seeking its selfish ends without regard to the welfare of others."[9]

Of all the organized minorities, labor undoubtedly
benefited most from the interest-group orientation of the
New Deal. "In fact, I think Labor has been given so much
by this Administration that is has grown arrogant and
cruel," Hiram Johnson wrote in 1937. "There was a happy
medium. . .but now every board is pro-labor, and Labor is
left to its own devices." Gerald P. Nye agreed with his
fellow Insurgent, and he singled out the National Labor
Relations Board for special vituperation. "The NLRB is a
kangaroo court," the North Dakota Senator proclaimed. "It
has such a pronounced C.I.O. bias that the average man
regards it as an adjunct. . . . The government should not
be dedicated to the penalization of any group or class; on
the contrary it should strive for a harmonious meeting of
minds which will enable us to go forward." Johnson went so
far as to predict that the New Deal's labor policies would

---

[9]Quoted in Otis L. Graham, Jr., *An Encore for Reform:
The Old Progressives and the New Deal* (New York, 1967),
pp. 69-70.

result in the emergence of "a dictator of the proletariat,
or a dictator otherwise. Lewis thinks he is going to be
it, and Roosevelt thinks he is going to command."[10]

The anti-sit-down strike amendment was not the only
controversial labor measure considered by the Senate in
1937. When the Supreme Court reversed itself and approved
the Washington minimum-wage law in March, Roosevelt immediately took advantage of this judicial change of mind
and proposed a fair labor standards bill. "We have promised
it," the President told Congress. "We cannot stand still."[11]
The bill sought to impose minimum-wage scales, set maximum-
hour schedules, and prevent the use of child labor in industries involved in interstate commerce. The measure also
called for the establishment of a five-man board, to be
appointed by Roosevelt, that would set the minimum standards allowed by the bill.

In June hearings on the bill began under the leadership
of Massachusetts' William P. Connery, Jr., in the House and
Alabama's Hugo Black in the Senate. Roosevelt hoped that
the Black-Connery bill, as the wages-and-hours proposal
subsequently came to be known, would prove to be so popular
that it would enable him to regain the initiative which
Congress had taken from him during the Court fight. The
measure, however, encountered the swift and determined

[10]Congressional Record, 75th Cong., 1st Sess., pp. 7734-
39; Johnson to Hiram Johnson, Jr., June 5, 1937, April 9,
1937, Johnson Papers, Part IV, Box 4.

[11]Samuel I. Rosenman (ed.), The Public Papers and Addresses of Franklin D. Roosevelt, VI (New York, 1941) 209-14.

opposition of Southern Democrats. South Carolina Senator
Cotton Ed Smith characterized the bill as just another of
the many Northern attempts to penalize the South for its
"kindly living conditions." Instead of regulating wages
and hours, Smith facetiously suggested that the New Deal
Democrats should go to the root of the problem and "call
in God and tell him that He must stop this thing of making
one section more advantageous than another." In the House,
Georgia Representative Edward "Goober" Cox left no doubt
that the South's fear of losing its low wage scale was the
real reason for its resistance to the measure. "I warn
John L. Lewis and his Communistic cohorts," Cox shouted,
"that no second 'carpet bag expedition' under the banner
of Soviet Russia will be tolerated."[12]

Southern sectionalism was not the only basis for opposition to the bill. Many Congressmen from rural districts
outside the South, including most of the Insurgents, opposed
the wages-and-hours measure because they believed it benefited only the urban centers of the nation. "If the bill
passes," Clifford Hope wrote, "it is going to be a pretty
bitter pill for the Democrats from the South and the agricultural sections of the Middle West to swallow." The
coalition of Congressmen opposing the fair-labor standards
proposal revealed the growing alienation of rural and small
town America from the increasingly urban-oriented New Deal.
Denied the cost of production for his products, the American

---

[12]*Congressional Record*, 75th Cong., 1st Sess., p. 7882;
Time, XXX (August 23, 1937), 12.

farmer resented legislation that would fix the wages of the urban laborer. In addition to giving preferential treatment to the working man, many farmers believed that the Black-Connery proposal would be detrimental to agricultural interests. "I think you recognize," a group of constituents reminded Norris, "that anything which increases the cost of manufactured goods results in a decrease of the purchasing power of Nebraska farmers." It is not so surprising under the circumstances that five of the Insurgents voted to recommit the bill to the Senate Committee on Education and Labor. After this motion was defeated by a vote of 48 to 36, Borah led a group of farm-state Senators who were successful in their attempt to exempt from the bill's provisions various agricultural workers and farm-related industries.[13]

Once agricultural workers had safely been exempted from the bill, most Insurgents were willing to admit that it was necessary for Congress to pass a provision for minimum wages and maximum hours. They still objected, however, to the New Deal's version of the labor standards bill because it sought to establish yet another bureaucratic agency to control the life of the individual citizen. "I feel that every man or woman who is worthy of hire is entitled to sufficient compensation to maintain a decent standard of living," Borah declared. "But to me this

---

[13]Hope to A. Lewis Oswald, August 9, 1937, Hope Papers, General Correspondence, 1937-37, Misc.-P; H. C. Filley to Norris, May 28, 1937, Norris Papers, Tray 18, Box 5; Congressional Record, 75th Cong., 1st Sess., p. 7954.

problem is one of method," he continued. ". . .I hesitate
to grant to any five men. . .the power /to/ practically control and determine the industrial interests of the different
communities of the United States." The Idaho Senator denounced the proposed Fair Labor Standards Board as "a little
NRA" and suggested that Congress should write a uniform
minimum wage into the law. "I feel, as a legislator,"
Borah concluded, "that I owe a duty to the minimum wage
employees in this country, and that I ought not to shift
that responsibility over to a board over whom I have no
control." Hiram Johnson also favored some sort of wages-
and-hours bill, but he too balked at the New Deal's proposed
method of enforcement. "I would be very glad to make a
minimum wage and prescribe hours," the California Insurgent
explained, "but to leave it to a board in Washington would
be one more way of turning over the economic life of the
country to the President for him to exercise at his own
sweet will. I decline to do this."[14]

The Insurgents, and particularly Wheeler, believed
that the Black-Connery bill was not stringent enough in
restricting the use of child labor since it permitted the
Chief of the Children's Bureau to make exceptions regarding
the use of child labor if employment did not interfere with

---

[14]Congressional Record, 75th Cong., 1st Sess., pp.
7793-94; Johnson to Hiram Johnson, Jr., August 1, 1937,
Johnson Papers, Part IV, Box 4. Wheeler claimed that the
Black-Connery bill, like most other New Deal legislation,
required Congress to delegate too much of its authority to
the executive branch of government: "The broad and extended
delegation of power to a new bureau under the Black bill. . .
is based on the theory of arbitrary rule by men, and most
completely circumvents the democratic rule by law." Congressional Record, 75th Cong., 1st Sess., p. 7665.

the child's education and health. "The provision now in the
bill," Wheeler maintained, "would permit the representatives
of the Children's Bureau to go into every home in America. .
and make an order with reference to a particular child and
say that it may work, but that another child in the same
household may not work." The Montana Senator, who was
firmly convinced that the Senate should never again give
unlimited powers to any New Deal administrative agency,
urged his colleagues to register their intent that child
labor be abolished altogether. To effect this, Wheeler
recommended that the Senate accept his substitute amendment forbidding employment of all children under sixteen
years of age and making it unlawful to ship in interstate
commerce any product manufactured by child labor. In the
end, all Insurgents except LaFollette and Norris heeded
Wheeler's advice.[15]

The ambivalent attitude of the Insurgents during the
controversies over the sit-down strikes and wages-and-hours
legislation was also evidenced during the debate regarding
appropriations for relief. Although they consistently
criticized the New Deal's "over-spending and debt-building"
relief policies, the Insurgents found it difficult to recon-
cile their abhorrence of an unbalanced budget with their
sympathy for the underprivileged. Borah thus declared that

---

[15]Interview with Burton K. Wheeler, Nov. 22, 1968;
Congressional Record, 75th Cong., 1st Sess., pp. 7932, 7947.
For a detailed account of the enactment of the wages-and-
hours bill, see George Edward Paulson, "The Legislative His-
tory of the Fair Labor Standards Act" (Ph.D. Thesis, Ohio
State University, 1959).

he favored reductions in governmental spending but not at
the expense of "distressed men and women seeking food."[16]
In 1937 the Insurgents' concern for the needy prevailed
over their penchant for economy.

Roosevelt also found himself in a quandary on the
relief issue, for he too favored a balanced budget. In
July, 1937, the President informed Garner that "if Congress
does not run wild, the budget for the coming year looks
like. . .a balanced budget." This news was in line with
Roosevelt's address to Congress on April 20, 1937, in which
he had promised a determined effort "to bring about a
balance of actual income and outgo." Although the President
recommended many economies, he also called for an increased
appropriation of $1.5 billion to fund the Works Progress
Administration (WPA)—the agency that had been established
to administer the Emergency Relief Appropriation Act of
1935. Roosevelt stated that he could not advocate a reduction in relief expenditures at a time when many Americans
had no buying power.[17]

Roosevelt's request for additional WPA funds touched
off a bitter debate in the Senate, and for the first time
Roosevelt was opposed by the Senate Democratic leadership
on a major New Deal measure. Byrnes thought that the
government should make budgetary reductions across the board

---

[16]New York Times, June 22, 1937, IV, p. 1; ibid.,
April 26, 1937, p. 3.

[17]Roosevelt to Garner, July 7, 1937, Roosevelt Papers,
PSF 62; Rosenman (ed.), Public Papers of FDR, VI, 163-68.

and particularly in the appropriations for the WPA. Because
Negroes received much of the relief money, Byrnes accused
the WPA of upsetting Southern race relations. Since he was
convinced that the economic emergency had passed, the South
Carolina Senator also argued that huge federal expenditures
for relief were no longer necessary. Byrnes, therefore,
moved to reduce the $1.5 billion requested by the President
to $1 billion. Failing to obtain sufficient support for
this reduction, he proposed an amendment requiring communities to pay for 40 per cent of the total cost of local
WPA projects. Byrnes contended that his amendment would
save millions of dollars by forcing local governments to
expel "career workers" from the relief rolls. The White
House was appalled by the 40 per cent proposal. "If it
is made a hard and fast rule," the President predicted to
newsmen, "there are going to be a great many cases where
hardship will result." To Roosevelt's disappointment, however, the Senate Committee on Appropriations attached the
Byrnes amendment to the administration's bill.[18]

Since Roosevelt believed it imperative that he be
allowed broad discretion in distributing relief funds, he
called upon the loyal Joseph T. Robinson to block passage
of the Byrnes amendment. The Majority Leader, however, was
not so willing to side with the President on the spending
issue as he had been on the fight over the sit-down resolution. "It seems to me that the time has about come—indeed,

[18]Rosenman (ed.), Public Papers of FDR, VI, 264.

it has already arrived," Robinson had said in April, "when
we should give careful consideration. . .to close the gap
between receipts and expenditures." Robinson, however,
agreed to sponsor a compromise amendment even though he
favored the Byrnes proposal and was angered by Roosevelt's
delay in appointing him (Robinson) to the vacancy on the
Supreme Court created by the retirement of Justice Van-
Devanter. The Robinson amendment reduced to 25 per cent
the contribution required from local communities, but it
gave the President the authority to waive this requirement
for bankrupt communities. Though the Robinson amendment
gave Roosevelt greater control over relief funds, the
Majority Leader claimed that he expected the 25 per cent
obligation to result in sizable savings for the Federal
Government. "Gentlemen may laugh about a 36-billion-dollar
debt hanging over the head of the Treasury if they wish to,
but I find it impossible to laugh about such a thing,"
Robinson declared in defense of his amendment. "We spend
and we spend and we spend. . . . We can't go on forever
doing it."[19]

It appeared in early June as though the Senate would
approve Robinson's 25 per cent amendment. "The plea for
economy coming from all over the country has taken posses-
sion of Congress," wrote a despondent George Norris. "In
my judgment, there will be a very stiff fight in the

[19]Time, XXIX (April 26, 1937), 11; Congressional
Record, 75th Cong., 1st Sess., p. 5956; "Robinson on Relief,"
Nation, CXLIV (June 26, 1937), 720; Nevin E. Neal, "A Bio-
graphy of Joseph T. Robinson" (Ph.D. Thesis, University of
Oklahoma, 1958), p. 412.

Senate. . . . The question of balancing the budget seems
uppermost in the minds of nearly everyone." Since the amendment allowed the President flexibility in cancelling the 25
per cent requirement for hard-pressed communities, Borah
believed that it was an ideal solution to a complex problem.
The Idaho Senator maintained that Congress must place some
restrictions on federal spending. "If the brakes are not
put on in Congress," he exclaimed, "there is no place where
they can be put on." Capper concurred and declared that
only "Congress can see to it that. . .governmental expenditures are kept within reasonable bounds." These remarks
prompted Alben Barkley, upon whom the administration, because
of Robinson's defection, was forced to rely for leadership
in the struggle, to respond that he never had expected to
see The Merchant of Venice re-enacted on the Senate floor
"with Uncle Sam playing the role of Shylock." Norris reminded his colleagues that although their desire for
economy was commendable, an unbalanced budget was preferable to permitting a large portion of the people to starve.
Carter Glass retorted that there had already been too many
"economic crimes" perpetrated by Congress in the name of
starving people "who never starved and freezing people who
never froze."[20] In the end, Barkley and Norris claimed
victory as the Senate defeated Robinson's amendment, 49 to

---

[20]Norris to Darwin J. Messerole, June 5, 1937, Norris
Papers, Tray 33, Box 6; Congressional Record, 75th Cong.,
1st Sess., pp. 5967-6031.

232

34. Borah and Capper were the only Insurgents to vote for
the amendment.[21]

Ostensibly, the large federal deficit was the major
cause for Insurgent dissatisfaction with New Deal relief
expenditures. There was, however, a more basic reason for
their uneasiness: the Insurgents believed that the New Deal
relief program was a threat to the continued existence of
American democracy because they thought it made a mockery
of the system of checks and balances and dislocated the
relationship between Washington and the state governments.
Hiram Johnson complained that in implementing its relief
policies the administration cavalierly circumvented the
Congress. "There is a great deal of impatience and irrita-
tion among thoughtful men in the Senate,. . .one of whom I
confess myself to be," the California Insurgent wrote, "in
yielding the purse of the nation, without disclosure or
knowledge of the uses to which the money shall be put."
Even more disconcerting than what Johnson thought was the
surrender of a sacred legislative prerogative was his belief
that the President used relief funds to increase his political and personal power. The California Senator thus accused Roosevelt of buying the 1936 election. "Any man,"
Johnson explained, "who could not be elected who. . .takes
out his checkbook and says, 'I will allot a few million
dollars to this particular place and a few million dollars

---

[21]Congressional Record, 75th Cong., 1st Sess., p. 6032.
A last-minute attempt by Byrnes to substitute his 40 per
cent plan also failed, by a vote of 58 to 25; Ibid., p.
6023.

to some other place,' and who carried with him Mr. Hopkins
to dole out relief in unstinted quantities, should retire
from politics."[22]

The Insurgents also believed that the New Deal's relief program was undermining the power of the state and local
governments. "We have made tramps and beggars of a once
proud union of states, counties, and municipalities,"
William Lemke declared. "All of these have their hands
out expecting something for nothing." To remedy the existing state of affairs, Nye proposed that the administration
should return certain types of relief to local governments.
LaFollette thought that implementation of Nye's suggestion
would mean disaster for the unemployed, but Borah believed
that such a policy was imperative. "If we are going to
maintain this great Government of ours," the Idaho Senator
warned, "we have got to have something in the nature of
local self-government."[23]

In addition to their belief that the "relief machine"
was contributing to the destruction of the traditional form
of government in the United States, the Insurgents resented
the fact that a large proportion of WPA funds was expended
in metropolitan centers. The Insurgents were especially
mindful of this fact in 1937 because early in the session
the President had threatened to veto a low-interest farm

---

[22]Johnson to Hiram Johnson, Jr., Feb. 10, 1935, Sept.
22, 1936, Johnson Papers, Part IV, Box 4.

[23]Progressive, Sept. 14, 1935, p. 3; Nye to Roosevelt,
Jan. 30, 1937, Roosevelt Papers, PPF 1614; Congressional
Record, 75th Cong., 1st Sess., p. 2494.

mortgage proposal on the grounds that it was inflationary.
Also, Secretary of Agriculture Henry Wallace had refused to
support a crop-loan measure favored by the Insurgents until
the Senate Agricultural Committee granted its approval to
an administration-sponsored production-control bill. "We
deny relief to drought-stricken farmers," Wheeler complained,
"but we give relief to the great city of New York." Despite their anger at Roosevelt and their aversion to cities,
however, the Insurgents did not vote to deny WPA relief
funds to the urban poor.[24]

After the WPA controversy had been resolved, the Senate turned its attention to a public-housing measure sponsored by New York's Robert Wagner. The bill stemmed from
the demands of urban pressure groups and received only mild
support from Roosevelt. "As little as I can gather from the
President's attitude," observed Harold L. Ickes, "he isn't
particularly interested in the Wagner bill. He indicated
that he would let it take its chances on the Hill."[25]
Roosevelt's indifference, however, did not restrain Wagner;
the New York Senator persisted in his efforts and finally
persuaded his colleagues to consider the bill, which called
for a $700-million government loan to municipalities for
slum clearance and low-cost housing.

The Wagner proposal encountered the determined opposition of Senators representing rural states. "I. . .predict

---

[24]Congressional Record, 75th Cong., 1st Sess., p. 773.

[25]Harold L. Ickes, The Secret Diary of Harold L. Ickes,
II (New York, 1954), 85.

that. . .at least half the money will find its way into New
York City or the immediately surrounding area and that that
municipality will not put up a red penny," Maryland Senator Millard Tydings proclaimed. Carter Glass demanded to
know "upon what theory of government it ever became the
business of the National Government. . .to tax all the
American people to clear up slums in certain specified parts
of the country." Many Senators were also unhappy because the
Wagner bill represented yet another departure from the administration's announced intention to balance the budget.
Finally, the Senate hesitated to establish another independent administrative agency, the United States Housing Authority (USHA), since this would give still greater power
to the executive branch.[26]

In an effort to cripple Wagner's housing proposal,
Senator Harry Byrd of Virginia attached an amendment limiting the construction costs under the bill to $4,000 per
unit or $1,000 per room. Wagner painstakingly pointed out
that such restrictions would render the bill practically
useless in the nation's urban areas. Unimpressed by Wagner's remarks, Borah announced that he favored Bryd's plan
because it would "provide sufficient safeguards. . .with
respect to expenditures." Frazier, similarly revealing a
singular ignorance of urban problems, described the Byrd
restrictions as reasonable. "I cannot understand, for the
life of me," the North Dakota Senator stated, "why it should

---

[26]Congressional Record, 75th Cong., 1st Sess., pp.
8194, 8266.

cost any more for materials and for the work to build an
ordinary liveable home in New York City than it does in the
smaller cities of the United States, or why it should even
cost as much, for in a large city. . .there is more competition among the firms which furnish the materials and among
contractors than in smaller cities." Not surprisingly all
the Insurgents except LaFollette and Norris voted in favor
of the Byrd amendment, and the entire Senate accepted it by
the slender margin of 40 to 39.[27]

Another amendment to Wagner's bill, sponsored by
Senator Tydings, limited the amount spent in any one state
to 20 per cent of the total appropriation. Since the Tydings
amendment was approved by a voice vote, it is impossible to
determine Insurgent sentiment on this question, although
they probably favored the amendment. Lining up against
Wagner, the Insurgents supported Senator Marvel Logan's
proposal to place the USHA in the Interior Department rather
than to grant it the status of an independent agency.
Frazier indicated that the Logan amendment would help to
eliminate "political graft" from relief work, and Borah
declared that the Senate either must halt the proliferation
of the federal bureaucracy or face a revolution. "I might
not live to see it," the Idaho Senator warned, "but I am
satisfied the day will come when the people will rise and
tear up a number of these bureaus by the roots." Only La-
Follette among the Insurgents voted against the Logan amendment. Thus, with regard to the Wagner measure, the

[27]Ibid., pp. 8363-64, 8196.

Insurgents sided with Senate conservatives to nullify an important piece of New Deal legislation. Since the housing bill did not directly feed a hungry citizenry, the Insurgents felt themselves free to vote their anti-urban, anti-spending, and anti-bureaucratic prejudices.[28]

Congress adjourned soon after it had passed a diluted version of the Wagner housing bill. After comparing the performance of the 75th Congress with that of previous New Deal Congresses, Arthur Krock dubbed the 1937 Senate "remarkable" because it had done "so very little legislating." The Senate, however, had passed some significant measures. In addition to the relief bill and the labor and housing bills, the Senate had approved a farm-tenancy measure and a neutrality law. The Bankhead-Jones Farm Tenancy Act created the Farm Security Administration, which, among other responsibilities, was to help Southern tenant farmers and submarginal farmers of the Midwest and Great Plains to purchase family-size farms. Wheeler, although conceding that the bill finally would do something for the "poor farmer," nevertheless agreed with William Lemke's charge that the bill scarcely touched the problem of rural poverty. "If a mountain ever labored to produce a mouse, this bill is it." Lemke bitterly exclaimed. "It is a joke and a camouflage."[29]

---

[28]Ibid., pp. 8364, 8357. For a good account of the debate on the housing bill, see Timothy L. McDonnell, The Wagner Housing Act: A Case Study of the Legislative Process (Chicago, 1957).

[29]New York Times, August 22, 1937, IV, 3; interview with Burton K. Wheeler, Nov. 22, 1968; Sidney Baldwin, Poverty and Politics: The Rise and Decline of the Farm Security Administration (Chapel Hill, North Carolina, 1968), p. 189.

The 1937 neutrality bill received an even less cordial
reception from the Insurgents, who claimed that the measure
permitted Roosevelt too much freedom in determining what
materials should be placed on a cash-and-carry basis during
a war crisis. The Insurgents preferred to have the Senate
write "broad mandatory controls" into the bill. "It seems
to me," Nye told the Senate, ". . .that whenever we leave
a discretion in providing a neutrality policy, we at once
issue an invitation to selfish corporations and selfish individuals to hammer away and to exert pressure on the one
holding such discretionary power." Hiram Johnson did not
doubt that the administration would inevitably succumb to
such pressure. "I think the President has adopted now the
views he held before Hearst got from him that amazing re-
cantation he made in 1932," a disturbed Johnson wrote
Raymond Moley, "and, of course, Hull believes that only if
we were part of the League all of our problems would eva-
porate and we could lean upon dear old England."[30]

"If we have done nothing else than make our President
pause for awhile," one Insurgent declared at the end of the
1937 session, "there has been something accomplished."[31]
The voting records of the Insurgents must indeed have caused
Roosevelt to "pause for awhile." On the four key roll calls
of the session, the Byrnes sit-down strike amendment, the

---

[30]Congressional Record, 75th Cong., 1st Sess., p. 1798;
Johnson to Moley, Nov. 1, 1937, Johnson Papers, Part III,
Box 17.

[31]Johnson to Edward J. Devlin, Oct. 22, 1937, Johnson
Papers, Part III, Box 17.

fair-labor-standards bill recommittal, the Robinson relief amendment, and the Byrd housing amendment, the Insurgents cast only 50 per cent of their vote in favor of the administration. Even more significant was their 67 per cent anti-New Deal vote on the two most obvious urban-oriented proposals, the wages-and-hours bill and the housing bill. When contrasted with the 96.8 per cent-favorable vote the Insurgents had given to the major New Deal legislation of 1935 and 1936, their 1937 voting record demonstrates the widening rift between Insurgent progressivism and New Deal liberalism.

The reasons for the growing Insurgent alienation from the New Deal were quite obvious. One factor was the marked urban orientation of much of the legislation of the 1937 session. "The way it looks to me," one Congressman wrote, "is that Roosevelt has put himself in a position where he and his group have become the party of the great cities and the industrial labor groups of the East." To some degree, the Insurgents voted against urban-oriented measures because they lacked knowledge of urban problems, but their opposition to much of the New Deal legislation after 1936 was more fundamentally the result of an anti-urban prejudice. "We must clean up and disinfect our great cities," Arthur Capper thus pleaded in Jeffersonian rhetoric. "They seem accursed."[32]

---

[32]Hope to R. J. Laubengayer, Nov. 13, 1936, Hope Papers, General Correspondence, 1936-37, I-Misc.; quoted in Graham, Encore for Reform, p. 98.

In addition to a general dislike of urban-oriented
legislation, most of the Insurgents were convinced that the
New Deal was increasingly bestowing privileges on urban
dwellers without granting equal favors to the farmers.
Capper, characteristically, wrote that Congress should not
continue "to appropriate billions of dollars for relief of
the unemployed industrial worker who is unemployed partly
because he is seeking a. . .higher standard of living than
that enjoyed by his farmer customer." Wheeler believed that
"city farmers" had even infiltrated the Department of Agriculture to block effective farm legislation. "The mess in
Washington," the Montana Insurgent told a Wisconsin audience,
"was created by young lawyers from Harvard and Columbia Law
Schools who have never practiced law or heard of Wisconsin
or Montana except in a geography book."[33]

The primary reason for the increasing Insurgent estrangement from the New Deal was not, however, its effort
to enact legislation of benefit to the cities but the administration's continuing reliance on welfare—state liberalism. This type of approach to solving the nation's problems, the Insurgents maintained, destroyed individual self-
initiative and independence. "The present administration is
as dumb on this subject as the Hoover administration,"
William Lemke wrote. ". . .fifty-four billion dollars have
been spent, and they have done nothing towards making men

---

[33] Capper to Milton Beutler, May 4, 1938, Arthur Capper
Papers, Agriculture, Co-ops-Farm Labor, Kansas State Historical Society, Topeka, Kansas; New York Times, Oct. 17,
1937, II, 3.

and women self-supporting." Hiram Johnson complained,

"Everyone is a materialist now. Constituents have a dif-

ferent way of regarding their representatives now. They

seem to think that the best man to represent them is the

man who can get the most money for some fool scheme, and

that man who gets little money for a local scheme is of

little consequence."[34]

In addition to stifling individual initiative, the

New Deal welfare programs, as most of the Insurgents saw

it, fostered the growth of a large federal bureaucracy and

concentrated too much authority in the executive branch of

government. The Insurgents believed that these administra-

tive developments were inimical to individual liberty. Ac-

coring to Borah, bureaucracy "straight-jacketed" and "regi-

mented" the nation's economic life and narrowed the in-

dividual's freedom of choice. The growth of a large federal

bureaucracy also added to the already great power in the

hands of the President. Johnson predicted in June, 1937,

that within "the next few years with the sit-down strikes

that /Roosevelt/ has been sympathetic with, with an unbalanced

budget, with the expenditure of funds running wild, with a

neutrality bill giving the President the war-making power,

and with the Supreme Court and Congress subservient to him,

---

[34]Lemke to Harold W. Metz, Nov. 19, 1938, William Lemke
Papers, The Orin G. Libby Manuscript Collection, University
of North Dakota Library, Grand Forks, North Dakota; Johnson
to Colonel Frank G. Snook, June 7, 1937, Johnson Papers,
Part III, Box 17. For an excellent contemporary account of
the reaction of Progressives to the "materialistic" New Deal,
see Edgar Kemler, The Deflation of American Ideals (Seattle:
American Library Edition, 1967).

we'll be very close to a Dictatorship." Wheeler confirmed that Roosevelt's "incessant reaching out for more power" explained much of the Insurgent opposition to the New Deal. "The time has come," the Montana Senator exclaimed, "when the people of this country should say there is a line beyond which no President of the United States should go, no matter how much we think of him."[35]

[35]Congressional Record, 75th Cong., 3rd Sess., p. 4194; Johnson to Hiram Johnson, Jr., Feb. 6, 1937, Johnson Papers, Part IV, Box 4; New York Times, Sept. 10, 1937, p. 15.

CHAPTER VII

INSURGENT PROGRESSIVISM AND THE WELFARE STATE, 1938

When Congressmen returned to their home districts in
September, 1937, they left behind them a record that fell
far short of Roosevelt's expectations. To be sure, Congress
had approved a relief bill and a diluted housing measure,
but other administration recommendations had not been enacted.
The Senate had passed a wages-and-hours bill, but the House
Rules Committee refused to accept it. The House, on the
other hand, had given its assent to Secretary of Agriculture
Wallace's farm bill only to have the measure obstructed by
the Senate Agriculture Committee. An executive reorganization proposal and a conservation bill calling for the creation of "seven little TVA's" had received only scant attention from the legislators.[1]

At first, a puzzled Roosevelt attempted to explain the
lackluster performance of Congress as the "usual 'off-year'
combination of heat, the jitters, and dissension." Later,
however, the President became angry; and convinced that he,
not Congress, represented the majority sentiment of the

---

[1]For an excellent account of the legislative obstruc-
tion of the regional conservation bill, see William E.
Leuchtenberg, "Roosevelt, Norris and the 'Seven Little
TVA's,'" Journal of Politics, XIV (August, 1952), 418-41.

nation, Roosevelt embarked on a cross-country trip to confirm
his analysis. Everywhere he went, the people greeted him
with unbounded enthusiasm. "They love Roosevelt," wrote one
reporter of the remarkable display of affection for the
President. Confident that the people were still behind him
and his program, Roosevelt called Congress into special
session in November to complete its unfinished business.[2]

In a special message to Congress, Roosevelt urged
approval of the fair-labor-standards bill, a new and permanent farm program, an executive reorganization measure,
and a regional planning proposal. "It is really important
that the major measures go through this year," the President
reminded Colonel House, "for they are all integral and necessary parts of a democratic picture which grows more logical
and simple the more we analyze it." Many Congressmen, however, did not share either the President's sense of urgency
or his humanitarian vision; when the special session adjourned a few days before Christmas, only the farm bill was
assured of passage. A Southern filibuster against an anti-
lynching measure and Congressional reluctance to consent to
any more "must" legislation combined in late 1937 to thwart
Roosevelt's desire to extend the New Deal.[3]

[2]Franklin D. Roosevelt to Colonel Edwin M. House,
June.16, 1937, Franklin D. Roosevelt Papers, PPF 222,
Franklin D. Roosevelt Library, Hyde Park, New York; Richard
L. Neuberger, "They Love Roosevelt," Forum, CI (January,
1939), 11-15.

[3]Roosevelt to House, June 16, 1937, Roosevelt Papers,
PPF 222; O. R. Altman, "Second and Third Sessions of the
Seventy-fifth Congress," American Political Science Review,
XXXII (December, 1938), 1099-1123.

Most of the Insurgents were opposed to the administration's farm bill, and they continued to insist that prosperity could be returned to agriculture only if the farmers were guaranteed the cost of production and if reciprocal trade agreements allowing importation of agricultural products were prohibited. In the end, however, the Hull-Wallace approach to the farm problem again triumphed, as Congress extended the Reciprocal Trade Agreements Act of 1934 for three years and passed a second Agricultural Adjustment Act (AAA). The new AAA embodied Wallace's scheme to store present surpluses for future emergency use—the concept of the ever-normal granary. It also established soil conservation as a permanent policy, authorized crop loans in a manner similar to Populism's subtreasury plan, offered crop insurance to certain wheat farmers, provided for farmer-approved marketing quotas on surplus agricultural products, and, of greatest importance, empowered the Secretary of Agriculture to assign to growers of staple crops acreage allotments in return for commodity loans and parity payments.

The Insurgent fight to change the New Deal farm program had begun in February, 1937, when the administration announced its intention to seek the approval of Congress for a continuation of the President's authority to negotiate reciprocal trade agreements. The Insurgents contended that the New Deal's policy of reciprocity violated the right of the American farmer to the domestic market. "So far as the reciprocal trade agreements are concerned, Roosevelt is

helping farmers. But not those in the United States,"
Arthur Capper declared. Frazier agreed and also reminded
the Senate that the manufacturing interests in the United
States, particularly the makers of farm machinery, benefited
immensely from reciprocity. As in the 1934 controversy over
the Reciprocal Trade Agreements Act, the Insurgents sought
to prevent the application of trade agreements to agricultural products. Failing to secure this objective, they
supported an amendment requiring that all reciprocity
treaties be ratified by a two-thirds vote of the Senate.
This attempt to regain a Senatorial prerogative also met
defeat; only LaFollette and Norris among the Insurgents
voted against it.[4]

Although the administration's 1938 farm bill emphasized control of the farm surplus through marketing quotas,
the Insurgents correctly believed that the measure continued the production-control approach of the Farm Relief
and Inflation Act. The Insurgents maintained that the New
Deal's reliance on production control as the means to increase farm prices was a proven failure. In addition, they
thought it immoral to impose a policy of scarcity on agriculture when people were hungry. "As long as we have, as
the President has said, one-third of the people of the United
States in a state of need and want," Borah contended, "we
are certainly not on the right road when we are reducing

---

[4]Congressional Record, 75th Cong., 1st Sess., pp.
1606-08; Capper to Cordell Hull, Oct. 27, 1937, Arthur Capper Papers, Agriculture, Reciprocal Trade-Wheat, Kansas
State Historical Society, Topeka, Kansas; New York Times,
Nov. 19, 1937, p. 7.

the quantity for which they are nightly praying." The Idaho
Senator also insisted that crop control was impossible to
enforce "without a copartnership with the Divine Being."
Frazier agreed with Borah, but he indicated that crop control might nevertheless be acceptable if it aided the
average farmer. He did not, however, believe that the administration bill fell into this category, since it was
really the "Farm Bureau Bill" that Frazier complained was
designed to benefit only the "corporation farmer."[5]

The major Insurgent complaint against the farm bill
was that it, like most New Deal legislation, sought to control the individual through the largess of the state. "It
is part of a set scheme to regiment everything," Hiram
Johnson wrote his son. "Farmers who accept the provisions
which rigidly make them farm just so many acres in such and
such a way, have bartered away for a few paltry dollars
their independence." Norris expressed similar reservations
about the bill's threat to the farmer's freedom, and Borah
urged the Senate to rewrite the proposal in order to prevent Wallace from placing agriculture under absolute bureaucratic control. "To impose upon the farmer the regulations

---

[5]*Congressional Record*, 75th Cong., 2nd Sess., pp. 165-
66, 401; William Lemke to Vincent F. Harrington, August 9,
1937, William Lemke Papers, Box 12, The Orin G. Libby Manuscript Collection, University of North Dakota Library, Grand
Forks, North Dakota. Lemke held the Farm Bureau partially
responsible for the New Deal's farm program. "All the rank
and file of the organization are for a cost-of-production
bill," he explained. "Unfortunately, some of their leaders
are not. Of course, Ed O'Neal /President of the American
Farm Bureau Federation/ is simply a catspaw of Mr. Wallace."
Lemke to H. M. Harden, Jan. 20, 1939, Lemke Papers, Box
14.

and rules prescribed by this bill," the Idaho Senator exclaimed, ". . .supposes that he has just escaped from the
home for the feeble-minded."[6]

To preserve the farmer's independence, the Insurgents
supported an attempt by California Senator William G. McAdoo
to substitute a cost-of-production amendment for the production-control portion of the farm bill. The Insurgents reasoned that fixing the price of agricultural goods would
permit the farmer to grow any quantity of the crop of his
choice free from governmental interference. Despite the
impassioned pleas of the Insurgents for its passage, the
Senate defeated the cost-of-production proposal by the
narrow margin of 46 to 40. All of the Insurgents except
Norris, who had sponsored the John A. Simpson cost-of-
production measure in 1933, voted for McAdoo's substitute
amendment.[7]

After their failure to attach a cost-of-production
amendment to the administration's farm bill, the Insurgents
joined an effort, led by Republican Senate Leader Charles L.
McNary, to limit the law's application to two years. The
Insurgents were especially concerned about the second AAA
bill because they realized that it was designed as the New
Deal's permanent agricultural policy. "I view it in a

[6]Johnson to Hiram Johnson, Jr., Feb. 12, 1938, Hiram
W. Johnson Papers, Part IV, Box 4, Bancroft Library, Uni-
versity of California, Berkeley; Congressional Record, 75th
Cong., 2nd Sess., pp. 803-10.

[7]Congressional Record, 75th Cong., 2nd Sess., pp. 986-
87.

totally different light," Borah informed his colleagues,
"than I would if it were purely an emergency measure."
Hiram Johnson declared that the Senate should reserve the
right to review legislation which "regiments the entire
farming community." All the Insurgents but LaFollette and
Norris supported the McNary amendment, but it failed by a
vote of 51 to 25.[8]

The Insurgents regarded the administration's support
of the second AAA as irrefutable evidence that Roosevelt was
not interested in "real agricultural legislation." Because
they had long been in the forefront of those advocating
agricultural reform, the Insurgents resented the President's
preference for the farm program drafted by "bureaucrats"
in the Department of Agriculture. "The farm bill, or rather
the monstrosity," William Lemke informed his constituents,
"demonstrates the overwhelming ignorance in the Department
of Agriculture. . . . The bill as passed is the kind that
Tammany and the other sidewalk farmers of the other large
cities want. It was passed by those who believe that the
farmers should feed them below the cost of production."
Wheeler was also bewildered by the administration's refusal
to grant the farmers the cost of production when everything
else in the country was subject to price-fixing. "Labor
organizations have price-fixing with the help of legislation,"

---

[8]Ibid., p. 1766. Actually, the second AAA farm bill
did not become law until the Senate approved the conference
report on Feb. 14, 1938. Five Insurgents, Borah, Johnson,
LaFollette, Nye, and Shipstead, voted against the final bill.
Congressional Record, 75th Cong., 3rd Sess., p. 1881.

the Montana Senator explained to reporters. "The same is
true of every large industry. Why not give the farmer the
same treatment?"[9]

The second AAA farm bill, which was approved by the
Senate a few days before it adjourned in December, 1937,
was the only one of the President's recommendations that was
assured of passage as the result of the action of the special
session of Congress. House Republican Leader Bertrand Snell
laughingly told reporters that the major accomplishments of
what administration critics called a "Goose-Egg" session
included Roosevelt's fishing trip in the Gulf of Mexico,
Vice-President Garner's hunting trip to Pennsylvania, and
a Congressional eating contest to decide the relative merits
of Maine and Idaho potatoes. The session was one of inordinate importance, however, because it gave strong evidence of the determination of Congress not to be dominated
by the President. Some Insurgents were not content simply
to reject administration recommendations but announced their
intention to regain many of the prerogatives that they had
relinquished earlier in the New Deal. "I think the thing
that most perils our form of government, democracy, has been
the yielding of the power of Congress under the stress of
emergency," Hiram Johnson stated in December. "The American
Congress. . .must, now that the emergency has passed, resume

---

[9]Lemke Newsletter, Dec. 22, 1937, Lemke Papers, Box
28; New York Times, Feb. 3, 1939, p. 28.

its powers."[10] Roosevelt would discover in the next two
years that many Congressmen shared Johnson's views.

In addition to a hostile Congress, the President, by
January, 1938, faced a deepening economic crisis. Industrial
production, profits, stock prices, and wages had all began
to decline sharply by September, 1937; and by the end of the
year two million people had been added to the ranks of the
unemployed. "In severity," one economist wrote in June,
1948, "the decline is without parallel in American economic
history." In the past, Roosevelt had been quick to credit
the New Deal for the nation's economic revival. Now the
administration had to endure the taunts of its critics that
the economic downturn was "Roosevelt's Recession." Baffled
by the sudden decline in the economy, the President at first
suggested no new remedies to deal with the crisis; in his
opening message to the 1938 Congress, he merely called
for the passage of the bills he had recommended to the
preceding session. "What the President is doing," Harold
L. Ickes recorded in his diary, "is to let Congress have
its head in the belief that it will need help and then will
come to him." Now that the New Deal's recovery program had
been proved vulnerable, however, many Congressmen preferred
that the administration give business a chance to extricate
the country from the recession. Congress could best aid the

[10]Time, XXXI (Jan. 3, 1938), 8; John R. Moore, "Senator Josiah W. Bailey and the 'Conservative Manifesto' of 1937," Journal of Southern History, XXXI (Feb., 1965), 21-39; New York Times, Dec. 23, 1937, p. 2.

recovery effort, Borah believed, by demonstrating to business that it will reduce taxes and curtail expenditures.[11]

The first measure taken up by Congress in 1938, a proposal to reorganize the executive branch, had nothing to do with the recession. Roosevelt first submitted his reorganization request to Congress in January, 1937, but it had been relegated to the background when the Court fight stalled all other legislation. The reorganization proposal authorized the President to issue executive orders to consolidate the various New Deal agencies and bureaus into twelve large cabinet-rank departments, including two new departments—Social Welfare and Public Works. These executive orders were to go into effect immediately and were to remain in force unless disapproved within sixty days by both Houses of Congress. The President could veto a disapproving vote of Congress, but the legislators could override his veto by the customary two-thirds vote.[12]

Although his relationship with the legislative branch had deteriorated considerably, Roosevelt anticipated little Congressional opposition to his reorganization plan. After all, the President noted, Congress had granted him similar powers under the Economy Act of 1933; and, he remarked,

[11]Samuel I. Rosenman (ed.), The Public Papers and Addresses of Franklin D. Roosevelt, VII (New York, 1941), 1-14; Kenneth D. Roose, "The Recession of 1937-38," Journal of Political Economy, LVI (June, 1948), 239-48; Harold L. Ickes, The Secret Diary of Harold L. Ickes, II (New York, 1954), 256; New York Times, Nov. 21, 1937, p. 21.

[12]For an excellent account of the entire reorganization controversy, see Richard Polenberg, Reorganizing Roosevelt's Government: The Controversy Over Executive Reorganization, 1936-1939 (Cambridge, Mass., 1966).

everyone appreciated "good management." The supposedly non-controversial reorganization bill, however, encountered fierce opposition in the Congress. Most of the Insurgents were among the opponents of the measure, and they saw in it what most disturbed them about the New Deal: large public expenditures, greater bureaucracy, and, most important, alleged executive usurpation of legislative prerogatives.

The first challenge to the reorganization bill came from a group of "economy" Democrats led by Virginia Senator Harry F. Byrd. In January, 1937, Byrd had gone on record as favoring executive reorganization if it resulted in "substantial economies and contributed to budget balancing possibilities." Roosevelt had replied that he also preferred a balanced budget but that he could not promise savings through reorganization. In an effort to connect reorganization and economy, Byrd in 1938 introduced an amendment requiring that reorganization result in a 10 per cent reduction in public expenditures. Agreeing with Byrd on the need for economy, all the Insurgents except LaFollette, Norris, and Nye supported the Byrd amendment, but the amendment failed by a vote of 28 to 36. The economy bloc then sought to "save" Comptroller General J. Raymond McCarl, whose office was to be abolished by the administration's bill. Byrd insisted that the Comptroller General prevented wasteful spending: "He has been like a policeman patrolling up and down the streets." New Dealers maintained, however, that "Watchdog McCarl" used his right of pre-audit to cause annoying delays in the enforcement of legislation. In the

end, Byrd's McCarl amendment was defeated by a vote of 47
to 36, with all the Insurgents except LaFollette and Norris
voting with the economizers.[13]

Although most of the Insurgents joined the Senate's
economy bloc in an attempt to convert the reorganization bill
into an anti-spending measure, they were more concerned
about curbing the growth of the federal bureaucracy. "The
problem which confronts us is the restraining and controlling of the remarkable bureaucratic growth in this country,"
Borah explained. The Idaho Senator believed that bureaucracy was burdensome to the taxpayer and destructive of
democratic government, and he warned his colleagues that it
was ridiculous to expect that the President alone would
accomplish a reduction in the number of federal agencies
when the executive department had been responsible for "bureaucracy run mad" in the first place. Borah stated it was
now time for Congress to assist in controlling the proliferation of the executive branch of government. Wheeler agreed
with Borah and cautioned that if Congress did not perform
this task, some "New York bureaucrat" would do it—and with
disastrous results.[14]

The Insurgents were disdainful of bureaucracy, bureaucrats, and academics, but the primary reason for their

---

[13]New York Times, Jan. 2, 1937, p. 4; Johnson to Hiram
Johnson, Jr., Feb. 26, 1938, Johnson Papers, Part IV, Box 4;
Congressional Record, 75th Cong., 3rd Sess., pp. 2594-96,
3748, 3999; Ickes, Secret Diary, II, 46.

[14]Congressional Record, 75th Cong., 3rd Sess., pp.
4194, 3018-23.

opposition to the executive reorganization bill was their
deeply-seated fear of any increase in presidential power
and their jealous regard for Congressional prerogatives.
Roosevelt's scheme to pack the Supreme Court had caused most
of the Insurgents to be distrustful of the President and
had made them wary of any plan that might lead to the augmentation of executive authority. "This is really the
companion bill to the Court bill of a year ago," Hiram
Johnson wrote of the reorganization proposal. "It is intended to give dictatorial powers to the President, to take
from the Congress what little power it now has, and transfer
it to the President." With totalitarianism on the rise in
Europe, the Insurgents worried that the reorganization bill,
like the Court plan, might lead to the establishment of one-
man rule in the United States. Wheeler told Congress that
the measure could only hasten the advent of dictatorship in
this country by making further delegations of power to the
President. "I say to the Senate," the Montana Insurgent
warned, "that it is far better to maintain the bureaus we
now have than to turn over dictatorial powers to the President and admit to the world that Congress is. . .incompetent
to function. I refuse to admit it."[15]

---

[15] Johnson to Hiram Johnson, Jr., Feb. 26, 1938,
Johnson Papers, Part IV, Box 4; New York Times, March 9,
1938, p. 4.

Still smarting over administration reprisals for his role in defeating the Court bill,[16] Wheeler readily consented to join Borah in leading a bipartisan coalition against the executive reorganization proposal. Partly as a way to humiliate Roosevelt, partly to retain some legislative authority, and partly to preserve his friendly relationships with certain "pet bureaus" such as the Bureau of Indian Affairs and the Forestry Bureau, Wheeler sponsored an amendment that would have prevented the President's reorganization orders from taking effect until approved by a majority vote in both Houses of Congress. If the Senate adopted his amendment, the Montana Insurgent maintained, it would demonstrate that Congress possessed "the courage to fulfill its role." Hiram Johnson enthusiastically endorsed Wheeler's amendment and claimed that it would prohibit the President from "ramming requests down Congress' throat." George Norris, who ultimately supported the administration bill because he "trusted Roosevelt," admitted that the assertion of Congressional independence was the attractive feature of the Wheeler amendment.[17]

---

[16]After the Court fight, the administration channeled all federal patronage to Montana to Wheeler's Democratic rivals. Interview with Burton K. Wheeler, Nov. 22, 1968; James A. Farley to Franklin D. Roosevelt, June 16, 1937, Roosevelt Papers, PPF 723; Richard T. Reutten, "Showdown in Montana, 1938: Burton K. Wheeler's Role in the Defeat of Jerry O'Connell," Pacific Northwest Quarterly, LIV (Jan., 1963), 19-29.

[17]Congressional Record, 75th Cong., 3rd Sess., pp. 3018-23, 3477, 3824. George Norris, who opposed Ickes' attempt to bring the Forestry Division into the Interior Department and any change in the independent status of the TVA, finally voted for the reorganization bill because he had

Roosevelt objected to the Wheeler amendment, contending that it would paralyze any attempt to reorganize the
executive branch. "If an amendment similar to the Wheeler
amendment is adopted," one White House aide announced, "we
may as well say goodby to reorganization." Robert LaFollette
also questioned the logic behind Wheeler's amendment by
reminding the Senate that dictatorships were prevalent only
because the world's democracies had failed to use governmental powers swiftly enough to alleviate the problems of
modern industrialism. James F. Byrnes, the Senate sponsor
of the reorganization bill, agreed with LaFollette, but he
conceded that Wheeler's amendment would be difficult to
defeat because Roosevelt's attitude toward the Supreme
Court, his failure to act to curb sit-down strikes, and his
advocacy of lump-sum relief expenditures had alienated many
Senators.[18]

The Wheeler amendment was put to a vote on March 18,
1938, and was defeated 39 to 43. All of the Insurgents
except LaFollette and Norris voted against the administration.

---

faith that Roosevelt "will not do a foolish, senseless
thing." "I could never understand why honest men, especially
members of Congress," Norris later wrote, "believed that
there was danger of the President's taking advantage of law
. . .to establish himself as a dictator. . . . I can see no
motive in such a course, except that they thought they saw
in the defeat of the Reorganization bill an opportunity to
destroy the influence of the President in the carrying out
of his program in other fields." Norris to John M. Leyda,
April 30, 1938, George W. Norris Papers, Tray 18, Box 5,
Library of Congress, Washington, D. C.

[18]Polenberg, Reorganizing Roosevelt's Government,
pp. 247-48; Congressional Record, 75th Cong., 3rd Sess.,
pp. 4195-96; James F. Byrnes, All In One Lifetime (New York,
1958), pp. 105-107.

Shipstead called the defeat of the Wheeler amendment a "blow
to democracy." Another Insurgent labeled the vote "a small
crack in the dike of democracy that will let through the
torrent. . .of dictatorship." In analyzing the defeat of
the Wheeler amendment, Borah declared that intense White
House lobbying had persuaded wavering Senators to vote
against the proposal. Hiram Johnson confirmed that the
votes had been promised on the Wheeler amendment but "over
night they were pulled down. . . . The overwhelming victory
for Roosevelt gave us a class of Senators worse than 'yes-
men,' all of them being members in high standing of A. K.,
Inc." The Insurgents still hoped that the bill could be
recommitted, but this effort also failed by a vote of 43
to 48. Johnson blamed this second defeat on the same
"Democrats who fought the Court Bill and are trying to
crawl back into good favor with the President on this bill."[19]

When the Senate passed the reorganization bill on
March 28, 1938, Roosevelt was elated. "It proves," he told
reporters, "that the Senate cannot be purchased by organized
telegrams based on direct misrepresentation." Roosevelt's
remarks, which were directed at the organized lobby that had
fought the bill, angered most of the Insurgents who denounced the President's use of the word "purchase" as

---

[19]Congressional Record, 75th Cong., 3rd Sess., p. 3645;
Shipstead News Release, March 28, 1938, Henrik Shipstead
Papers, Box 25, Minnesota Historical Society, St. Paul, Min-
nesota; Polenberg, Reorganizing Roosevelt's Government, pp.
130-145; Johnson to Hiram Johnson, Jr., March 26, 1938;
Johnson Papers, Part IV, Box 4; Johnson to Frank P. Doherty,
March 24, 1938; April 11, 1938, Johnson Papers, Part III,
Box 17; Congressional Record, 75th Cong., 3rd Sess., p. 4204.

"unjust, and outrageous." The President's remarks did not help him in the House either. "It really did stir the animals up," Representative Clifford Hope later recalled. And it was in the House that Roosevelt's reorganization bill was to be defeated. Rather than sending the bill to the conference committee, opponents in the Senate arranged to send it directly to the House.[20] Democratic Representative John O'Connor of New York, chairman of the House Rules Committee, had assured a doubting Hiram Johnson that the House would recommit the Senate bill; and this prediction proved correct, as the House recommitted the proposal by a vote of 204 to 196. "The outcome of the fight on the Reorganization bill was glorious!," the California Senator exalted to one of his friends. "It was more relished because we little expected it. To think of 108 Democrats voting to recommit the Bill seems incredible."[21]

Roosevelt was as surprised as Johnson was at the House's decision to recommit the bill. "Someday in the next forty-four years I hope a Reorganization Bill will pass," the angry President wrote. "I think the first effort

---

[20]Time, XXXI (April 11, 1938), 11; Congressional Record, 75th Cong., 3rd Sess., p. 4368; Hope to Harry Sharp, March 31, 1938, Clifford R. Hope Papers, Legislative Correspondence, 1937-38, R-V, Kansas State Historical Society, Topeka, Kansas. Since the House had already approved two parts of the reorganization plan during the 1937 session, the Senate bill could have been sent directly to a conference committee. However, a series of parliamentary errors and the hostility of several top-ranking Democrats to the bill, most notably Key Pittman, prevented this course of action.

[21]Johnson to Frank P. Doherty, April 11, 1938, Johnson Papers, Part III, Box 17; Congressional Record, 75th Cong., 3rd Sess., pp. 5121-24.

was made forty-four years ago." Roosevelt, as a matter of
fact, contributed to his own defeat by making certain strategic blunders. Hoping to dispel any notion that he favored
one-man rule, the President had released a statement at
1:00 A.M. on March 31, denying that he had any intention
of becoming a dictator. The statement backfired and only
succeeded in accentuating the public's fear of a dictatorship.[22] A week earlier Roosevelt had removed the Chairman
of the TVA in a manner that invited his critics to charge
that he had acted arbitrarily. Frank Gannett's National
Committee to Uphold Constitutional Government, a group of
modern-day Paul Reveres, and Father Charles E. Coughlin
seized upon these two incidents as evidence of the President's love of power. The Reveres marched on Washington,
and Coughlin demanded that Americans wire their Senators
"to stop the Reorganization Bill as Washington stopped
George III." The public response to the radio priest's
demand was remarkable: 300,000 telegrams poured into the
nation's capital within two days. Clifford Hope reported
that the President's "Don't-Want-to-be-a-Dictator" statement

---

[22]Roosevelt to Colonel William Gorham Rice, April 15,
1938, Roosevelt Papers, PPF 5310. For a copy of the President's "Don't-Want-to-be-a-Dictator" statement, see Rosenman
(ed.), Public Papers of FDR, VII, 179-81. The letter read
as follows:
    "As you well know I am as much opposed to American
Dictatorship for three simple reasons:
    A. I have no inclination to be a dictator.
    B. I have none of the qualifications which would make
me a successful dictator.
    C. I have too much historical background and too much
knowledge of existing dictatorships to make me desire any
form of dictatorship for a democracy like the United States
of America."

and the ensuing national reaction definitely stiffened opposition to the bill in the House. "This letter given out in the wee hours of the night had a decided effect on the result," Hiram Johnson wrote to his son. "It seems impossible that the President would have written the word 'I' so many times, and no word of. . .our hatred of dictatorships. Well, as in the last year, in the Court fight, 'He was just too damned smart.'"[23]

Roosevelt's political maneuvering was not, however, alone responsible for the defeat of his executive reorganization plan. Like many Senators, members of the House wanted to curb excessive federal spending, to halt the growth of the federal bureaucracy, to retain friendly relationships with certain pet bureaus, and to restrict presidential power. William Lemke proclaimed that the House wanted to reorganize the executive branch for the sake of effecting economy and eliminating bureaucrats. "But no one is foolish enough to believe that this will be done under the present bill," he told his constituents. "This bill is a camouflage. Its only purpose is to concentrate more power in the Executive, and power once surrendered to the Executive is never recovered without a struggle."[24]

---

[23]_Time_, XXXI (April 4, 1938), 10-11; Hope to B. T. Robinson, April 6, 1938, Hope Papers, Legislative Correspondence, 1937-38, R-V; Johnson to Frank P. Doherty, April 11, 1938, Johnson Papers, Part III, Box 17.

[24]Lemke Newsletter, April 13, 1938, Lemke Papers, Box 28; Polenberg, _Reorganizing Roosevelt's Government_, Chapt. VIII.

Quite apart from their stated reasons for opposing the executive reorganization bill, House members were angered because they felt neglected. The House was therefore anxious to demonstrate its independence as it had done in 1935 by rejecting the death-sentence provision of the public utility holding company bill. "The minute that most of the old line Democrats feel that the President has begun to lose the confidence of the country, they are going to run out on him so fast that it will be amazing," Clifford Hope had predicted in April, 1937. "They feel as they do. . .because of their personal resentment of the way they are being treated at the White House."[25]

Defeated in his efforts to secure executive reorganization, Roosevelt, as of April, 1938, still had not decided how to cope with the economic recession. "The week went, lock, stock and barrel, to Garner. . .and the other conspirators, with hardly a turn of the hand against them at the White House," Tommy Corcoran complained on April 14. Stanely High, another White House advisor, wrote that "for the time being, the New Deal is a crusade that has lost its Richard." As in 1935, before the "second hundred days," Roosevelt appeared to be uncertain as to the direction in which he should move. His aides, again as in 1935, offered

---

[25] Samuel G. Blythe, "New Deal Politics," Saturday Evening Post, CCVII (Sept. 22, 1934), 9; Hope to Floyd H. Nichols, April 20, 1937, Hope Papers, General Correspondence, 1936-37, Misc.-P; James T. Patterson, Congressional Conservatism and the New Deal (Lexington, Ky., 1967), chapt. 5. Arthur Krock maintained the House action on the "death sentence" resulted from a desire "to resume its place as a free legislative unit." New York Times, July 5, 1935, p. 12.

him conflicting advice: Secretary of the Treasury Morgenthau
and Vice-President Garner wanted a balanced budget—"You
ought to cut until the blood runs," Garner informed the President; but Hopkins and Ickes, "the spenders' union," pleaded
for increased government spending. Roosevelt's sympathies
were with the budget balancers, but his humanitarian tendencies made agreement with the spenders inevitable. On
April 14, about a week after the House had voted to recommit
the reorganization bill, the President sent Congress a multi-
billion dollar spending program. "Viewed from every angle
today's purchasing power—the citizen's income of today—
is not sufficient to drive the economic system at higher
speed," Roosevelt informed the Congress. ". . .I believe we
have been right in the course we have chartered. I propose
to sail ahead. I feel sure your help is with me."[26]

　　　Congress, however, had other ideas about how to cure
the recession: it preferred to let business do the job.
As an inducement to private enterprise, many Congressmen
concluded that business should receive a measure of tax
relief. To Byrnes, Garner, and Harrison this meant repeal
of the undistributed corporate-profits tax. In late
February, 1938, Byrnes invited Bernard M. Baruch to testify
before his special Committee on Unemployment. Blaming unemployment on the government's punitive policies with regard
to private capital, Baruch predicted that the repeal of the

---

[26]Corcoran to Sager Bruoh, April 14, 1938, Roosevelt
Papers, PSF 51; Stanley High, "Fog Over Washington," Saturday
Evening Post, CCX (April 9, 1938), 27; Ickes, Secret Diary,
II, 280; Rosenman (ed.), Public Papers of FDR, VII, 221-
33.

undistributed profits tax and modification of the capital
gains tax would give business incentive to alleviate the
recession. A few days later the House approved a tax bill
that largely followed Baruch's suggestions except for the
retention of the principle of the undistributed profits
tax.[27]

In the Senate, Finance Committee chairman Pat Harrison
was determined to enact Baruch's recommendations to the
letter. Following the House's lead, the Finance Committee
in late March eliminated the undistributed profits tax
altogether and substituted a flat 18 per cent tax on corporate income. In addition, Harrison saw to it that the
progressive tax on capital gains was lowered and that
special exemptions were given to small business firms.
Garner quickly forced the bill through the Senate, boast-
ing, "We passed 224 pages of tax bill in twenty minutes—
not bad." A jubliant Harrison declared that the Senate had
offered capital "the fullest inducement to get busy and
help itself out of the depression." Roosevelt, however,
regarded the Senate tax bill as completely unacceptable.
The President instructed the conference committee to retain
the principle of taxation in proportion to the ability to
pay, but this plea fell on deaf ears as the committee members approved the Senate's weakened capital gains tax along
with the House's face-saving undistributed profits tax.[28]

---

[27]Time, XXXI (March 14, 1938), 13; Congressional
Record, 75th Cong., 3rd Sess., p. 3269.

[28]Time, XXXI (April 18, 1938), 18; Rosenman (ed.),
Public Papers of FDR, VII, 214-19. Although the conference

The _Nation_ accused the Congress of enacting a tax law
that "would have graced the days when Andy Mellon ran the
Treasury as an outpost of big business." The Insurgents had
favored slight revisions in the undistributed profits tax
to aid small businesses, but they also regarded the Revenue
Act of 1938 as a surrender to the economic royalists. "I
think a corporation should pay something for the privilege
of incorporating," said George Norris in expressing the
typical Insurgent sentiment. "There is no reason why they
should be permitted to accumulate large surpluses without
being taxed for it." Although their estrangement from the
administration was nearly complete by 1938, the Insurgents
were not willing to abandon their belief in the efficacy of
progressive taxation laws. LaFollette and Borah attempted
to amend the 1938 tax bill by raising the tax rates on personal incomes and by removing all exemptions on future
issues of federal securities. The Senate agreed to the
latter, only to have it deleted by the conference committee.[29]

Congress not only sought to aid business by lowering
taxes but also by reducing the President's request for
necessary government expenditures. "Priming the pump,"
John J. O'Connor argued, "won't do any good if there's no

---

committee retained at least the principle of the undistributed-profits tax, even this "principle" was removed in
1939.

[29]"Victory For Hysteria," _Nation_, CXLVI (April 16,
1938), 428; _New York Times_, April 6, 1938, p. 13; _Congres-
sional Record_, 75th Cong., 3rd Sess., pp. 5162, 5181.
Roosevelt considered the 1938 tax bill so distasteful that he
allowed it to become law without his signature.

water in the well." Norris also questioned the ability of
the government to continue a program of long-term public
spending. "This cannot go on forever," the Nebraska Insurgent wrote, "and there will come a time when even the
federal government will have to cease." Arthur Capper
worried that increased government spending would interfere
with the recovery efforts of business. "If our army of
unemployed is to go back to useful work," the Kansas Senator explained, "it will have to be done largely by private
enterprise."[30]

Despite the widespread sentiment for economy, Roosevelt's pump-priming proposal encountered only minor opposition in Congress. The House, which only a month earlier
had blocked Roosevelt's reorganization bill, speedily approved the spending program, authorizing expenditures
slightly above the $3 billion requested by the President.
One Representative told reporters that although many Congressmen were reluctant to vote for the measure, they
realized that the acute unemployment situation necessitated
increased appropriations for relief. The Senate offered
somewhat greater resistance to increased spending than the
House did, but in the end the Appropriations Committee
added more than $300 million to the administration bill,
primarily in the form of farm parity payments. Not wanting to oppose the farm bloc, Senators overwhelming approved
this version of the pump-priming bill by a vote of 60 to 10,
with Hiram Johnson being the only Insurgent in opposition.

[30]New York Times, April 15, 1938, p. 1; ibid., May 23,
1938, p. 2; Norris to Henry P. Nielson, April 18, 1938,
Norris Papers, Tray 33, Box 6.

One reporter caustically observed that Congress quickly lost
its desire to balance the budget when the President proposed
a large spending program in an election year.[31]

Although the Insurgents voted for the pump-priming
bill, they regarded Roosevelt's advocacy of large government
expenditures as evidence of the bankruptcy of the New Deal.
Doubting the long-range usefulness of public spending, the
Insurgents regretted that the resumption of spending was
the only remedy the President could offer to cure the recession. Hiram Johnson believed that Roosevelt was too stubborn to admit that government spending had failed to restore
prosperity. Borah also questioned Roosevelt's reliance on
spending, especially when, in the Senator's opinion, the
President could have chosen a more effective and fundamental
method of reform by enforcing the Sherman Antitrust Act.
"Under the present economic set-up," the Idaho Insurgent
complained, "the spending program will be in the nature of
a subsidy to the monopolistic controlled interests. If we
do not solve this problem, we will be struggling along here
for a long time to come with the purchasing power of the
masses constantly decreasing."[32]

---

[31]Congressional Record, 75th Cong., 3rd Sess., p. 6836;
Hope to J. L. Harkleroad, April 20, 1938, Hope Papers, Legislative Correspondence, 1937-38, N-P; New York Times, June
4, 1938, p. 1; Congressional Record, 75th Cong., 3rd Sess.,
p. 8152; Time, XXXI (June 27, 1938), 10-11.

[32]Johnson to Hiram Johnson, Jr., April 16, 1938,
Johnson Papers, Part IV, Box 4; Borah to E. E. Allen, April
22, 1938, William E. Borah Papers, Box 644, Library of
Congress, Washington, D. C.

Actually, Roosevelt had decided to accompany the resumption of government spending with an investigation of monopoly. Shortly after he announced his spending program, the President sent Congress a special message urging the creation of a committee to conduct a thorough study of the concentration of economic power. Most of the Insurgents thought Roosevelt's anti-monopolistic position was another example of the administration's indecisiveness regarding its relationship to big business. "The promotion of the two ideas of the N.R.A. and the new anti-trust legislation are inconsistent and worse. What treason!" exclaimed Hiram Johnson. "In the eyes of some of our officials today, although. . .I cannot believe it, consistency is the vice of fools." Borah scoffed at the necessity of conducting such an investigation when everyone already knew that monopoly existed in the United States. At the President's insistence, Borah, however, agreed to serve on the committee, but he also perspicaciously predicted that the findings "would reach the dust of the upper shelf in the form of ten or twenty volumes which few will ever consult."[33] Nor were the Insurgents overly enthusiastic about the Justice Department's antitrust campaign. Although Thurman Arnold, head of the Antitrust Division, turned out to be the most vigorous trust buster

---

[33]Rosenman (ed.) Public Papers of FDR, VII, 305-20; Johnson to Howard C. Rowley, August 1, 1938, Johnson Papers, Part III, Box 18; New York Times, April 30, 1938, p. 2. "I really think Borah should be made to serve," Roosevelt wrote Garner about the make-up of the monopoly-investigatory committee. "This is his pet hobby anyway." Roosevelt to Garner, June 14, 1938, Roosevelt Papers, PSF 62.

in the nation's history, he regarded the antitrust laws as
symbols of "economic meaninglessness" on which "men like
Senator Borah have founded their political careers." Unlike
the Insurgents, Arnold was not concerned about the social
evils of bigness per se but rather with protecting the consumer from inefficient corporations. To the Insurgents,
therefore, this last New Deal attempt to come to grips with
the problem of monopoly appeared to be woefully inadequate,
and they favored the passage of the rigid antimonopoly bill
sponsored by Borah and Wyoming's Joseph O'Mahoney.[34]

Because of the Insurgents' criticism of government
deficit financing and their belief that the proposed investigation of monopoly was inadequate, most observers were
incredulous at the nearly unanimous Insurgent vote for the
New Deal's largest spending bill. The Insurgents, however,
were well aware of the political consequences of voting
against a measure that included a substantial appropriation
to increase parity payments and to fund the Farm Security
Administration. The Insurgents, also, could not ignore the

---

[34]Thurman Arnold, The Folklore of Capitalism (New
Haven, 1937), pp. 207-08, 217; Jerome Cohen, "The Forgotten
T.N.E.C.," Current History, N.S., I (1941), 45-50. The Borah-
O'Mahoney bill would have required that all corporations
engaged in interstate commence be licensed by the FTC. In
order to obtain these licenses corporations could not employ
child labor or obstruct organization of their employees, and
they had to observe all antitrust laws and refrain from
stock-watering and other malpractices. Failure to maintain
these standards would result in revocation of a corporation's
license to do business. See Ellis W. Hawley, The New Deal
and the Problem of Monopoly (Princeton, 1966), Part IV.
Hawley maintains that the Insurgents were incorrect in their
belief that Roosevelt called for a monopoly investigation
in 1938 to "sidetrack the rigid Borah-O'Mahoney bill."
Hawley, The New Deal and the Problem of Monopoly, pp. 372,
410-14.

fact that the recession made an increase in relief spending imperative. Even Hiram Johnson, who was the only Insurgent to record himself against the bill on the final roll call, admitted that his humanitarianism had almost led him to vote for the proposal. "I do not doubt that a vast number of. . . unemployed require assistance, and I would give this to them," Johnson informed his son. "But the only way we could protest mixing up an equal amount of money for Ickes and Roosevelt to play with, to 'prime the pump', as they put it, but to prime the polls, in reality, was by voting against the bill."[35]

It was this suspicion that the administration would use relief funds to "prime the polls" that most disturbed the Insurgents in their reaction to the 1938 spending bill.[36] "If we are going to appropriate money to be turned over to the executive branches to be used for the slaughtering of Senators because someone doesn't like the color of their hair," said Burton K. Wheeler, who realized that the administration wanted him out of the Senate, "then we ought to know about it." With no assurances forthcoming from the White House that the administration would not play politics

---

[35]Capper to B. F. Abmeyer, Sept. 20, 1938, Capper Papers, Agriculture, A.A.A.-Co-ops; Johnson to Hiram Johnson, Jr., June 4, 1938, Johnson Papers, Part IV, Box 4.

[36]The Insurgents objected that the 1938 bill, like all New Deal spending measures, placed considerable power in the hands of Roosevelt. "It simply enables the expenditure of a billion dollars or more at the sweet will of the President," complained Hiram Johnson. "But Congressmen and Senators dare not oppose it. . .for fear of subjecting themselves to the charge that they won't relieve human misery." Johnson to Hiram Johnson, Jr., June 4, 1938, Johnson Papers, Part IV, Box 4.

with relief funds, the Insurgents unanimously voted to in-
corporate into the pump-priming bill two amendments, one
sponsored by New Mexico's Carl Hatch and the other by
Vermont's Warren Austin, designed to prevent the use of
relief appropriations for political purposes. Both amendments failed to gain Senate approval, however, partly because
it was rumored that Roosevelt opposed them. "I cannot
believe your opposition to legislation of this kind," an
incredulous George Norris wrote the President. "I believe
the /Hatch/ bill is a giant step towards the purification
of politics and Government." Following Senatorial rejection
of the Hatch and Austin amendments, Hiram Johnson solemnly
warned his colleagues that Roosevelt "is now out to get
every man who was against him on his attempt to pack the
Supreme Court."[37]

There is a good deal of evidence to indicate that
Johnson's warning was not to be taken lightly. The opposition of members of his own party to the Court plan had infuriated Roosevelt. "The President will never forgive them
for the bitter defeat of major importance that he suffered,"
one Insurgent predicted. Farley also revealed that Roosevelt was eager for revenge. As soon as the 1937 session
ended, the President revealed his displeasure with his

---

[37]New York Times, May 26, 1938, p. 5; Norris to
Roosevelt, July 26, 1939, Roosevelt Papers, PSF 54; Johnson
to Hiram Johnson, Jr., May 28, 1938, Johnson Papers, Part IV,
Box 4. Actually, not only the rumored opposition of Roosevelt to the Hatch bill was responsible for the Senate's defeat of the measure in 1938. Many Senators, particularly the
Democrats, did not want to see the patronage possibilities
offered by the relief organizations in their states removed.

opponents. On his Western trip, he purposely snubbed three
Democrats who had played key roles in the defeat of the Court
plan: he ignored Wheeler and Nebraska's Edward Burke and
tried to avoid O'Mahoney. "He took no pains to hide his
anger," George Creel recalled. "Resentment crystallized
into the desire to crush all who conspired against the
throne." In early May, 1938, Florida's Claude Pepper, who
carried official White House endorsement, easily captured
that state's Senatorial primary. Since there was speculation that Pepper had benefited from a timely infusion of
WPA funds into his state, his victory set a precedent which
"put the fear of God in the hearts" of other anti-administration Democrats.[38]

After Congress adjourned in 1938, Roosevelt publicly
announced his intention to purge some conservative Democrats
from Congress. "As head of the Democratic Party, charged
with the responsibility of carrying out the definitely
liberal declaration of principles set forth in the 1936
platform," the President told the nation in a fireside chat,
"I feel that I have every right to speak in those few instances where there may be a clear issue between candidates
for a Democratic nomination involving these principles."

---

[38]Johnson to Hiram Johnson, Jr., August 14, 1937,
Johnson Papers, Part IV, Box 4; James A. Farley, Jim Farley's
Story (New York, 1948), p. 95; George Creel, Rebel At Large
(New York, 1947), p. 295; Hope to Richard W. Robbins, May 17,
1938, Hope Papers, Official Correspondence, 1937-38, P-R.
Pepper's victory served as a catalyst for House passage of
the Fair Labor Standards Act. See Patterson, Congressional
Conservatism, pp. 242-46; Paul Y. Anderson, "Roosevelt's New
Bandwagon," Nation, CXLVI (May 14, 1938), 551-52; and Johnson
to Hiram Johnson, Jr., May 28, 1938, Johnson Papers, Part IV,
Box 4.

Roosevelt hoped to replace conservative Democrats with liberal Democrats, and he actively intervened in several state
primaries in an attempt to accomplish this objective.[39]

In previous New Deal elections, particularly in 1934,
the Insurgents had urged Roosevelt to promote a realignment of parties along liberal and conservative lines. In
1938, however, most Insurgents opposed the President's attempted purge of conservatives. Some Insurgents, such as
Borah, Capper, Frazier, Nye, and Shipstead, inconsistently
declared that Roosevelt's intervention in local politics was
a violation of states rights. Others, most notably Johnson
and Wheeler, regarded the purge as another example of the
President's ready disposition to augment his personal power.
By 1938, moreover, most of the Insurgents believed that New
Deal reformism, in the main, did not reflect their ideas of
liberalism. Thus, it was evident that when Roosevelt called
for the election of liberals to the 1939 Congress, he no
longer included Insurgents in that category. The New Deal
had transformed the Democratic party into an organization in
which labor unions, urban political machines, and ethnic
minority groups were heavily represented. The response to
the demands of these groups in the 75th Congress convinced
most of the Insurgents that New Deal legislation was destructive of their conception of American democracy. "The

---

[39]Rosenman (ed.), Public Papers of FDR, VII, 391-400.
Roosevelt concentrated his purge efforts on Iowa Senator
Guy Gillette, Indiana Senator Frederick Van Nuys, Georgia
Senator Walter George, Maryland Senator Millard Tydings,
South Carolina Senator "Cotton" Ed Smith, and New York Repre-
sentative John J. O'Connor.

New Deal Administration is on the wrong track," said Arthur

Capper in a typical Insurgent indictment of the New Deal.

"It is attempting to attain worthwhile objectives by that

deceptive short cut—regimentation of the individual; con-

centration of all powers of the Federal Government in the

hands of the Executive; and substitution of a central govern-

ment at Washington for state and local government."[40]

Because of their lack of trust in Roosevelt and their

negative attitude toward much of the recent New Deal legis-

lation, it is not surprising that the Insurgents deplored

the President's efforts in 1938 to liberalize the Democratic

party. What is surprising is that they assumed an active

role in seeking to thwart Roosevelt's attempted purge. Al-

though not running for reelection himself, Wheeler promised

his personal aid to any Insurgent or Democrat marked for

elimination by the administration. Hiram Johnson and Gerald

Nye also voiced support of the Democrats Roosevelt opposed.[41]

The Insurgents in 1938 were, however, actually less

concerned about aiding Democrats Roosevelt had marked for

purging than in supporting Republican candidates. Thus in

California, Johnson endorsed the anti-labor, conservative

Republican Philip Bancroft for the Senate. "If to be a

conservative at heart means backing Bancroft. . .I plead

guilty," the California Senator frankly admitted. "If to

be a liberal means that you must be for any crack-pot scheme

[40]Johnson to Harry Flood Byrd, August 13, 1938, Johnson Papers, Part III, Box 18; Capper Radio Address, 1938,
Capper Papers, General Correspondence, New-OPA.

[41]New York Times, May 26, 1938, p. 5.

proposed by any half-baked economist, and that you must advocate any plan, however bizarre, that will mean ruin to the
country, then I am a conservative at heart." Capper, "for
the sake of the personal and the economic liberties of the
individual," urged his constituents to elect the entire GOP
ticket in his state. In North Dakota, Frazier and Nye allied
themselves with Republican conservatives to obtain financial
support for Nye's reelection. Even the Farmer-Laborite
Henrik Shipstead indicated that he intended to vote for GOP
candidates in the 1938 Minnesota elections.[42]

In Idaho and Montana two Insurgents engineered their
own purge. In Idaho, Borah led a Republican-conservative
Democratic coalition to victory over incumbent Senator James
P. Pope in the Democratic primary. Pope had been one of the
chief sponsors of the 1938 farm bill and was an avid inter-
nationalist, and since Borah did not favor the second AAA
and was an avowed isolationist, he encouraged Idaho Republicans to "cross-over" to the Democratic primary in an attempt to replace Pope with the conservative Congressman D.
Worth Clark. On primary day more than 80,000 Republicans
deserted their own primary to give Clark a narrow margin of
victory. Pope confirmed to Roosevelt that Borah was responsible for persuading Clark to enter the Senate race

---

[42]Johnson to Walter P. Jones, Sept. 26, 1938, Johnson
Papers, Part III, Box 18; Capper Radio Address, 1938, Capper
Papers, General Correspondence, New-OPA; Wayne S. Cole,
Senator Gerald P. Nye and American Foreign Relations (Min-
neapolis, 1962), pp. 148-49; Sister Mary Rene Lorentz,
"Henrik Shipstead: Minnesota Independent, 1923-1946" (Ph.D.
Thesis, Catholic University of America, 1963), p. 55.

against him and that the Idaho Senator was "deeply involved" in the Republican scheme to vote in the Democratic primary.[43]

In Montana, Wheeler conducted a successful purge of Democratic Representative Jerry O'Connell. After the Court fight, the President let it be known that he hoped O'Connell, a loyal administration supporter, would defeat Wheeler for the Senate in 1940. In the 1938 Congressional primary O'Connell stated that Roosevelt had instructed him "to go out and fight like hell to defeat Senator Wheeler's machine so he wouldn't be back in 1940." Wheeler quietly attempted to derail his rival in the Democratic primary, but his effort fell some 6,000 votes short. In the general election, the Montana Senator and his wife openly attacked O'Connell and endorsed his Republican opponent. The result was one of the most stunning upsets in Montana political history, as the anti-Semitic, conservative Republican Dr. Jacob Thorkelson gained nearly an 8,000-vote margin over O'Connell. The election was a remarkable personal victory for Wheeler, but the Montana Senator was forced to ally himself with his former enemy, the Anaconda Copper Company, to accomplish it.[44] This indicated the lengths to which he was willing to go in order to embarrass Roosevelt.

---

[43] Patterson, Congressional Conservatism, pp. 268-70; Pope to Roosevelt, Sept. 28, 1938, Roosevelt Papers, PSF 51.

[44] New York Times, Sept. 2, 1937, p. 7; July 20, 1938, p. 2. Reutten, "Showdown in Montana," pp. 19-29; Kenneth Romney to Marvin McIntyre, Nov. 17, 1938, Roosevelt Papers, OF 300 (Montana Politics).

In deciding to intervene in local primaries Roosevelt
embarked on a futile vendetta. Having been an eyewitness to
the failure of Wilson's "great and solemn referendum" in
1920, the President should have known that it was extremely
difficult to transform a decentralized political party into
a national organization that was primarily responsive to
presidential leadership.[45] Except for the ouster of the
chairman of the House Rules Committee, John J. O'Connor of
New York City, whose defeat was secured with virtually no
Presidential assistance, Roosevelt's attempt to liberalize
the Democratic party proved to be a decided blow to both
his personal prestige and his legislative program. Not only
did conservative Democrats defeat their liberal opponents
in the Senatorial primaries, but the New Deal suffered another
setback as the Republicans made heavy gains in the 1938 elections. The GOP won thirteen new governships, captured eight
additional seats in the Senate, and gained a remarkable
eighty-one seats in the House.[46]

---

[45]James M. Burns, Deadlock of Democracy: Four-Party
Politics in America (Englewood Cliffs, N. J., 1963), pp. 151-
76, takes an opposing view and argues that Roosevelt could
have affected an ideological realignment of parties during
his first two terms had he committed himself to that end
early in the New Deal.

[46]Joseph Boskin, "Politics of an Opposition Party: The
Republican Party in the New Deal Period, 1936-1940" (Ph.D.
Thesis, University of Minnesota, 1959), pp. 200-08; Harry W.
Morris, "The Republicans in a Minority Role, 1933-1938"
(Ph.D. Thesis, State University of Iowa, 1960), pp. 281-82;
"The Republican Party: Up from the Grave," Fortune, XX,
(August, 1939), 33-36; Milton Plesur, "The Republican Come-
back of 1938," Review of Politics, XXIV (Oct. 1962), 525-
62.

Most of the Republican gains came in the Midwest and West, where low corn and wheat prices served as catalysts for a revolt against Roosevelt and the New Deal. Since many of the farmers in these regions were not satisfied with the second AAA, they used the 1938 elections to register their disapproval of the administration's agricultural policies. Both the Senate sponsors of the 1938 farm bill, George McGill of Kansas and James P. Pope of Idaho, sustained defeat. F. Ryan Duffy, the defeated Democratic Senator from Wisconsin, testified that dissatisfaction with both the second AAA and the reciprocity treaties caused many citizens to vote straight Republican tickets. There were, however, other factors responsible for the Republican sweep in the farm states. Many voters were upset by Roosevelt's attempt to pack the Supreme Court and by his apparent tolerance of the sit-down strikes. It was the recession, though, that probably accounted for most of the administration's losses. Distressed about the state of the economy, a portion of the electorate voiced its disapproval of New Deal policies that they thought were alien to the middle-class value system of most Americans. Having lost confidence in the administration's ability to restore prosperity, these voters indicated their rejection of alleged politics in the distribution of relief, too much executive authority, and continued deficit financing.[47]

[47]Duffy to Marvin H. McIntyre, Nov. 29, 1938, Roosevelt Papers, PPF 443; Paul Y. Anderson, "What the Election Means," Nation, CXLVII (Nov. 19, 1938), 527; Philip LaFollette, Elmer Benson, and Frank Murphy, "Why We Lost," Nation, CXLVII

279

Even though many of their former conservative enemies
had succeeded in solidifying their hold on the Republican
party, most of the Insurgents were elated over the GOP
revival in the 1938 elections. Henrik Shipstead saw the
elections as a rebuke to Roosevelt's "insolent interference
in local politics." Arthur Capper interpreted the election
as a popular mandate for Congress to dismantle parts of the
New Deal, especially "wasteful spending and farm regimentation." Wheeler said the election result demonstrated the
nation's approval of the Senate's attempts to curb presidential authority during the 75th Congress. "The people
want the Congress to become the Legislative Branch once
more instead of the mere echo of the Executive," the Montana
Insurgent declared. "Now Congress ought to take back
practically all the powers granted to the Executive during
the hysteria of the depression." Hiram Johnson agreed with
Wheeler. "We must stop this delegation of power /before7
there is no freedom left," the California Senator wrote. "I
look forward to the next session as one which will try men's
souls and put them to the acid test."[48]

(Dec. 3, 1938), 586-90; L. H. Robbins, "White Hails a 'Revolt' of the Middle Class," New York Times Magazine, VIII
(Nov. 20, 1938), 24. "What it boils down to apparently is
the following," Henry Wallace wrote to Roosevelt. "Republicans from farm sections benefited by voting for the farm
legislation. Democrats from the same kind of regions, however, did not benefit to the same extent because they were
hooked up all along the line with huge government spending,
and the farmers and the small town people recur again and
again to the thought that we have got to stop spending, and
moreover they don't like people on relief." Wallace to
Roosevelt, Dec. 15, 1938, Roosevelt Papers, PSF 22.

[48]New York Times, Dec. 29, 1938, p. 2; ibid., Dec. 25,
1938, p. 2; Time, XXXII (Nov. 21, 1938), 12-13; Johnson to
Richard M. Tobin, Dec. 12, 1938, Johnson Papers, Part III,
Box 18.

CHAPTER VIII

CONCLUSION: INSURGENT PROGRESSIVISM
VERSUS NEW DEAL LIBERALISM

As the opening of the 76th Congress neared in January, 1939, it was evident that Roosevelt and the New Deal would face a hostile Congress. Clifford Hope believed that by working with conservative Democrats the Republicans would be able to obstruct any of the more radical bills advocated by the administration. Aware of the mounting Congressional opposition to himself and to his program, the President attempted to re-establish a good working relationship with Democratic party leaders. In a series of meetings in December, 1938, Roosevelt promised not to ask for any more "must" legislation and agreed to keep his legislative lieutenants informed of his intentions. Despite these conciliatory gestures by the President, George Norris predicted that Congress would not allow any major extension of the New Deal. "The present attitude of all members of the Senate, and the House of Representatives as well, and in fact the entire country," the Nebraska Insurgent indicated, "is not favorable to any change."[1]

---

[1] Hope to Nettie Barrett, Dec. 14, 1938, Clifford R. Hope Papers, Legislative Correspondence, 1938-39, A-B Kansas State Historical Society, Topeka, Kansas; Time, XXXIII

There were two changes in New Deal policy desired by
many Congressmen—a reduction of relief spending and a
curtailment of presidential power. Early in January Roosevelt received a first-hand indication of the sentiment in
Congress for economy. When the President delivered his
annual message to the Congress, his mention of balancing
the budget was greeted with a thunderous ovation. This
anti-spending outburst, however, did not deter Roosevelt
from requesting a lump-sum appropriation of $8.75 million
for WPA in fiscal 1939. The House demonstrated its interest
in economy by cutting Roosevelt's request by $1.5 million
before passing the proposal. This was the first New Deal
relief-appropriation bill that the House had reduced below
White House requests. One reporter noted that "Representatives swelled their chests with pride," and he predicted
that the Senate would cut another $1.25 million from the
bill.[2]

The "economy clique" on the Senate Appropriations
Committee, Alva Adams, Jimmy Byrnes, and Carter Glass,
wanted to make further cuts, but they decided that to
reduce the House figure might impair the changes of passing

(Jan. 2, 1939), 5; Norris to Theodore H. Skinner, March 26,
1938, George W. Norris Papers, Tray 78, Box 6, Library of
Congress, Washington, D. C.

[2]Floyd M. Riddick, "First Session of the Seventy-
sixth Congress," American Political Science Review, XXXIII
(Dec., 1939), 1022-43; Time, XXXIII (Jan. 16, 1939), 12;
Samuel Rosenman (ed.), The Public Papers and Addresses of
Franklin D. Roosevelt, VIII (New York, 1941), 36-53; Con-
gressional Record, 76th Cong., 1st Sess., p. 343; Time,
XXXIII (Jan. 23, 1939), 11.

the measure. The committee bill included two slight modi-
fications in the House version that made the measure more
acceptable to Roosevelt. The bill now specified that relief
rolls could not be cut more than 5 per cent by April 1,
and it authorized the President to ask Congress for additional funds if an emergency arose. The full Senate began
debate on the proposal on January 24. With McNary leading
a united group of Republicans and Harrison leading the conservative Democrats, the Senate defeated an attempt by
Majority Leader Alben W. Barkley to restore the $1.5 mil-
lion to the bill.[3] The vote was close, 47 to 46, with five
Insurgents siding with the administration. "I am for
economy," Borah declared in explaining his affirmative
vote, ". . .but there are plenty of places to cut Federal
appropriations without taking it out of the hides of the
poor, helpless people on relief." Capper, who voted against
the bill, reasoned that Roosevelt could always request more
funds if he needed them, and he rejoiced that things were
"Looking a lot better around Washington." Hiram Johnson
agreed. "It is a happy augury," the California Senator wrote
his son, ". . .for it has taught a lot of weak-kneed Senators that they can stand up and vote as their consciences
dictate without falling dead."[4]

---

[3]For McNary's and Harrison's roles respectively, see
Walter K. Roberts, "The Political Career of Charles Linza
McNary, 1924-1944" (Ph.D. Thesis, University of North Carolina,
1953), pp. 257-58; and Robert S. Allen, "WPA—or the Dole,"
Nation, CXLVIII (Jan. 28, 1939), 111-12.

[4]New York Times, Jan. 19, 1939, p. 1; James T. Patterson, Congressional Conservatism and the New Deal (Lexington,

After the Barkley amendment was defeated, the Senate
quickly approved the House's $7.25 million relief bill.
This did not end the executive-legislative controversy over
WPA funds, however, for two weeks later Roosevelt demanded
that Congress grant him the $1.5 million it had just deleted.
The President accompanied this request with a statement
forecasting increased hardship for the unemployed unless
Congress consented to appropriate the additional money. In
the House, the relief bill became a pawn in a battle over
appropriations between urban and rural Congressmen. Just
prior to a vote on the $1.5 million request, urban Democrats
vetoed a farm-subsidy proposal deemed necessary by rural
legislators. This action infuriated William Lemke, who
criticized "City Congressmen" for never supporting meaning-
ful farm legislation in return for the farm bloc's cooperation in enacting the New Deal's urban-oriented measures.
Concurring with Lemke's assessment, the rural-dominated
House Subcommittee on Relief Appropriations sliced one-half
million dollars from the WPA bill. A few days later the
House again ignored Roosevelt's recommendations for emergency
relief spending and instead granted him only $1 million.[5]

Ky., 1967), p. 296; Johnson to Hiram Johnson, Jr., Jan. 29,
1939, Hiram W. Johnson Papers, Part IV, Box 4, Bancroft
Library, University of California, Berkeley. Borah, Frazier,
LaFollette, Norris, and Wheeler among the Insurgents voted
to restore the $1.5 million to the Senate bill, but Capper,
Johnson, Nye, and Shipstead voted against it. Congressional
Record, 76th Cong., 1st Sess., p. 887.

[5]Rosenman (ed.), Public Papers of FDR, VIII, 83-85;
Congressional Record, 76th Cong., 1st Sess., p. 4825; Lemke
to William G. Goodwin, June 15, 1939, William Lemke Papers,
Box 16, The Orin G. Libby Manuscript Collection, University

Realizing the futility of championing the full $1.5 million request in the Senate, Barkley advised his colleagues to acquiesce in the House bill. Senate liberals were furious over Barkley's position. "There /is̅/ no one to crack the whip or keep the votes lined up," LaFollette complained. Florida's Claude Pepper, a rabid New Dealer, decided to revolt against the Senate's Democratic leadership and announced that he would conduct the floor fight for the administration. Brandishing a letter from Roosevelt outlining the need for the full $1.5 million, Pepper pleaded for the support of his colleagues in voting more relief funds. Hiram Johnson, however, declared that he would not vote for any more lump-sum relief expenditures in the name of human misery when "petty politics have been played with human beings, who could not help themselves, whose very subsistence, and next meal indeed, depended on the man over them." Many other Senators believed that there had been too many "crises" and "emergencies" during the past six years and declared that they wanted a "breathing-spell." The Senate easily defeated the Pepper amendment by a vote of 49 to 28. This time only LaFollette, Norris, and Wheeler among the Insurgents voted with the administration forces.[6]

---

of North Dakota Library, Grand Forks, North Dakota; New York Times, April 1, 1939, p. 1.

[6]Harold L. Ickes, The Secret Diary of Harold L. Ickes, II (New York, 1954), 612; Patterson, Congressional Conservatism, pp. 302-05; Johnson to Hiram Johnson, Jr., Jan. 14, 1939, Johnson Papers, Part IV, Box 4; Time, XXXIII (March 27, 1939), 13-14; Congressional Record, 76th Cong., 1st Sess., p. 4109.

Although most Insurgents obviously disliked some aspects of the New Deal's relief and spending policies, they readily discarded their scruples about economy when it came to the governmental subsidies to agriculture. In addition to the $8.75 million appropriation for WPA, the President's January budget message had included an $8.4 million request for farm programs in fiscal 1940. The farm bill had been bottled up in the House earlier by urban Congressmen who resented the action of their rural colleagues in paring WPA funds. In the Senate, however, even the economizers on the Appropriations Committee could not resist the demands of the farm bloc. After the committee added nearly $4 million to the farm bill, the Senate, with unanimous Insurgent support, overwhelmingly approved the measure. Only a month after most of them had opposed a request for additional relief expenditures, all the Insurgents thus voted for an inflated farm bill. Capper argued that farm subsidies were essential expenditures since agriculture was the basis of all national prosperity. Wheeler was more candid in his explanation. "I don't like government spending," the Montana Senator proclaimed, "but as long as we allow labor and industry to fix the price of things the farmer has to buy, we must continue to increase farm subsidies."[7]

---

[7]Congressional Record, 76th Cong., 1st Sess., p. 5294; Capper Radio Address, March 13, 1939, Arthur Capper Papers, Agriculture, Reciprocal Trade-Wheat, Kansas State Historical Society, Topeka, Kansas; interview with Burton K. Wheeler, Nov. 22, 1968.

Insurgent inconsistency on the matter of public spending was also demonstrated with regard to the so-called lend-
spend bill. In late June, 1938, with the country still
feeling the effects of the recession, Roosevelt suggested
that Congress appropriate $3.86 billion for a series of
self-liquidating construction projects. The spenders within
the administration considered this sum too small an allotment to stimulate a lethargic economy, but the Congressional
conservatives viewed the amount as too large a burden for
an already bankrupt treasury. In the Senate, Harry F. Byrd
led an effort to slash the appropriation; by the time the
bill came to a vote, he had managed to cut more than $1.4
billion from the President's original request. These reductions proved to be remarkably selective. One historian
has noted that the economy bloc had carefully left alone
the provisions for rural electrification and farm security
so that the bill looked suspiciously like another farm
bill. On July 31 the Senate finally approved its handiwork
by a vote of 52 to 28.[8] The bill then went to the House
Rules Committee where it was pared even further before the
full House rejected it altogether. "This vote marked the
end of an era," Clifford Hope wrote. "It was the first

[8]Rosenman (ed.), Public Papers of FDR, VIII, 372-75;
Patterson, Congressional Conservatism, pp. 320-21; Congres-
sional Record, 76th Cong., 1st Sess., p. 10512; Henrik
Shipstead Speech, July 1, 1939, Henrik Shipstead Papers,
Box 26, Minnesota Historical Society, St. Paul, Minnesota.

clear-cut repudiation by Congress of the theory that we can spend ourselves into prosperity."[9]

The 76th Congress, indeed, had demonstrated its deep hostility toward continued governmental spending for relief. To some extent the Insurgents shared this anti-spending sentiment—47 per cent of the total Insurgent vote had been cast against the two WPA supplemental appropriations bills of the session. Their knowledge of the sad plight of much of the American farm community and their genuine concern for all needy citizens, however, usually prevented most of the Insurgents from joining their more conservative colleagues in seeking blanket reductions in relief expenditures. This sympathy for the underprivileged did not, however, silence Insurgent criticism of New Deal relief legislation. Most of them continued to object to the lack of Congressional control over the distribution of relief funds, and some of them suspected that the administration was using relief money for political purposes. Since every Insurgent favored a balanced budget, their most persistent criticism of the New Deal's relief policy was that it added to the mounting federal deficit without attempting to increase the government's revenue. For the most part, the Insurgents thus supported the efforts of LaFollette to levy higher taxes on

---

[9]Hope to Perry White, August 3, 1939, Hope Papers, Legislative Correspondence, 1938-39, Farm-G; Congressional Record, 76th Cong., 1st Sess., p. 10717.

large corporate and personal incomes to aid in the financing of necessary relief appropriations.[10]

If the voting record of the Insurgents on the issues of public spending was ambivalent, their support of measures designed to curb executive power and to regain legislative prerogatives was unequivocal. Nothing demonstrated this better than the battle over the Reorganization Act of 1939. Soon after the 1938 elections, Roosevelt informed North Carolina Representative Lindsay Warren of his desire to push again for some sort of executive reorganization bill. "It is my thought that if we can dress up the old. . .bill in a new suit of clothes," the President wrote Warren, "a lot of people who voted against us before might in the new Congress come back to us." Warren agreed but advised that the original reorganization measure would have to be "drastically curtailed." Roosevelt readily accepted this advice and suggested that Warren and some of his fellow Congressmen redraft the proposal. The subsequent House bill deleted all the objectionable features of the original proposal by retaining the Comptroller-General and authorizing the President to submit reorganization plans subject to a veto by a majority of both Houses of Congress. This diluted version of the executive reorganization bill easily swept through the House in a 246 to 153 vote.[11]

---

[10]Robert M. LaFollette, Jr., "Taxes Should Be Higher— But Fewer and Direct," Saturday Evening Post, CCX (June 11, 1938), 23, 32, 34; New York Times, June 25, 1937, p. 20.

[11]Roosevelt to Warren, Nov. 16, 1938, Franklin D. Roosevelt Papers, PSF 51, Franklin D. Roosevelt Library, Hyde Park, New York; Richard Polenberg, Reorganizing

Observers who predicted swift Senate action on the
bill neglected to consider Burton K. Wheeler's hatred of
centralized power and his personal desire to embarrass
Roosevelt. "I think the Senate this next session will be
more independent than it has been during the last six
years," Wheeler had predicted in late 1938. "This doesn't
mean that the Senate is going to oppose any and all New
Deal legislation. It does mean that we are not going to
be a lot of Charley McCarthys." Wheeler reintroduced his
amendment requiring both Houses of Congress to approve
reorganization plans before they could go into effect.
Wheeler's amendment carried by the margin of 45 to 44, with
all the Insurgents except LaFollette and Norris voting in
the affirmative. Byrnes immediately offered a motion to
reconsider, which succeeded because Borah refused to vote
for anything resembling cloture. "This was something of a
blow to those of us who had been fighting all along, and it
was more than a blow coming, as it did, from Borah," wrote
an exasperated Hiram Johnson. "Had Borah. . .voted to table
the motion, the matter would have been ended, and no power
could resurrect it."[12]

The administration mustered enough strength the next
day to defeat Wheeler's proposal, 46 to 44. The two new

Roosevelt's Government (Cambridge, Mass., 1966), chapt. IX;
J. M. Ray, "The Defeat of the Administration Reorganization,"
Southwestern Social Science Quarterly, XX (Sept., 1939),
115.

[12]New York Times, Oct. 16, 1938, p. 1; Paul Y. Anderson, "Reorganization and Bunk," Nation, CXLVI (April 9,
1938), 406-07; Johnson to Hiram Johnson, Jr., March 26,
1939, Johnson Papers, Part IV, Box 4.

administration votes came from Missouri's Harry Truman, who
had been absent on the previous day, and New Mexico's Dennis
Chavez. Chavez had initially voted for the Wheeler amendment, but he quickly announced that he had changed his mind
when he was assured that the Forestry Service was protected
from any reorganization plan. The Insurgents, who had had
no respect for Chavez since his appointment to replace
Bronson Cutting in 1935, discounted as a falsehood the New
Mexico Senator's explanation for his sudden switch. "The
Administration bought Chavez, the half-breed from New Mexico,"
sneered Johnson, ". . .so the fat was in the fire, and
Wheeler's amendment was beaten."[13]

Defeated in its bid to curb Roosevelt's power to reorganize the executive branch, the Senate moved to restrict
presidential authority in several other areas. Late in the
session most of the Insurgents successfully combined with
Republicans and conservative Democrats to deny the President
the power to devalue the dollar, a right he had received
under the Thomas amendment to the AAA in 1933. The 1939
Congress further extended its control over the executive
branch of government by enacting the Hatch Act to regulate
state primary elections and by commissioning House

[13]Johnson to Hiram Johnson, Jr., March 26, 1939, John-
son Papers, Part IV, Box 4; Congressional Record, 76th
Cong., 1st Sess., pp. 3050-51; 3093; Ickes, Secret Diary,
II, 603.

investigations of the WPA and the NLRB. Congress also abolished the undistributed-profits tax.[14]

There can be no doubt that the 76th Congress had declared its independence from Franklin D. Roosevelt and, to
a lesser extent, from the New Deal. "Clark Gable or John
Barrymore, Rudy Vallee or Joe Dimaggio could have done as
well in the White House as Franklin D. Roosevelt," William
Allen White wrote in August, 1939. In his second term,
according to White, the President had won no major clash
with Congress and was so badly weakened politically that he
could not unite the Republican progressives and the Democratic liberals behind his programs and had succeeded in
uniting only the Republican and Democratic conservatives.
Roosevelt himself partially agreed with White's assessment. In the midst of the controversy over the second
WPA deficiency appropriation bill, he privately admitted that he had all but given up hope that Congress would
enact any of his suggestions into law. "I recommend what
I think is needed," he told Josephus Daniles, "and leave it
to them to cut so deep that people will go hungry or be
denied work which is needed." To Pennsylvania's Democratic
Senator Joseph E. Guffey, the President acknowledged that a
bipartisan coalition of conservatives in the Congress had
halted the advance of the New Deal. "Isn't it a pity!" he
lamented. "Why is it that Democrats have to hook up with

---

[14]Congressional Record, 76th Cong., 1st Sess., p. 7867;
Allen Seymour Everest, Morgenthau, The New Deal and Silver
(New York, 1950), pp. 69-75; "Saved by the Bell," Nation,
CXLIX (Aug. 12, 1939), 163-64.

reactionary Republicans?" Despite the obvious shackling of
Roosevelt by Congress and its obstruction of the New Deal,
Burton K. Wheeler still exhorted the American public to
continue its study of "the effects of all existing legislation" in an effort to prevent "financial and political
bankruptcy—dictatorship."[15]

In 1932 many of the Insurgents had labored ardently for
Roosevelt's election, and until late 1936 most of them lauded
Roosevelt's performance as President. "We're nearer our
philosophy of government that we have ever been in my lifetime in this nation,"[16] exclaimed Hiram Johnson during the
President's first term. In Roosevelt's second term, however,
many Insurgents thought of Roosevelt as a would-be dictator,
and they denounced much of the New Deal for allegedly contributing to the destruction of American government and the
erosion of American society.

After the initial enthusiasm for the Roosevelt reforms,
most of the Insurgents eventually become alienated from the
New Deal. "Man oh man," sighed Gerald P. Nye, "if only it
could have ended after four years."[17] The Insurgents, to be
sure, never embraced the philosophy of the First New Deal,

---

[15]New York Times, Aug. 20, 1939, p. 30; Roosevelt to
Daniels, April 14, 1939, Roosevelt Papers, PPF 86; Roosevelt
to Guffey, August 1, 1939, Roosevelt Papers, PSF 62; New
York Times, Dec. 9, 1939, p. 10.

[16]Johnson to Hiram Johnson, Jr., April 1, 1933,
Johnson Papers, Part IV, Box 4.

[17]Gerald P. Nye Lecture Series, "North Dakota and the
New Deal," (University of North Dakota, Nov. 15, 1967),
Tape MR 69-3 (1), Roosevelt Papers.

but they enthusiastically welcomed the attack upon the corporate and financial interests by what they regarded as a
Second New Deal. Even this brief flurry of "antimonopolistic"
legislation in 1935, however, was not altogether consonant
with the undiluted brand of Insurgent progressivism. The
Insurgents still complained about the expansion of the power
of the federal government, incessant executive experimentation, and large government deficits. They consoled themselves at first, however, with the thought that many of the
New Deal's objectionable features were to be only temporary
in nature.

The 1936 election served to strengthen the apprehen-
sions of the Insurgents concerning Roosevelt and the New
Deal. Their immediate worry was that the President, with
his overwhelming electoral victory and with a heavy Democratic majority in Congress, would feel himself free from
all restraints in the exercise of executive authority;
Roosevelt's espousal of the Court plan only a few months
later proved to the Insurgents that their fears in this
regard were well-founded. The composition of Roosevelt's
majority in 1936 was also a significant factor in leading to
the disaffection of the Insurgents with the New Deal. The
legislative demands of the new Democratic coalition, including as it did urban dwellers, labor unionists, and ethnic
minority groups, resulted in the institutionalization of
many of the characteristics that the Insurgents most disliked about New Deal reformism. According to most of the
Insurgents, federal housing programs, increased government

spending, and minimum wage laws all expanded presidential power, circumscribed the daily life of the individual, and created a more divided society.

"When Roosevelt took office," William E. Leuchtenberg has written, "the country, to a very large degree, responded to the will of a single element; the white, Anglo-Saxon, Protestant, property-holding class. Under the New Deal, new groups took their place in the sun. It was not merely that they received benefits they had not received before but that they were 'recognized' as having a place in the commonwealth." As representatives of rural regions or small towns, the Insurgents sometimes found it difficult to comprehend the novel and pragmatic response of the New Deal to the demands of urban dwellers and labor unionists. For many Insurgents, the bedlam in Washington during the 1930's proved to be both confusing and discouraging. As a Democratic member of the United States Senate, Wheeler complained of the mental and political frustration involved in having to favor one piece of legislation on a particular day and then being forced to move in an entirely different direction a few days later. "Once liberals were against monopolies and price fixing, but. . .no one can say definitely what will be the outcome of all this confusion," the Montana Senator complained. Most of the Insurgents urged the administration to plot a specific course of action and then stay with it. In addition to making their lives intellectually less complicated, the Insurgents maintained that a consistent policy of reform would contribute

295

to economic recovery and would make less likely the passage
of what they regarded as the more bizarre pieces of New Deal
legislation.[18]

The belief that the administration, particularly
during Roosevelt's second term, catered to the interests of
the large cities was certainly a factor in the growing Insurgent disquiet about the New Deal. Many of the Insurgent
votes against the administration during Roosevelt's second
term were motivated by a rural bias. Despite the large
amounts of money received by the agricultural areas in
parity payments and other farm subsidies, most of the Insurgents insisted that the urban-oriented legislation of
the New Deal benefited the metropolitan areas at the expense of the agricultural states. The Insurgents, who
regularly voted for special legislation for farmers,
believed that urban-oriented measures deprived their rural
districts of federal funds. Because of their rural
predilections and their innate anti-urban prejudices, the
Insurgents often held legislation designed to alleviate
urban problems responsible for the New Deal's shortcomings.
Describing "almost all the great cities" as "reeling with graft,"
Wheeler thus asserted that "the way to balance the budget is
for New York, Chicago, Butte, and other cities to look

---

[18]William E. Leuchtenberg, Franklin D. Roosevelt and
the New Deal, 1932-1940 (New York, 1963), p. 332; Otis L.
Graham, Jr., An Encore for Reform: The Old Progressives and
the New Deal (New York, 1967), p. 166; New York Times, IV,
May 9, 1937, 10; Bernard Sternsher, "The New Deal 'Revolution,'" Social Studies, LXVI (April, 1966), 157.

after their own needs instead of coming down to Washington and putting pressures on Congressmen."[19]

Moreover, the Insurgents were by no means convinced that the increased amount of urban-oriented legislation after 1936 was motivated solely by the altruistic desire of the New Deal to relieve human suffering; some Insurgents were convinced that the legislation was designed to insure the perpetuation of Franklin D. Roosevelt in office. "The way the big city machines have been clicking in behalf of the New Deal Administration has me worried," a friend wrote Arthur Capper. "It is my opinion that if these machines continue unhindered we in the small towns or on the farms will have less than nothing to say about elections. Is there nothing Congress can do about breaking up these machines and exposing the rotteness which is bound to be at the core of them?" Capper responded to this plea by introducing a Constitutional amendment to exclude aliens from the population in the apportionment of seats for the House of Representatives. The Kansas Senator hoped that his amendment would eliminate at least thirty-three representatives from the states of New York, Pennsylvania, Illinois, Massachusetts, and California, "whose seats would then very properly go to other states." The opposition of the Insurgents to the "urban spirit" of the New Deal might not have been as pronounced had they approved of the administration's farm program. For the most part, however, they agreed with

---

[19] New York Times, Oct. 16, 1937, p. 6; ibid., Feb. 18, 1939, p. 5.

William Lemke, who claimed that "city radicals" had even
drafted the New Deal's agricultural legislation, which, as
he saw it, did nothing but "place 88,000 inspectors on the
farmer's shoulders."[20]

The Insurgents complained even more persistently about
the collectivist approach to reform followed by the New Deal
than they did about what they regarded as its confusion and
its catering to urban dwellers. Insurgent progressivism
envisioned the state as playing the role of a policeman,
moving intermittently against "special privilege" to preserve equality of opportunity and individual freedom of
choice; but it did not include the welfare-state liberalism
of the New Deal, the permanent and large-scale government
involvement in the daily lives of the people. This did not
mean that the Insurgents opposed all governmental intervention in the economy, for they had been among the first
and most fervent advocates of federally financed relief
programs to aid in the war against poverty. By the late
1930's, however, they had become convinced that the government's largess was more harmful than helpful, and they
wished that President Franklin D. Roosevelt would somehow
magically transform himself into the budget-balancing
Governor of New York who had been so prominent in the 1932
campaign. Far from making the poor self-supporting, the
Insurgents contended that New Deal reformism had resulted

---

[20] George C. Cook to Capper, Nov. 13, 1940, Capper
Papers, General Correspondence, New-OPA; New York Times,
Feb. 3, 1939, p. 8; Lemke to Frank Nechas, June 20, 1939,
Lemke Papers, Box 16.

in the formation of a cumbersome federal bureaucracy whose
paternalism further eroded individual self-reliance. "The
New Deal marked a complete turn-around of American attitudes,"
recalled Gerald P. Nye. "Before this there was an emphasis
on individual freedom and thrift. The New Deal was the. . .
beginning of a welfare state. People now place as much
dependence on Government as upon themselves, and in some
instances, even more dependence."[21]

In addition to its allegedly being detrimental to individual liberty, the New Deal's welfare-state liberalism,
according to the Insurgents, incited class against class.
They were willing to admit that the New Deal had been in-
strumental in checking some of the more obvious corporate
and financial abuses, but, in the end, they believed that
it had created forms of special privilege just as dangerous
as those it had destroyed. The Insurgents also maintained
that the various New Deal agencies fostered and protected a
myriad of special interest groups; as evidence of this, they
pointed in particular to the CIO's relationship to the NLRB.
The institutionalization of diverse interest groups, most
Insurgents believed, encouraged each group to continue its
demands upon government for special favors. The ensuing
acrimonious competition among these organized groups for
public funds made it difficult to attain a harmonious society
united in the pursuit of the national interest. "The old

---

[21]New York Times, April 25, 1938, p. 2; Lemke to L.
O. Harnrick, April 23, 1938, Lemke Papers, Box 13; Gerald P.
Nye Lecture Series, "North Dakota and the New Deal," (Uni-
versity of North Dakota, Nov. 15, 1967), Tape MR 69-3 (1),
Roosevelt Papers.

statesman has passed," sighed Hiram Johnson, "and the time
when men were judged by the service to the country as a
whole is gone." To most of the Insurgents, the results of
the New Deal's broker-state politics were disastrous. "The
methods employed appeared to have been brewed in the caldron
of economic ignorance and class hatreds," declared Henrik
Shipstead. ". . .Prejudices generated by the New Deal leave
our people more divided than at any time throughout our
whole history. A house so divided cannot long stand."[22]

Although the Insurgents found themselves increasingly
at odds with much of the welfare-state legislation recommended by the administration during Roosevelt's second term,
their criticisms were directed less against the legislation
as such than against the large expansion of the federal
government's authority which had occurred under the New
Deal. To be sure, most of the Insurgents had begun their
Congressional careers as advocates of federal intervention
in the economy, mainly to destroy trusts, to aid agriculture,
and to harness water power, but they believed that federal
authority had expanded so greatly under the New Deal that the
Roosevelt administration possessed as much power as the
despotic governments of some of the contemporary European
states. Sounding like Lord Acton, Borah lamented in November, 1939, that "the centralization of political power inevitably tends toward the corruption of that power."

---

[22] Johnson to Colonel Frank G. Snook, June 7, 1937,
Johnson Papers, Part III, Box 17; Shipstead to E. M.
Ferguson, March 28, 1939, Shipstead Papers, Box 2.

By the late 1930's this fear of concentrated governmental power caused many Insurgents to attack Big Government
with all the vigor and ferocity they earlier had directed
against Big Business. "My own feeling," one Insurgent claimed,
"is that while the times, the issues, and the leaders have
changed, my basic outlook has remained the same." Most Insurgents echoed this claim of consistency, but many of them,
in their criticism of the powerful state erected by the New
Deal, sounded like reactionary conservatives. "Businessmen
of the nation," Burton K. Wheeler said in exhorting his
former enemies, "must bear the responsibility of seeing that
the United States does not abandon democracy for a state
resembling Fascist Italy or Nazi Germany." Henrik Shipstead charged the New Deal with destroying the traditional
form of American government. "The Federal Government is a
creature of the States with limited authority from the
sovereign States," the Minnesota Senator claimed in language
reminiscent of John C. Calhoun. "When the Federal Government ignores this fact, the pillars of a people's government,
founded on the sovereignty of the people of the States, are
torn down, one by one."[23]

Not only did some of the Insurgents sound like the
conservatives they had formerly criticized so vehemently,
but also most of their individual voting records during the
75th and 76th Congresses were distinctly anti-New Deal. On

---

[23]New York Times, Nov. 15, 1939, p. 14; Burton K.
Wheeler, Yankee From the West (Garden City, N. Y., 1962),
p. 428; New York Times, June 12, 1937, p. 5; Henrik Shipstead Speech, undated, Shipstead Papers, Box 22.

eighteen key roll calls during the 1937-1939 period, the Insurgents recorded themselves agains the New Deal 66.2 per
cent of the time. On the same roll calls, the ten "most
conservative" Senate Democrats and the Republican Senatorial
membership voted against the New Deal 81.6 and 96.2 per cent
of the time, respectively. Although the Insurgents as a
group did not oppose the administration as much as the
"irreconcilable" Democrats or "reactionary" Republicans
did, the individual voting records of most of them for the
years 1937-1939 are conservative enough to warrant including
them as members of the bipartisan congressional coalition
that so effectively blocked much of the legislation proposed by Roosevelt during his second term.[24]

The anti-New Deal voting records of most Insurgents
not only indicated their disapproval of welfare-state
liberalism and a concomitant expansion of government authority, but it also demonstrated their fear of the concentration of power in the hands of Franklin D. Roosevelt.
Many of the Insurgents accused the President of using power
for purely political and personal ends. "The Administration
stands indicted because is has placed its desire for power
ahead of the general problem of unemployment," declared
Arthur Capper. Hiram Johnson agreed with his fellow Insurgent. "He is sure of just one thing, and that is the
politics of the situation," the California Senator said of
the President. "Through thick and thin he will stand with

---

[24]For a compilation of individual Insurgent voting
records from 1937-1939, see Appendix B.

the labor unions and those upon relief or working for the W.P.A., no matter what the right or wrong may be, knowing that his political fortunes can only thus thrive." Johnson maintained that Roosevelt bordered on being a megalomaniac and that his insatiable hunger for power was motivated by more than just a desire to perpetuate himself in office. "This President of ours is so anxious to lead the world. . . that he will go to any lengths," Johnson informed his son. "It does not make any difference that his position is illogical or injurious to the country, he thinks that he can make history, and by golly, he is going to do it at all hazards."[25]

By 1939 some of the Insurgents were obsessed with the belief that Roosevelt wanted to become a dictator. Since Congress, in their view, had thwarted the President's dictatorial designs by rejecting the Court plan and the first reorganization proposal, some of the Insurgents believed that Roosevelt would attempt to consummate his longing for absolute power by involving the country in a foreign war. "I am entirely satisfied that the President desires to take us into war," Johnson warned in May, 1939. "We have kept up such an agitation for keeping out that he has not dared to do it, as yet; but, if he could get us

---

[25]*New York Times*, June 26, 1939, p. 5; Johnson to Hiram Johnson, Jr., March 5, 1938, March 19, 1939, Johnson Papers, Part IV, Box 4.

out of here, even for a short period of time, by some act,
the nature of which we cannot now conceive, he would make
war necessary."[26]

Even prior to Johnson's prediction Roosevelt had tried,
in the opinion of Gerald P. Nye, to involve the United
States in the European war. On January 11, 1939, Senator
Key Pittman announced the administration's desire for a
repeal of the arms embargo and for other revisions in the
neutrality laws allowing more presidential discretion in
conducting the nation's foreign affairs. Nye contended
that Roosevelt was definitely "drifting from a strict 'keep
out of war policy'. . .at precisely the time when he was
failing in domestic policy." The Senate, with the Insurgents playing a leading role, was able to block a change
in the neutrality laws this time, but after Germany in-
vaded Poland on September 1, 1939, Roosevelt called a
special session of Congress which granted him the requested
neutrality revisions by a vote of 63 to 30. Choosing to
ignore the threat a Nazi-dominated Europe would pose to
the national security of the United States, Hiram Johnson
held the conservative Democrats responsible for the
President's victory. "There is a certain class of Democrats, the kid-glove group from the Southern states, who
have always felt uneasy since the purge last year, and have
been looking for a more comfortable seat in the Democratic

[26]Johnson to John Bassett Moore, May 12, 1939, Johnson
Papers, Part III, Box 18.

party," the California Senator wrote. "They found it this
year on the war issue."[27]

Roosevelt's support for a policy of aid to the Allies
after the war in Europe broke out was not the initial cause
for the estrangement of most of the Insurgents from the
President and the New Deal, but it served as the final
determinant of the break between them. Most of the Insurgents saw in Roosevelt's foreign policy beginning in 1939
the same thirst for power they had come to see in some of
his domestic legislation. They feared that the administration's foreign policy would serve further to strengthen
the state's control over the individual and would further
magnify the power of the presidency. It was the differing
attitudes about the power of the state and the power of the
presidency that really distinguished the Insurgents' brand
of progressivism from the New Deal's brand of liberalism.
"I wonder sometimes," Hiram Johnson could thus write in
January, 1939, "if we, who've continued in the faith which
we originally have chosen, and who have not deviated from
it at all, are doomed to see the world pass us by. As I
listen to the so-called 'liberals' of today, who trembled
and shook when liberalism was not fashionable, and who have
no understanding of it now, except that it means following

---

[27]Wayne S. Cole, "Senator Key Pittman and American
Neutrality Policies, 1933-1940," Mississippi Valley Historical Review, XLVI (March, 1960), 644-62; Congressional
Record, 76th Cong., 2nd Sess., Appendix, pp. 89-91; Johnson
to Hiram Johnson, Jr., Oct. 28, 1938, Johnson Papers, Part
IV, Box 4. All the Insurgents except Norris voted against
the administration in its efforts to revise the neutrality
legislation in 1939.

where power is the greatest, we may be pardoned a cynical

grin. However, there is nothing to do but with stout heart

go on for the end."[28]

The charges by most of the Insurgents that the Roose-

velt administration disregarded the traditional American

system of values and eroded the traditional form of American

government were, of course, exaggerated, for, if anything,

the New Deal can justly be regarded as the savior of the

nation's capitalistic-democratic structure. Regardless of

the factual basis for people's beliefs, however, it is what

they think to be true that is important, and by 1939 most

of the Insurgents thought of Roosevelt and the New Deal as

being destructive of individual freedom. To Harold L.

Ickes, it was surprising that so many of the Insurgents,

acting as "blocs of one," agreed that much of the New Deal

legislation during Roosevelt's second term was ruinous to

the type of society they envisioned for America. "I suppose

that Borah, Johnson, and company are too old to change

their ways," the septuagenarian Ickes wrote in 1939, "and

they have gone much farther to the right than /they/ were

ever to the left."[29]

Being avowed independents, not all the Insurgents

turned against the New Deal as "Borah, Johnson, and company"

did. In fact, both LaFollette and Norris continued to be

dependable supporters of the administration—during the

---

[28]Johnson to Franklin Hickborn, Jan. 5, 1939, Johnson Papers, Part III, Box 18.

[29]Ickes to Raymond Robins, Sept. 18, 1939, Raymond Robins Papers, Box 28, State Historical Society of Wisconsin, Madison, Wisconsin.

1937-1939 period LaFollette and Norris voted in favor of
New Deal legislation 76.5 per cent and 93.7 per cent of the
time, respectively.[30] LaFollette's major disagreement with
New Deal legislation was in the area of agricultural policy;
the Wisconsin Senator believed that the cost-of-production
approach rather than production control was the way to raise
the prices of farm commodities. Norris primarily objected
to what he regarded as the President's partisan acceptance
of the spoils system.

The expansion of their progressivism to include welfare-
state liberalism explains, to a large degree, the affinity
of LaFollette and Norris for most of the New Deal's legislative program. By the 1930's both men believed that the
primary function of "a progressive form of government" was
to provide relief to the underprivileged classes of the
nation. In fact, LaFollette's conception of the duty of
the state was to the left of that of many New Dealers. "If
private employment fails," the Wisconsin Senator stated
twelve years before the enactment of the Full Employment Act
of 1946, "then the government should provide every person
able and willing to work with a job at decent wages."[31]

---

[30]Excluding LaFollette and Norris, the Insurgents as a
group voted against the New Deal 81.2 per cent of the time
during Roosevelt's second term.

[31]Norris to Claude Pepper, August 28, 1939, Roosevelt
Papers, PSF 62; New York Times, August 13, 1934, p. 4. Both
LaFollette and Norris realized that the failure of the New
Deal meant a return to Hooverism, a state of affairs desired
by neither man. LaFollette, a much younger man than most of
the other Insurgents, recognized almost from the start of his
Senatorial career the need for a national welfare state to
solve the nation's unemployment and urban crises. See

LaFollette and Norris, moreover, never distrusted
Roosevelt as most of the other Insurgents eventually did.
Frequent conferences at the White House throughout the 1930's
accounted for much of the faith and respect both men held
for the President. "I have had many confidential conferences
with Mr. Roosevelt," Norris wrote in August, 1939, "and
while he has made mistakes,. . .the cry that is being made
by his enemies that he is trying to set himself up as a
'dictator' is entirely without foundation. . .and utterly
foolish." Roosevelt also regularly praised Norris and
LaFollette. He lauded Norris as the personification of all
that was good about American liberalism, and it was rumored
that he preferred LaFollette as either his successor or
running mate in 1940.[32] Also, by the mid-1930's both
LaFollette and Norris had concluded that the Republican
party was a hopelessly reactionary organization, and they
usually made decisions free from the restraints of partisanship. By 1940 most of the Insurgents had completely rejected Roosevelt and the New Deal and had reaffirmed their
allegiance to the GOP, but Norris in that year headed the

Mauritz A. Hallgren, "Young Bob LaFollette," Nation, CXXII
(March 4, 1931), 235; Mark Rhea Byers, "A New LaFollette
Party," North American Review, CCXXXVII (May, 1934), 407;
and Wallace S. Sayre, "Left Turn in Wisconsin," New Republic,
LXXX (Oct. 24, 1934), 300-02.

[32]Norris to Pepper, August 28, 1939, Roosevelt Papers,
PSF 62; George W. Norris, Fighting Liberal: The Autobiography of George W. Norris (Collier Books Edition: New York,
1961), p. 18. "If Roosevelt thought of any of the Progressives as his successor," Arthur M. Schlesinger, Jr., has
written, "it was certainly the quiet, tough-minded Senator
from Wisconsin." Schlesinger, The Politics of Upheaval
(Boston, 1960), p. 136.

National Committee of Independent Voters for Roosevelt, and
LaFollette, despite his disagreement with the administration's foreign policy, supported Roosevelt because of the
New Deal's domestic accomplishments.[33] For these two Insurgents, unlike their colleagues, the New Deal appeared
to be consistent with the Progressive tradition rather than
being a break with the nation's reform past.

---

[33]Donald R. McCoy, "The Progressive National Committee
of 1936," Western Political Quarterly, IX (June, 1956), 455;
Roger T. Johnson, Robert M. LaFollette, Jr. and the Decline
of the Progressive Party in Wisconsin (Madison, Wisc., 1964),
chapt. 11.

APPENDIX A

SELECTIVE AMENDMENTS INDICATIVE OF INSURGENT UNEASINESS

WITH THE FIRST NEW DEAL—73rd CONGRESS, SENATE

Amendment
Number   Issue

Agricultural Adjustment Act

1. Motion striking out Norris amendment, which would have
    given the farmer the cost of production. Passed 48-
    33. Vote no is anti-New Deal.

2. Frazier amendment, reducing interest rate to $1\frac{1}{2}$ per
    cent on farm loans. Defeated 25-44. Vote aye is
    anti-New Deal.

3. Wheeler amendment, free silver at 16-1. Defeated 33-
    43. Vote aye is anti-New Deal.

Gold Reserve Act

4. Wheeler amendment, free silver at 16-1. Defeated 43-
    45. Vote aye is anti-New Deal.

Civil Works Emergency Relief Act

5. Cutting amendment, increasing the appropriation by
    $1.5 billion. Defeated 10-58. Vote aye is anti-New
    Deal.

6. LaFollette amendment, increasing the appropriation by
    $500 million. Defeated 14-52. Vote aye is anti-New
    Deal.

Internal Revenue Act (1934)

7. LaFollette amendment, raising individual income taxes
    in the higher brackets. Defeated 36-47. Vote aye is
    anti-New Deal.

8. Murphy amendment, redefining capital gains and losses, and taxation of same. Defeated 36-42. Vote aye is anti-New Deal.

9. Motion striking out Borah amendment, forbidding consolidated corporation returns. Passed 40-37. Vote no is anti-New Deal.

10. Borah amendment, forbidding tax exemptions on dividends of subsidiary companies. Defeated 33-39. Vote aye is anti-New Deal.

Securities Exchange Act

11. Costigan amendment, requiring the Federal Trade Commission to administer the act. Defeated 29-51. Vote aye is anti-New Deal.

12. Bulkley amendment, requiring more stringent margin requirements. Defeated 30-48. Vote aye is anti-New Deal.

Reciprocal Trade Agreements Act

13. Johnson amendment, forbidding reciprocal tariff agreements covering agricultural products. Defeated 33-54. Vote aye is anti-New Deal.

14. Johnson amendment, forbidding a reduction of tariffs on agricultural products. Defeated 32-53. Vote aye is anti-New Deal.

15. Johnson amendments, requiring Congressional approval of trade agreements. Defeated 29-46. Vote aye is anti-New Deal.

Senator	Per Cent Anti-New Deal	Anti-New Deal 1	2	3	4	5	6	7	8	9	10	11	12	13	14	15	Pro-New Deal 1	2	3	4	5	6	7	8	9	10	11	12	13	14	15
Borah	73.3	x	–	–	x	–	–	x	x	x	x	x	x	x	x	x	–	x	x	–	x	x	–	–	–	–	–	–	–	–	–
Capper	78.6	o	x	x	x	–	–	x	x	x	x	x	x	x	x	–	o	–	–	–	x	x	–	–	–	–	–	–	–	–	x
Costigan	75	x	o	x	x	x	x	x	x	o	x	x	x	–	–	–	–	o	–	–	–	x	–	o	–	o	–	–	x	x	x
Couzens	46.7	–	x	x	–	–	x	x	o	–	x	x	x	–	–	–	x	–	–	x	x	x	–	x	x	–	–	–	x	x	x
Cutting	100	x	x	x	x	x	x	x	x	x	x	x	x	x	x	x	–	–	–	–	–	–	–	o	–	–	–	–	–	–	–
Frazier	100	x	x	x	x	x	x	x	x	x	x	x	x	x	x	x	–	–	–	–	–	–	–	–	–	–	–	–	–	–	–
Johnson	69.2	–	–	–	–	x	x	x	x	x	x	x	o	x	–	x	x	x	x	x	–	–	–	o	–	–	–	o	–	–	–
LaFollette	86.7	x	x	x	x	x	x	x	x	x	x	x	x	–	–	x	–	–	–	–	–	–	–	–	–	–	–	x	x	x	–
Norbeck	100	x	x	x	x	x	o	o	o	o	o	x	o	x	x	o	–	–	–	–	o	o	o	o	o	–	–	o	–	–	o
Norris	73.3	x	–	x	x	x	x	x	x	x	x	x	x	x	x	–	–	x	–	–	–	–	–	–	–	–	–	x	x	x	x
Nye	100	x	x	x	x	x	x	x	x	x	x	x	x	x	x	x	–	–	–	–	–	–	–	–	–	–	–	–	–	–	–
Shipstead	93.3	x	x	x	x	x	x	x	x	x	x	x	x	x	x	–	–	–	–	–	–	–	–	–	–	–	–	–	–	–	x
Wheeler	75	x	x	x	x	x	x	x	o	o	o	x	x	–	–	–	–	–	–	–	–	–	–	o	o	o	–	x	x	x	x

APPENDIX B

The key roll calls used to compile the degree of opposi-
tion of each Insurgent to the administration during the 1937-
1939 period were: 1937—O'Mahoney Reciprocal Trade Agree-
ments Amendment, Byrnes Anti-Sit-Down Strike Amendment,
Robinson Relief Amendment, Court Plan Recommittal, Fair Labor
Standards Recommittal, Byrd Housing Amendment, and the McAdoo
Cost-of-Production Amendment; 1938—AAA Conference Report,
Wheeler Executive Reorganization Amendment, Byrd Economy-
Executive Reorganization Amendment, Byrd Comptroller-General
Amendment, and the Hatch WPA Amendment; 1939—Barkley WPA
Amendment, Wheeler Executive Reorganization Amendment, Pep-
per WPA Amendment, Gold Devaluation, the Lend-Spend Bill,
and Neutrality Revision.

The "ten most conservative" Senate Democrats were:
Josiah Bailey of North Carolina, Edward Burke of Nebraska,
Harry Byrd of Virginia, Royal Copeland of New York, Peter
Gerry of Rhode Island, Carter Glass of Virginia, Rush Holt
of West Virginia, Edwin Johnson of Colorado, Cotton Ed
Smith of South Carolina, and Millard Tydings of Maryland.
(See James T. Patterson, Congressional Conservatism and the
New Deal /Lexington, Ky., 1967/, pp. 347-51.)

The Republican Senators, excluding those whose tenure
began in January, 1939, were: Warren Austin of Vermont,
Styles Bridges of New Hampshire, James Davis of Pennsyl-
vania, Ernest Gibson of Vermont, Frederick Hale of Maine,
Henry Cabot Lodge of Massachusetts, Charles McNary of Oregon,
Frederick Steiner of Oregon, John Townsend of Delaware,
Arthur Vandenberg of Michigan, and Wallace White of Maine.

INSURGENT VOTING RECORDS, 1937-1939: BASIC DATA

Name	State	Anti-Adminis-tration Votes (%)	Sec-tion[1]	Age in 1937	Tenure
Johnson	California	100	W	71	1917--
Capper	Kansas	88.9	W	72	1919--
Shipstead	Minnesota	85.7	MW	56	1922--
Nye	North Dakota	82.3	W	44	1924--
Borah	Idaho	75	W	72	1907--
Frazier	North Dakota	72.2	W	62	1922--
Wheeler	Montana	64.7	W	55	1922--
LaFollette	Wisconsin	23.5	MW	42	1925--
Norris	Nebraska	6.3	W	76	1913--

[1]Sections defined as follows: East (E): New England, New York, New Jersey, Pennsylvania, Delaware; Border (B): Maryland, West Virginia, Missouri, Kentucky; South (S): Old Confederacy; Midwest (MW): Old Northwest, Minnesota, Iowa; and West (W): the rest.

BIBLIOGRAPHICAL NOTE

The following bibliographical note does not contain all the sources previously cited in the text and in the footnotes but is intended to include only those published and unpublished sources which were especially helpful in the preparation of this work.

Manuscript Sources

This study relies most heavily on manuscript collections. The two most important collections among the Insurgents' personal papers were those of George W. Norris and Hiram W. Johnson, located in the Library of Congress and the Bancroft Library of the University of California, Berkeley, respectively. Both men candidly recorded their opinions of New Deal legislation and of President Franklin D. Roosevelt. The Norris Papers contain lengthy letters detailing the Nebraskan's reasons for accepting most of the New Deal reforms as both necessary and proper extensions of progressivism. The Johnson Papers, particularly "The Diary of Hiram W. Johnson," recount with stark clarity the California Senator's distrust of Roosevelt and his rejection of much of New Deal liberalism as both an unnecessary and dangerous departure from the progressive past.

The personal correspondence of the other Insurgents
is not so revealing as that of Norris and Johnson but is
nevertheless valuable in ascertaining Insurgent views of
various New Deal programs. The William E. Borah Papers
(Library of Congress) are most helpful in the areas of
antitrust and monetary policy; the Arthur Capper Papers
(Kansas State Historical Society, Topeka) and the Peter
Norbeck Papers (Richardson Archives, University of South
Dakota) reflect Insurgent views of agricultural policy; the
Edward P. Costigan Papers (Western History Library, University
of Colorado) and the Robert M. LaFollette, Jr., Papers in the
collection of LaFollette Family Papers (Library of Congress)
are most revealing on the subjects of labor legislation,
taxation, and unemployment relief; the James Couzens Papers
(Library of Congress) present Insurgent attitudes on banking
reform; the Bronson M. Cutting Papers (Library of Congress)
have a good deal of material on veterans' legislation; and
the Henrik Shipstead Papers (Minnesota Historical Society,
St. Paul) are useful on the subject of labor legislation.

Of course, the Franklin D. Roosevelt Papers (Franklin D.
Roosevelt Library, Hyde Park, N. Y.) contain crucial material
on the President's relationship to progressivism and the
Insurgents influence on the New Deal. The following manuscript
collections provided useful information in spots: Thomas R.
Amlie Papers (State Historical Society of Wisconsin, Madison);

John J. Blaine Papers (State Historical Society of Wisconsin);
John Carmody Papers (Franklin D. Roosevelt Library); Morris
L. Cooke Papers (Franklin D. Roosevelt Library); Raymond
Clapper Papers (Library of Congress); Democratic National
Committee Papers (Franklin D. Roosevelt Library); Clifford
R. Hope Papers (Kansas State Historical Society); William
Lemke Papers (the Orin G. Libby Manuscript Collection,
University of North Dakota Library); Charles L. McNary Papers
(Library of Congress); R. Walton Moore Papers (Franklin D.
Roosevelt Library); Diaries of Henry Morgenthau, Jr.,
(Franklin D. Roosevelt Library); John F. Neylan Papers
(Bancroft Library); Progressive National Committee of 1936
Papers (Library of Congress); Raymond Robins Papers (State
Historical Society of Wisconsin); Chester Rowell Papers
(Bancroft Library); Albert G. Schmedeman Papers (State
Historical Society of Wisconsin); Henry G. Teigan Papers
(Minnesota Historical Society); Arthur H. Vandenberg Papers
(Bentley Historical Library, University of Michigan); William
Allen White Papers (Library of Congress); and the Howard Y.
Williams Papers (Minnesota Historical Society).

Other Primary Sources

The New York Times, the Progressive (the LaFollette newspaper in Wisconsin), and the San Francisco Examiner, all of
which I consulted for years 1932-1940, are invaluable sources
for New Deal issues and for matters that most concerned the

Insurgents. The Congressional Record is essential for the
same purposes and also for Insurgent voting records.
Current History, Nation, Newsweek, New Republic, Saturday
Evening Post, and Time provide useful supplementary material.

Autobiographies, Biographies, and Memoirs

The following autobiographies, biographies, and memoirs
were of particular interest for this study: LeRoy Ashby,
Spearless Leader: William E. Borah and the Progressive Move-
ment in the 1920's (Urbana, 1972); Harry Barnard, Independent
Man: The Life of Senator James Couzens (New York, 1958);
Edward C. Blackorby, Prairie Rebel: The Public Life of William
Lemke (Lincoln, Neb., 1963); John M. Blum, From the Morgenthau
Diaries: Years of Crisis, 1928-1929 (Boston, 1959); John M.
Blum, From the Morgenthau Diaries: Years of Urgency, 1938-
1941 (Boston, 1965); James MacGregor Burns, Roosevelt: The
Lion and the Fox (New York, 1956); Wayne S. Cole, Senator
Gerald P. Nye and American Foreign Relations (Minneapolis,
1962); Gilbert C. Fite, Peter Norbeck: Prairie Statesman
(Columbia, Mo., 1948); Frank Freidel, Franklin D. Roosevelt:
Launching the New Deal (Boston, 1973); Fred Greenbaum Fighting
Progressive: A Biography of Edward P. Costigan (Washington,
D. C., 1971); J. Joseph Huthmacher, Senator Robert F. Wagner
and the Rise of Urban Liberalism (New York, 1971); Harold L.
Ickes, The Secret Diary of Harold L. Ickes, 3 vols. (New York,
1953-1954); Fred L. Israel, Nevada's Key Pittman (Lincoln, Neb.,

1963); Claudius O. Johnson, Borah of Idaho (New York, 1936);
Roger T. Johnson, Robert M. LaFollette, Jr., and the Decline
of the Progressive Party in Wisconsin (Madison, 1964); Arthur
Krock, Memoirs: Sixty Years on the Firing Line (New York,
1968); Richard Lowitt, George W. Norris: The Persistence of
a Progressive, 1913-1933 (Urbana, 1971); Richard Lowitt,
George W. Norris: The Triumph of a Progressive, 1933-1944
(Urbana, 1978); Patrick J. Maney, "Young Bob" LaFollette: A
Biography of Robert M. LaFollette, Jr., 1895-1953 (Columbia,
Mo., 1978); Donald R. McCoy, Landon of Kansas (Lincoln, Neb.,
1966); Marion C. McKenna, Borah (Ann Arbor, 1961); Raymond
Moley, After Seven Years (New York, 1939); George W. Norris,
Fighting Liberal: The Autobiography of George W. Norris (New
York, 1945); James T. Patterson, Mr. Republican: A Biography
of Robert A. Taft (Boston, 1972); Homer E. Socolofsky, Arthur
Capper: Publisher, Politician, and Philanthropist (Lawrence,
Kans., 1962); Bernard Sternsher, Rexford G. Tugwell and the
New Deal (New Brunswick, 1964); David P. Thelan, Robert
LaFollette and the Insurgent Spirit (Boston, 1976); Ray Tucker
and Frederick R. Barkley, Sons of the Wild Jackass (Boston,
1932); Rexford G. Tugwell, The Democratic Roosevelt: A Biography
of Franklin D. Roosevelt (Garden City, N. Y., 1957); and Burton
K. Wheeler, Yankee From the West (Garden City, N. Y. 1962).
Current Biography and the Dictionary of Biography provide
interesting and informative sketches of some Insurgents.

Published Secondary Sources

Among the most valuable secondary works for this study were the following: Joseph Alsop and Turner Catledge, The 168 Days (Garden City, N. Y., 1938) is an excellent contemporary account of the Court fight; Paul K. Conkin, The New Deal (New York, 1967), William E. Leuchtenberg, Franklin D. Roosevelt and the New Deal, 1932-1940 (New York, 1963), and Arthur M. Schlesinger, Jr., The Age of Roosevelt, 3 vols. (Boston, 1957-1960) are superior surveys and stimulating interpretations of the New Deal era; Otis L. Graham, Jr., An Encore for Reform: The Old Progressives and the New Deal (New York, 1967) is an excellent study which, although not emphasizing the Insurgent Progressives in the United States Senate in the 1930's, stresses the discontinuity between most aspects of the progressive movement and the New Deal; Ellis W. Hawley, The New Deal and the Problem of Monopoly (Princeton, 1966) and Theodore Rosenof, Dogma, Depression, and the New Deal: The Debate of the Political Leaders over Economic Recovery (Port Washington, N. Y., 1975) provide good analyses of the economic thought and policies of New Dealers and other political leaders in the 1930's, Richard Hofstadter, The Age of Reform: From Bryan to F.D.R. (New York, 1955) and Russel B. Nye, Midwestern Progressive Politics (East Lansing, Mich., 1959) emphasize the agrarian orientation of progressivism; James Holt, Congressional Insurgents and the Party System, 1909-1916

320

(Cambridge, Mass., 1967) presents a good deal of background information on the Insurgents' early congressional careers; Edgar Kemler, The Deflation of American Ideals (Washington, 1941) claims that the progressives held a "moral approach" to reform while the New Dealers favored an "engineering approach;" Donald R. Matthews, U. S. Senators and Their World (New York, 1960) is a brilliant study of the history and the "workings" of the Senate; and James T. Patterson, Congressional Conservatism and the New Deal: The Growth of the Conservative Coalition in Congress, 1933-1939 (Lexington, Ky., 1967) and Richard Polenberg, Reorganizing Roosevelt's Government: The Controversy Over Executive Reorganization, 1936-1939 (Cambridge, Mass., 1966) are of inordinate value for their revelations about the legislative process and about Congressional-Executive rivalry during the New Deal years.

Unpublished Ph.D. Theses

The following theses were of particular interest for this study: Joseph Boskin, "Politics of an Opposition Party: The Republican Party in the New Deal Period, 1936-1940" (University of Minnesota, 1960); Howard A. DeWitt, "Hiram W. Johnson and American Foreign Policy, 1917-1941" (University of Arizona, 1972); John J. Fitzpatrick, "Senator Hiram W. Johnson: A Life History, 1866-1945" (University of California, Berkeley, 1975); Sister Mary Rene Lorentz, "Henrik Shipstead:

Minnesota Independent, 1923-1946" (Catholic University of America, 1963); Harry W. Morris, "The Republicans in a Minority Role, 1933-1938" (State University of Iowa, 1960); Nevin E. Neal, "A Biography of Joseph T. Robinson" (University of Oklahoma, 1958); Walter K. Roberts, "The Political Career of Senator Charles L. McNary, 1924-1944" (University of North Carolina, 1954); Arthur W. Schatz, "Cordell Hull and the Struggle for the Reciprocal Trade Agreements Program, 1932-1940" (University of Oregon, 1966); and Paul L. Silver, "Wilsonians and the New Deal" (University of Pennsylvania, 1964).

Miscellaneous

My understanding of the interrelationships between Insurgent progressivism and New Deal liberalism was enhanced by scholarly articles in Agricultural History, American Historical Review, American Political Science Review, Capitol Studies, Journal of American History, Mid-America, Political Science Quarterly, and Western Political Quarterly. I am grateful to Alfred M. Landon and Burton K. Wheeler for granting me interviews and for responding to my letters.

INDEX

Adams, Alva, B., 281
Agricultural Adjustment Act (AAA)
  of 1933, and domestic allotment
  plan, 50-51; and Norris-Simpson
  cost-of-production amendment,
  52-53; and inflation, 54; and
  Thomas amendment, 54; passage
  of, 55; and Insurgents, 50-55,
  51n, 52n; and unconstitution-
  ality of processing tax, 123,
  166; of 1938, provisions of,
  245; and McAdoo cost-of-production amendment, 248; and
  McNary amendment, 248-249;
  passage of, 249n; and Insurgents, 246-250; of 1939; and
  supplementary appropriation,
  285. See also Soil Conservation and Domestic Allotment
  Act; Insurgents, and primacy
  of agriculture
Agricultural legislation, 1920's,
  20-23
Agricultural Marketing Act, 27
American Farm Bureau Federation,
  21, 50, 247, 247n
Amlie, Thomas R., 102, 103n,
  134, 144, 147
Arnold, Thurman, 268-269
Ashurst, Henry F., 171, 187-188
Bailey, Josiah W., 90, 174
Bancroft, Philip, 274
Bankhead-Jones Farm Tenancy Act
  of 1937, and creation of FSA,
  237
Bank Holiday, 40
Banking Act of 1935, provisions
  of, 114; and Insurgents, 114-
  115, 115n; mentioned, 16, 105

Barkley, Alben W., 172n, 200-201,
  231, 282, 284
Baruch, Bernard M., 263-264
Black-Connery bill. See wages and
  hours legislation
Black, Hugo L., 192n, 200, 202,
  223
Blaine, John J., 4
Borah-O'Mahoney bill, 269, 269n
Borah, William E., early career
  of, 6-8; political philosophy
  of, 6-7; independence of, 6, 43
  305; on trusts, 6, 11, 57, 107,
  131, 267-269, 268n; supporter of
  Bryan, 9; on McNary-Haugen bills,
  27n; on Agricultural Marketing
  Act, 27; endorses Hoover in 1928,
  27; endorses Hoover in 1932, 32,
  135; on Emergency Banking Act of
  1933, 43; fearful of presidential
  power, 43, 46, 59-60, 74, 299; on
  Economy act of 1933, 44, 46;
  critical of federal bureaucracy,
  46, 59, 226, 236, 241, 247-248,
  254, on primacy of agriculture,
  48; opposes AAA, 51, 51n; on inflation, 54, 62, 64, 121; opposes
  NIRA, 58, 58n, 59-60, 78, 94; on
  Gold Reserve Act, 63; on tax reform, 68-69, 118-121; on World
  Court, 89; on federal relief, 92,
  227-228, 231, 233, 267, 282, 283n;
  on holding company bill, 107-108;
  on Banking Act of 1935, 114; on
  Second New Deal, 129; on New Deal
  liberalism, 130, 135; on Republican
  party, 134-135; on Democratic
  party, 135; on reorganization of
  GOP, 135-137; candidate for GOP

322

nomination in 1936, 137-139; on GOP platform, 139; on Landon, 139, 156, 157; and F. D. Roosevelt in 1936, 156-157, 156n; on Court reorganization plan, 170, 192; on judicial reform, 173; on GOP strategy and Court fight, 176, 185, 193, 194-195n; on sit-down strikes, 221; on wages and hours bill, 225-226; on deficit spending, 231, 235, 267; on Wagner housing bill, 235-236; on New Deal program of agricultural scarcity, 246-247, 248-249n; on Recession of 1937-1938, 251-252; opposes executive reorganization bill, 254, 256, 258, 289; on undistributed-corporate-profits tax, 265; on elections of 1938, 273, 275-276; mentioned, 4, 4n, 175n, 305
Bourne, Jonathan, 4
Brandeis, Louis D., 68, 100-101, 104, 109, 112, 122, 167, 174, 189-190, 194n
Brandeisians, political philosophy of, 100-101; and struggle with "planners," 100-101, 101n; and Insurgents, 101n; and holding company bill, 108-109; and wealth tax bill, 122. *See also* Second New Deal
Bristow, Joseph L., 4
Brookhart, Smith W., 4, 21, 52, 82-83
Bryan, William Jennings, 9, 54, 129
Burke, Edward R., 178, 202, 272
Burns, James MacGregor, 81
Butler, Pierce, 167
Byrd, Harry F., 90, 178, 235-236, 253, 286
Byrnes, James F., 109, 191, 219-220, 228-230, 257, 263, 281, 289
Cannon, Joseph G., 17

Capper, Arthur, on Norris, 5; early career of, 8-9; endorses Hoover in 1932, 32; on Economy Act of 1933, 44; on NIRA, 57; on reciprocal trade agreements, 77-78, 245-246; on World Court, 89; on trusts, 107; on Wealth Tax Act of 1935, 122; on undistributed-corporate-profits tax, 127n; endorses Landon in 1936, 157-158; on deficit spending, 157, 266, 282, 283n, 296; and anti-urban views of, 239-240, 296; on elections of 1938, 273, 275, 279; on New Deal liberalism, 273-275, 279, 296, 301; on primacy of agriculture, 285; and F. D. Roosevelt, 301; mentioned, 4, 4n, 175n
Cardozo, Benjamin N., 167
Chavez, Dennis, 87- 88, 290
Civil Works Emergency Appropriation Act of 1934, 66. *See also* Relief
Clapp, Moses, 4
Clapper, Raymond, 133, 157
Clark, Bennett Champ, 94, 178
Clark, D. Worth, 275
Clayton Antitrust Act, 15-16
Cohen, Benjamin V., 101
Commager, Henry Steele, 1
Congressional-Executive rivalry, and AAA, 52-53, and NIRA, 59-60; and inflation, 63-64; and veterans' legislation, 65-66, 98; and relief expenditures, 92, 231-233, 280-284; and Court reorganization plan, 192-193, 206-210; and "Dear Alben" letter, 200-201; and executive reorganization bills, 255-262, 288-290; and undistributed-corporate-profits tax repeal, 264, 291; and lend-spend bill, 286-287; and Gold Devaluation, 290; and Hatch Act, 290-291
Congress of Industrial Organizations (CIO), 215, 217-218, 220, 298